No Waste, Great Taste!

THE ULTIMATE

MEDITERRANEAN

DIET

COOKING FOR ONE

COOKBOOK

175 Healthy, Easy, and Delicious Recipes Made Just for You

Kelly Jaggers, Author of *The Everything® Mediterranean Instant Pot® Cookbook*

Adams Media
New York London Toronto Sydney New Delhi

Adams Media
An Imprint of Simon & Schuster, Inc.
100 Technology Center Drive
Stoughton, Massachusetts 02072

First Adams Media trade paperback edition June 2023

ADAMS MEDIA and colophon are trademarks of Simon & Schuster.

For information about special discounts for bulk purchases, please contact Simon & Schuster Special Sales at 1-866-506-1949 or business@simonandschuster.com.

The Simon & Schuster Speakers Bureau can bring authors to your live event. For more information or to book an event, contact the Simon & Schuster Speakers Bureau at 1-866-248-3049 or visit our website at www.simonspeakers.com.

Interior design by Julia Jacintho
Interior layout by Kellie Emery
Interior images © 123RF/tanjakrstevska, mallinka, chelovector
Photographs by Kelly Jaggers

Manufactured in the United States of America

2 2023

Library of Congress Cataloging-in-Publication Data
Names: Jaggers, Kelly, author.
Title: The ultimate Mediterranean diet cooking for one cookbook / Kelly Jaggers.
Description: Stoughton, Massachusetts: Adams Media, [2023] | Series: Ultimate for one | Includes index.
Identifiers: LCCN 2023006522 | ISBN 9781507220450 (pb) | ISBN 9781507220467 (ebook)
Subjects: LCSH: Cooking, Mediterranean. | Cooking for one. | LCGFT: Cookbooks.
Classification: LCC TX725.M35 J343 2023 | DDC 641.59/1822--dc23/eng/20230301
LC record available at https://lccn.loc.gov/2023006522

ISBN 978-1-5072-2045-0
ISBN 978-1-5072-2046-7 (ebook)

CONTENTS

INTRODUCTION | 4

CHAPTER 1: MEDITERRANEAN DIET
MADE FOR ONE | 5

CHAPTER 2: BREAKFAST | 11

CHAPTER 3: DIPS AND SNACKS | 33

CHAPTER 4: SALADS AND SOUPS | 54

CHAPTER 5: SIDE DISHES | 75

CHAPTER 6: PASTA DISHES | 97

CHAPTER 7: VEGETARIAN MAIN DISHES | 117

CHAPTER 8: SEAFOOD | 141

CHAPTER 9: POULTRY DISHES | 163

CHAPTER 10: PORK, LAMB, AND BEEF DISHES | 184

CHAPTER 11: DESSERTS | 207

US/METRIC CONVERSION CHARTS | 229

INDEX | 231

INTRODUCTION

Are you are looking for a lifestyle that can reduce stress, increase energy, and improve your overall health? The Mediterranean diet has been shown to improve vitality and health with a focus on plant-based eating and slowing down to enjoy life. Less diet and more lifestyle, this way of eating focuses on colorful, seasonal, and flavorful dishes featuring grains, pastas, nuts, seeds, olive oil, and fruits and vegetables. The only drawback to this healthy plan is that most Mediterranean diet dishes are designed to feed a large group, often around six to eight people! If you are cooking for one, that can lead to *a lot* of food (and money!) wasted—a thought that may have you reaching for a takeout menu. What if it did not have to be this way?

In *The Ultimate Mediterranean Diet Cooking for One Cookbook*, you will find 175 healthful and delicious recipes designed for one! For breakfast, you can find options like a Berry and Yogurt Smoothie and Eggs Florentine with Greek Yogurt Hollandaise (Chapter 2). Lunch and dinner options include recipes for light and fresh dishes like Mediterranean Couscous Salad (Chapter 4) and elegant Shrimp Pasta with Basil and Feta (Chapter 8). Hearty Three-Bean Vegetarian Chili (Chapter 7) or Feta and Spinach–Stuffed Chicken Breast (Chapter 9) are good choices when you crave something comforting. If it's sweets you crave, how about Dark Chocolate Mousse or Baked Stuffed Apple (Chapter 11)? Any time of day, any meal you want, this book has you covered!

But before you pull out your pasta maker and head to your local farmers' market, take a look at the first chapter to learn about the Mediterranean diet and lifestyle, including which foods are good for you to eat every day and which should be eaten less frequently, and the basics of cooking for one. You'll discover how to shop smartly for common Mediterranean diet ingredients you'll need, and how to avoid buying large quantities that you won't. And you'll find tips for meal prep so you can take the stress out of weekday meal planning, as well as information on substitutions and how to stock your kitchen.

When you have accessible ingredients and easy, delicious recipes on hand, you can create and enjoy a fabulous meal for one in no time. Whether you live alone, you're a parent who wants to keep on the heathy eating path while the kids enjoy their own favorites, or you have a partner who travels, *The Ultimate Mediterranean Diet Cooking for One Cookbook* is for you! So sit back, relax, and enjoy some nourishing meals made just for one!

CHAPTER 1

MEDITERRANEAN DIET MADE FOR ONE

Mediterranean Diet Basics 6

Mediterranean Cooking for One 7

Shopping Smartly 7

Fresh Ingredients and Pantry Staples 8

Meal Prep and Avoiding Food Waste 9

The Mediterranean diet combines delicious meals that are largely plant-based, slowing down at meal time to really savor your food, a daily glass of wine, and daily movement to create a happier, healthier you! The pleasure found in preparing and eating a meal is one of the hallmarks of the lifestyle; however, most recipes for the Mediterranean diet are designed to create six to eight servings, which can be a challenge if you are cooking only for yourself. Rather than have the same meal day after day, or throwing out unwanted leftovers, this book will show you how you can cook perfectly portioned meals for one person so you can enjoy a wide variety of dishes each week.

In this chapter you will discover more about the Mediterranean diet and how to enjoy all its benefits while cooking for one. You will find advice for stocking your pantry, how to utilize the bulk section of your store, how to buy and store foods, and ways to meal prep so even on busy days you can enjoy delicious, healthful, and relaxing meals. A list of equipment, tips, and ideas for meal prep are included to help make your weekly shopping, prep work, and cooking a breeze!

Mediterranean Diet Basics

If you think about the Mediterranean diet like a pyramid, at the base there are the foods you will eat daily and create most of your meals around. As you move up the pyramid, you will find foods you can enjoy daily in moderation, foods that should be eaten a few times a week, and at the top, foods to be enjoyed occasionally, as in once or twice per month.

The Base—Daily Foods

The base of the Mediterranean diet is filled with a variety of plant-based foods like grains, oats, pasta, bread, legumes, nuts, seeds, olive oil, and seasonal fruits and vegetables. These will form the basis for your meals, and when meal planning for the week, you will want to plan at least two meals per day that are fully plant-based. Thinking of a dinner plate, you want these foods to make up at least three-quarters of your meal.

Level 2—Weekly Foods

This level of the pyramid is filled with foods you can enjoy multiple times per week. Here you will find fish and seafood that is grilled, broiled, sautéed, stewed, or poached. Seafood and fish dishes are prepared with lots of fresh herbs, spices, and citrus to enhance their natural flavors. Deep-fried fish and seafood should be enjoyed very rarely. Examples of fish and seafood to incorporate into your diet include salmon, steelhead trout, cod, whitefish, clams, mussels, crab, and shrimp. On your dinner plate, these foods will fill one-quarter of the plate.

Level 3—Foods in Moderation

Moving up the pyramid, you find foods you will enjoy in moderation. This level incudes lower-fat dairy items, eggs, nuts, seeds, and poultry. Think about ways to use these foods to their best advantage. A beautifully fluffy Farmer's Omelet (see Chapter 2) for breakfast, a yogurt-based dressing on a salad, or a grating of cheese over pasta are examples of ways to get the most out of your dairy and eggs. Poultry, either roasted, grilled, stewed, or steamed/poached, should be enjoyed on a weekly basis. On your dinner plate, the dairy should be a garnish, while eggs and poultry take up one-quarter of the plate.

Level 4—Monthly Foods

The peak of the pyramid is where you find red meats, processed foods, and sweets. Being at the top of the pyramid means these foods are to be enjoyed occasionally, and in the case of red meat, as a smaller part of a more plant-focused meal. When it comes to sweets and desserts, fruit-based desserts offer nutrition in addition to sweetness, as does gelato, which is milk-based and has calcium and protein.

Other Elements of the Mediterranean Diet

In addition to the colorful, seasonal, and flavorful meals enjoyed on the Mediterranean diet, there are other elements to enjoy. Taking a daily walk or bike ride, slowing down at meal time to really savor your food, and enjoying a daily glass of red wine with dinner are part of the Mediterranean lifestyle that help reduce stress and improve overall mood.

Mediterranean Cooking for One

Cooking for yourself can be a real pleasure when you have the right tools and techniques. Starting with the right tools and knowing how to utilize your grocery store and ways you can stock your pantry will mean you have everything you need for a delicious meal whenever you want it.

The Right Tools for the Job

The right tools make all the difference, especially when you are cooking for one. Smaller pots, pans, and dishes will ensure that the recipes you make come out just right. Using the wrong-sized dishes and pots can affect the cooking time and leave you with an unexpected result. In the list that follows, you will find the types of pots, pans, and other tools used to develop the recipes in this book. You probably have most of these at home now, but anything you are missing can be purchased in most home goods stores, thrift stores, or online. And sometimes items can do double duty, such as blenders and food processors (it isn't always necessary to have each one).

- ¼ rimmed sheet pan
- ½ rimmed sheet pan
- 1-quart saucepan with lid
- 2-quart saucepan with lid
- 5" × 3" mini-loaf pan
- 6" baking or au gratin dish
- 6" casserole dish
- 6" cake pan

- 6" pie pan
- 8" ovenproof skillet with lid
- 8" nonstick pan
- Blender
- Chef's knife
- Colander
- Digital scale
- Digital instant-read thermometer
- Food processor
- Hand mixer
- Measuring cups
- Measuring spoons
- Microwave-safe bowl and mug
- Mixing bowls
- Nonstick griddle
- Parchment or a silicone baking mat
- Paring knife
- Serrated knife
- Silicone or rubber spatula
- Slotted spoon
- Strainer
- Tongs
- Whisk
- Wire rack
- Wooden spoons

Shopping Smartly

Cooking for one means that you need to think about ways to get the ingredients you need in the right amounts. Some items, like fresh meat and seafood, are easily stored in the freezer and dry goods can be held in your pantry long term, but what about specialty items? Check the bulk section for ingredients you may not need to stock up on regularly. There you can find a variety of nuts, dried fruits, spices, and flours that can be purchased in smaller amounts.

For fresh herbs and other aromatics, you may not need to use a whole bunch for one meal. You can put fresh herbs in water, like a bunch of flowers, and store them in your refrigerator. Check out the produce section of your grocery store for items like freeze-dried herbs and aromatics. You can find freeze-dried items like minced garlic, shallots, and most common culinary herbs available. They taste fresh and flavorful when used in cooking, dressings, and sauces and they keep for months, so you don't have to worry about throwing away wilted herbs you did not use.

Fresh Ingredients and Pantry Staples

Mediterranean cooking relies on wholesome, colorful ingredients that nourish the body and soul. The following are lists of foods, condiments, and ingredients to keep in mind when planning your weekly meals. The list is not comprehensive of the entire Mediterranean diet but includes commonly used ingredients, many of which are found in this book's recipes.

Dairy

- Brie
- Cottage cheese
- Feta
- Goat cheese
- Low-fat dairy milk or alternative milk
- Low-fat Greek yogurt
- Parmigiano-Reggiano cheese

- Part-skim mozzarella cheese
- Ricotta cheese

Fresh Proteins

- Bass
- Chicken
- Clams
- Cornish game hens
- Crab
- Eggs
- Lobster
- Mussels
- Oysters
- Red meat
- Salmon
- Sardines
- Shrimp
- Tofu (silken and firm)
- Trout
- Tuna
- Turkey
- Whitefish

Fresh Produce

- Apples
- Artichokes
- Asparagus
- Avocados
- Bananas
- Berries
- Brussels sprouts
- Carrots
- Cauliflower
- Citrus fruit
- Cucumbers
- Dates
- Eggplant

- Figs
- Garlic
- Green beans
- Green onions
- Greens
- Herbs
- Kale
- Kiwi
- Lettuce
- Melon
- Mushrooms
- Onions
- Pears
- Potatoes
- Sweet potatoes
- Tomatoes
- Zucchini

Pantry Staples

- Beans (canned and dry)
- Broth (chicken, seafood, and vegetable)
- Brown rice
- Buckwheat
- Bulgur
- Canned tuna
- Dried fruits
- Flour (all-purpose and whole-wheat)
- Herbs, dried
- Honey
- Lentils (canned and dry)
- No-sodium-added canned vegetables
- Nuts and nut butters
- Olive oil (regular and extra-virgin)
- Olives (canned or jarred)
- Peas (canned and dry)
- Pickles
- Polenta

- Pure maple syrup
- Quinoa
- Roasted red peppers
- Rolled oats
- Seeds and seed butters
- Spices (dried and ground)
- Vinegar
- Whole-grain bread
- Whole-grain pasta

Freezer Items

- Frozen fruit
- Frozen vegetables

Meal Prep and Avoiding Food Waste

Having a plan for your weekly meals has a myriad of benefits. It reduces decision fatigue, reduces food waste, lowers stress at meal time, saves money, and gives you greater control over the variety of foods you enjoy. Instead of trying to figure out what to cook at the last minute, and perhaps ordering takeout, you have a plan and ingredients ready to go.

Planning Ahead

Take a few minutes once a week to create a weekly menu for yourself of foods you love. With a weekly plan, you know what ingredients you will need to buy, which you can pull from your pantry or freezer, and which ingredients and meals you can prep in advance for busy days. Check your weekly grocery store circulars to see what is fresh and on sale to help build your menu.

Taking a little time once a week to plan will keep you on track, relaxed, and satisfied.

Keep an Inventory

Before you start your weekly meal plan, do a quick pantry, refrigerator, and freezer inventory. What meals can you build with these ingredients? What are you missing to make a complete meal? What pantry items are you running low on and need to restock? Keeping track of your pantry, refrigerator, and freezer means you have the ingredients you need to make delicious meals almost anytime, you won't find yourself missing a vital ingredient when you start cooking, and you will be less likely to rebuy items you already have.

Use Your Freezer

Are chicken breasts on an amazing deal, but they only come in the family pack? Is there is a buy-one-get-one deal on your favorite whole-grain bread? Do the onions you love come in at less per pound when you buy a 5-pound bag? Use your freezer to hold these foods longer. Freezer bags and airtight containers can be used to portion out the extra food into individual packs. Label the foods you are storing with the name and date and put them in the freezer. Make a note of the food you have stored away so you can use it in the weeks to come.

You can also buy prepared frozen fruits and vegetables that are cut and ready for cooking. Stocking up on vegetables in the freezer is a great way to have a colorful variety on hand without the worry of spoilage. You can also chop and freeze leftover vegetables and fruit from your weekly cooking to use later. Frozen vegetables retain most of their essential nutrients, and frozen fruits and vegetables are frozen at the peak of the season so they will taste their best.

Prep Ahead

Take an afternoon once or twice a week to do a bit of meal prep. Making a pasta salad, cooking some grains, preparing some snacks, and chopping fruits and vegetables ahead of time will save you time and effort on busy days when you might otherwise ring for takeout. Preparing salads, soups, and breakfast items ahead of time are great ways to be ready when time is tight. Think about recipes you can have ready to slide into a hot oven or toss into a hot skillet on busy days so you can have a comforting meal when you need it. Baked pasta and vegetable dishes are great to have prepped and ready for the oven. A batch or two of overnight oats in the refrigerator will keep you out of the fast-food drive-thru when time is tight.

You don't have to prep all at once, either. When you have time, prep one or two things and put them in the refrigerator or freezer for another day. Make lunches a day or two ahead on Sunday night for the work week ahead. While dinner for tonight is baking, chop the vegetables for tomorrow. You do not need to spend a whole day in the kitchen to successfully prepare your weekly meals. Remember, cooking should be a pleasure, not a chore, and being strategic means that on days when cooking would not be a pleasure, you are set up for success!

CHAPTER 2

BREAKFAST

Greek Yogurt Parfait 12

Almond Date Oatmeal 13

Red Pepper and Feta Omelet.................14

Baked Egg with Dill and Tomato 15

Egg Poached in Tomato Sauce
    (Shakshuka)..16

Spinach and Mozzarella Frittata.............18

Chickpea Hash with
    Hard-Boiled Egg..................................19

Fruit and Nut Overnight Oatmeal 20

Avocado Toast with Balsamic-Marinated
    Tomatoes...21

Whole-Grain Pancakes with
    Berry Sauce 23

Farmer's Omelet 24

Ricotta Berry Toast..................................25

Baked Egg in a Bell Pepper....................26

Berry and Yogurt Smoothie.................. 27

Spanakopita Frittata................................28

Eggs Florentine with Greek
    Yogurt Hollandaise 30

Blueberry Almond Butter
    Smoothie Bowl 32

A well-balanced breakfast sets you up with the energy you need to get your day started, and adds a little pleasure to your morning routine. A satisfying breakfast will help keep you full, focused, and happy until lunch. With a wide variety of options on the Mediterranean diet, such as eggs, oats, pancakes, yogurt, and avocado toast, there is bound to be something to satisfy almost any craving while providing your body with all of the healthy fats, fiber, and protein it needs to thrive.

This chapter features recipes for when you can enjoy a slow and leisurely breakfast, as well as recipes that can be enjoyed on the go. Each recipe is designed to create one serving, so there are no leftovers to put away. If you are short on time, why not blend up a Berry and Yogurt Smoothie packed with fruit and almond butter to keep you satisfied. If you have a little more time, make a batch of Whole-Grain Pancakes with Berry Sauce. Want something with fresh vegetables? Try a Farmer's Omelet. With breakfast options this good, you will look forward to getting out of bed every morning!

GREEK YOGURT PARFAIT

PREP TIME: 10 MINUTES | COOK TIME: 3 MINUTES | SERVES: 1

 Greek yogurt—a staple on the Mediterranean diet—is regular yogurt that has been strained to give it a thicker texture and tangier flavor. It is loaded with protein, which helps you feel full. You can make this parfait up to three days ahead. Use any fresh berries you like.

INGREDIENTS

2 tablespoons sliced almonds

1 tablespoon dried cherries

¼ teaspoon ground cinnamon

1 (5.3-ounce) cup plain low-fat Greek yogurt

1 teaspoon honey

¼ teaspoon pure vanilla extract

¼ cup fresh blueberries

2 medium strawberries, hulled and diced

1. In an 8" skillet over medium heat, cook almonds, stirring constantly, until lightly toasted, about 3 minutes. Set aside and cool to room temperature.

2. In a small bowl, add toasted almonds, cherries, and cinnamon and toss well to coat. Set aside.

3. In another small bowl, add yogurt, honey, and vanilla. Mix well to combine.

4. In a small serving bowl or parfait dish, add ⅓ of yogurt mixture, ½ of nut mixture, and ½ of blueberries and strawberries. Repeat these steps, ending with a layer of yogurt. Serve immediately, or cover and refrigerate up to three days. Serve chilled.

PER SERVING

Calories: 264

Fat: 9g

Sodium: 50mg

Carbohydrates: 30g

Fiber: 3g

Sugar: 24g

Protein: 18g

ALMOND DATE OATMEAL

PREP TIME: 5 MINUTES | COOK TIME: 11 MINUTES | SERVES: 1

 Oats are a Mediterranean breakfast staple and a nutritional powerhouse, with benefits that include controlling blood sugar, lowering bad cholesterol, and improving gut health. They are also loaded with antioxidants, vitamins, and minerals your body needs. Plus, oats taste great, so having a healthy breakfast is also a pleasure!

INGREDIENTS

1 cup unsweetened almond milk

½ cup rolled oats

¼ cup chopped pitted dates

⅛ teaspoon sea salt

2 tablespoons natural almond butter

1 teaspoon honey

1. In a 1-quart saucepan, add almond milk, oats, dates, and salt. Stir to combine, then place over medium-low heat. Cook, stirring constantly, until mixture comes to a low boil, about 4 minutes. Reduce heat to low and cook until almond milk is almost fully absorbed, about 2 minutes. Remove pot from heat, cover with a lid, and let stand 5 minutes.

2. Remove lid from pot and add almond butter and stir well. Transfer oats to a small bowl and drizzle honey over top. Enjoy immediately.

Storing Oats

Rolled, or old-fashioned, oats have a shelf life of up to twelve months if stored in an airtight container in a cool, dry place. Oats should have a pleasant, nutty aroma and should be a pale golden color. Any discoloration, off odors, or visible mold mean the oats are bad and should be discarded.

PER SERVING

Calories: 494
Fat: 23g
Sodium: 375mg
Carbohydrates: 70g

Fiber: 11g
Sugar: 30g
Protein: 13g

RED PEPPER AND FETA OMELET

PREP TIME: 10 MINUTES | COOK TIME: 7 MINUTES | SERVES: 1

 This omelet features colorful herbs and vegetables as well as tangy feta cheese for a breakfast that starts your day with a serving of healthy vegetables and good fats to keep you full. Crumbled goat cheese or part-skim mozzarella are good substitutes for feta.

INGREDIENTS

2 teaspoons olive oil, divided

½ cup loosely packed baby spinach

2 medium button mushrooms, trimmed and sliced

2 large eggs

⅛ teaspoon sea salt

¼ cup crumbled feta cheese, divided

¼ cup chopped jarred roasted red peppers, drained and patted dry

4 medium cherry tomatoes, quartered

1 tablespoon chopped fresh chives

⅛ teaspoon freshly cracked black pepper

1. In an 8" nonstick pan over medium heat, add 1 teaspoon olive oil. Let oil heat briefly, then swirl pan to evenly coat. Add spinach and mushrooms and cook until mushrooms are tender, about 4 minutes. Transfer to a bowl and set aside, then return pan to heat.

2. In a small bowl, add eggs and whisk 1 minute or until eggs are foamy. Add salt and whisk to combine.

3. Add remaining 1 teaspoon olive oil to pan and let it heat briefly, then swirl pan to coat. Add eggs to pan and reduce heat to low. Let pan stand 20 seconds or until eggs start to set, then use a spatula to gently push edges of eggs to the center of the pan while tilting the pan so uncooked eggs move to edges. Cook about 2 minutes.

4. Once bottom of eggs are just set and top is just slightly wet, add spinach and mushrooms, 3 tablespoons feta, and roasted red peppers.

5. Remove pan from heat and fold top ⅓ of omelet down, then fold in half so toppings are folded inside eggs. Transfer to a plate and top with remaining 1 tablespoon feta, tomatoes, chives, and black pepper. Enjoy immediately.

PER SERVING

Calories: 356	Fiber: 2g
Fat: 25g	Sugar: 7g
Sodium: 988mg	Protein: 20g
Carbohydrates: 10g	

BAKED EGG WITH DILL AND TOMATO

PREP TIME: 5 MINUTES | COOK TIME: 14 MINUTES | SERVES: 1

 You can prepare this dish up to the point of adding the egg up to two days ahead of time. When you are ready to bake, just add the egg and proceed as directed. You can swap the tomatoes out for diced roasted red peppers, zucchini, or squash, or you can try frozen mixed vegetables.

INGREDIENTS

1 teaspoon olive oil, divided

3 tablespoons finely chopped green onions (green part only)

½ clove garlic, peeled and minced

½ cup chopped Roma tomatoes

1 large egg

¼ teaspoon chopped fresh dill

¼ teaspoon freshly cracked black pepper

1. Preheat oven to 375°F and brush a 6" baking dish with ½ teaspoon olive oil. Add green onions to bottom of dish and set aside.

2. In an 8" skillet over medium heat, add remaining ½ teaspoon olive oil and swirl pan to evenly coat. Once oil is hot, add garlic and cook 10 seconds, then add tomatoes and sauté until they start to soften, about 2 minutes. Transfer tomato mixture to prepared baking dish.

3. Crack egg into center of dish, then sprinkle dill and black pepper over top.

4. Bake 12–15 minutes or until egg whites are set and yolk is set to your preference. Serve hot.

Benefits of Eggs

Eggs are packed with nutrition and offer a number of health benefits. They are nutritionally dense and are an excellent source of choline, selenium, and vitamin B_{12}. They are a complete protein, meaning eggs have all nine essential amino acids, so they can help your body with tissue regeneration and building muscle.

PER SERVING

Calories: 134

Fat: 9g

Sodium: 77mg

Carbohydrates: 6g

Fiber: 2g

Sugar: 3g

Protein: 8g

EGG POACHED IN TOMATO SAUCE (SHAKSHUKA)

PREP TIME: 5 MINUTES | COOK TIME: 18 MINUTES | SERVES: 1

 The dish Shakshuka is originally from North Africa, where it is enjoyed for breakfast and lunch. If you don't have fresh tomatoes, you can use ¾ cup diced or crushed canned tomatoes, and you can also add a tablespoon of crumbled feta cheese for a garnish.

INGREDIENTS

1 teaspoon olive oil

¼ cup chopped yellow onion

¼ cup chopped red bell pepper

1 clove garlic, peeled and minced

3 medium plum tomatoes (about ¼ pound), seeded and diced

2 teaspoons tomato paste

¼ teaspoon crushed red pepper flakes

¼ teaspoon ground cumin

¼ teaspoon smoked paprika

1 large egg

1 teaspoon dried parsley

1 (½"-thick) slice sourdough bread, toasted

1. Heat an 8" skillet over medium heat. Add olive oil and let it heat briefly, then swirl pan to coat. Add onion and bell pepper and cook until just tender, about 3 minutes.

2. Add garlic, tomatoes, tomato paste, red pepper flakes, cumin, and paprika. Cook, stirring often, until tomatoes soften and start to break down, about 5 minutes. Use the back of a spatula to help break down tomatoes if needed. Let sauce simmer, stirring often, until it is a medium thickness, about 5–6 minutes.

3. Use a spatula to make a well in the center of sauce and crack egg into it. Reduce heat to medium-low, cover pan, and cook 5–7 minutes or until egg is cooked to your preference.

4. Once egg is cooked, remove lid and add parsley for garnish. Transfer to a plate and enjoy with toasted bread.

PER SERVING

Calories: 266

Fat: 10g

Sodium: 318mg

Carbohydrates: 32g

Fiber: 6g

Sugar: 12g

Protein: 12g

SPINACH AND MOZZARELLA FRITTATA

PREP TIME: 5 MINUTES | COOK TIME: 14 MINUTES | SERVES: 1

A frittata is an elegant way to start your day. This version is packed with spinach and potatoes to start your day with plenty of nutrients. To limit prep time, this recipe calls for bagged frozen shredded hash brown potatoes. If you prefer to grate a potato fresh, just squeeze out the excess water before cooking.

INGREDIENTS

1 teaspoon olive oil

¼ cup frozen shredded hash brown potatoes

¼ cup diced yellow onion

1 clove garlic, peeled and minced

1 cup loosely packed baby spinach

¼ cup shredded part-skim mozzarella cheese

¼ teaspoon freshly cracked black pepper

2 large eggs, beaten

1. Preheat broiler.

2. In an 8" ovenproof skillet over medium heat, add olive oil and let it heat briefly, then swirl pan to coat. Add shredded hash brown potatoes in an even layer. Let cook without stirring for 4–5 minutes or until potatoes start to turn golden. Use a spatula to break up potatoes, then add onion. Cook until onion starts to soften, about 3 minutes. Add garlic and spinach and cook, stirring often, until spinach wilts, about 1 minute.

3. Spread vegetables into an even layer and top with mozzarella and black pepper. Add eggs and gently swirl pan to ensure eggs form an even layer. Reduce heat to medium-low and cook 3–4 minutes or until bottom of eggs are just set.

4. Transfer pan to oven and broil 3–5 minutes or until top of frittata is set and lightly browned. Remove from oven and cool 3 minutes before serving.

PER SERVING

Calories: 317

Fat: 17g

Sodium: 323mg

Carbohydrates: 18g

Fiber: 2g

Sugar: 3g

Protein: 20g

CHICKPEA HASH WITH HARD-BOILED EGG

PREP TIME: 5 MINUTES | COOK TIME: 8 MINUTES | SERVES: 1

 Chickpeas are a healthy breakfast food because their high fiber content helps you stay full all morning! The fiber is good for your digestion and also helps with blood sugar regulation, and because chickpeas are rich in nutrients like choline, they may also help keep your brain sharp.

INGREDIENTS

1 teaspoon olive oil

¼ cup chopped yellow onion

¼ cup chopped zucchini

¼ cup chopped red bell pepper

1 clove garlic, peeled and chopped

¼ teaspoon ground cumin

¼ teaspoon freshly cracked black pepper

½ cup canned chickpeas, rinsed and drained

1 large hard-boiled egg, sliced

⅛ teaspoon sea salt

⅛ teaspoon smoked paprika

1. In an 8" skillet over medium heat, add olive oil and let it heat briefly, then swirl pan to coat. Add onion, zucchini, and bell pepper. Cook until softened, about 4 minutes. Add garlic, cumin, and black pepper and cook until fragrant, about 30 seconds. Stir in chickpeas and cook until heated through, about 3 minutes.

2. Transfer chickpea mixture to a plate and top with sliced egg, then sprinkle with salt and paprika to garnish. Serve immediately.

Storing Cooked Chickpeas

Cooked chickpeas can be kept in the refrigerator for up to five days. To store chickpeas, rinse them under cool water, then transfer them to a clean storage container with a tight-fitting lid. Chickpeas tend to dry out, so add enough water to just cover the chickpeas, add a drizzle of olive oil, or store them in their canning liquid.

PER SERVING

Calories: 396

Fat: 12g

Sodium: 434mg

Carbohydrates: 62g

Fiber: 21g

Sugar: 8g

Protein: 19g

FRUIT AND NUT OVERNIGHT OATMEAL

PREP TIME: 6 HOURS 5 MINUTES | COOK TIME: 0 MINUTES | SERVES: 1

Overnight oats are a great breakfast on a busy morning. Any mix of dried fruits and nuts works here, so use what you like best. If you want a warm breakfast, just pop your oats in the microwave for 45 seconds or until warm throughout. This dish can be made up to three days in advance.

INGREDIENTS

½ cup rolled oats

⅓ cup unsweetened almond milk

¼ cup plain low-fat Greek yogurt

2 teaspoons honey

¼ teaspoon pure vanilla extract

¼ teaspoon ground cinnamon

2 tablespoons chopped toasted pecans, divided

½ large banana, peeled and sliced

2 large strawberries, hulled and diced

1. In a small bowl, add oats, almond milk, yogurt, honey, vanilla, and cinnamon. Stir until well combined. Place half of mixture into a 1-cup Mason jar.

2. Add 1 tablespoon pecans and banana slices, then remaining oat mixture. Top with strawberries and remaining 1 tablespoon pecans.

3. Cover jar and refrigerate at least 6 hours or overnight. Serve chilled.

PER SERVING

Calories: 413   Fiber: 9g
Fat: 15g   Sugar: 26g
Sodium: 78mg   Protein: 13g
Carbohydrates: 62g

AVOCADO TOAST WITH BALSAMIC-MARINATED TOMATOES

PREP TIME: 35 MINUTES | COOK TIME: 0 MINUTES | SERVES: 1

 Avocados are an important ingredient to add to a Mediterranean diet for good reason—they are an excellent source of potassium, monounsaturated fats, and folate, so they are great for helping lower blood pressure and cholesterol and improving brain health.

INGREDIENTS

6 medium cherry tomatoes, sliced in half

1 teaspoon balsamic vinegar

1 teaspoon extra-virgin olive oil

⅛ teaspoon Aleppo pepper

1 (½"-thick) slice whole-grain bread, toasted

⅓ cup mashed avocado

1 tablespoon finely minced red onion

¼ teaspoon freshly cracked black pepper

⅛ teaspoon flaky sea salt

1. In a small bowl, combine tomatoes, balsamic vinegar, olive oil, and Aleppo pepper. Mix well and let stand at room temperature 30 minutes.

2. On toasted bread, spread avocado in an even layer. Top with tomatoes cut side up and sprinkle with red onion, black pepper, and salt. If any marinade remains in bowl, drizzle on top. Serve immediately.

Storing Cut Avocado

A large avocado yields about three servings. A cut avocado can be placed directly in the refrigerator uncovered for up to one day. For storage longer than a day, place plastic wrap directly against the flesh to stop it from drying out; they should keep three to four days like this. To store any longer than that, you should dice and freeze.

PER SERVING

Calories: 262

Fat: 16g

Sodium: 306mg

Carbohydrates: 24g

Fiber: 9g

Sugar: 6g

Protein: 6g

WHOLE-GRAIN PANCAKES WITH BERRY SAUCE

PREP TIME: 10 MINUTES | COOK TIME: 11 MINUTES | SERVES: 1

This recipe makes two pancakes—just the right amount for a breakfast for one person. Whole-wheat pastry flour has a fine texture that will help keep these pancakes light and fluffy while still adding fiber and other nutrients. If you don't have it, you can use equal parts regular whole-wheat flour and all-purpose flour.

INGREDIENTS

2 large strawberries, hulled and diced

¼ cup blueberries

2 tablespoons pure maple syrup

½ cup whole-wheat pastry flour

1 teaspoon baking powder

¼ teaspoon baking soda

¹⁄₁₆ teaspoon sea salt

1 large egg, beaten

¼ cup 1% milk

2 teaspoons olive oil

1 teaspoon packed light brown sugar

¼ teaspoon pure vanilla extract

1. In a 1-quart saucepan over medium-low heat, add strawberries, blueberries, and maple syrup. Cook until mixture starts to simmer and fruit is soft, about 5 minutes. Stir well, then remove from heat and set aside.

2. Preheat a nonstick griddle over medium-low heat.

3. In a medium bowl, add flour, baking powder, baking soda, and salt and whisk well to combine. Make a well in the center and add egg, milk, olive oil, brown sugar, and vanilla. Mix until just combined and only small lumps remain, about ten strokes. Let stand 3 minutes.

4. Lightly coat griddle with nonstick cooking spray or brush lightly with olive oil. Pour half of batter onto prepared griddle. Cook 2 minutes or until top of pancake is bubbling and edges look dry, then flip and cook 1–2 minutes more or until the center of pancake springs back when gently pressed. Transfer to a plate and repeat with remaining batter.

5. Serve pancakes immediately with berry sauce over top.

PER SERVING

Calories: 551
Fat: 14g
Sodium: 320mg
Carbohydrates: 89g

Fiber: 10g
Sugar: 38g
Protein: 15g

FARMER'S OMELET

PREP TIME: 10 MINUTES | COOK TIME: 8 MINUTES | SERVES: 1

 When cooking for one, you may end up with a lot of leftover vegetables in your crisper. This omelet is the perfect way to use them all up! Feel free to toss in chopped vegetables like zucchini, squash, spinach, or broccoli florets—whatever you have on hand.

INGREDIENTS

2 teaspoons olive oil, divided

¼ cup chopped yellow onion

¼ cup chopped green bell pepper

¼ cup chopped red bell pepper

3 large button mushrooms, trimmed and chopped

2 large eggs

1 teaspoon freeze-dried chives

¼ teaspoon freshly cracked black pepper

¼ cup shredded part-skim mozzarella cheese

⅛ teaspoon Aleppo pepper

1. In an 8" nonstick skillet over medium heat, add 1 teaspoon olive oil and let it heat briefly, then swirl pan to coat. Add onion, bell peppers, and mushrooms. Sauté until vegetables are soft, about 5 minutes. Transfer cooked vegetables to a bowl and set aside.

2. Carefully wipe out pan with a paper towel and return to heat. Add remaining 1 teaspoon olive oil and swirl pan to coat. In a small bowl, beat eggs with chives and black pepper until well combined. Add eggs to pan and reduce heat to low. Let pan stand 20 seconds or until eggs start to set, then use a spatula to gently push edges of eggs to the center of the pan while tilting pan so uncooked eggs move to edges, then cook about 2 minutes.

3. Once bottom of eggs are just set and top is just slightly wet, add cooked vegetables and mozzarella.

4. Remove pan from heat and fold top ⅓ of omelet down, then fold in half so toppings are folded inside eggs. Transfer to a plate and sprinkle Aleppo pepper over top. Serve immediately.

PER SERVING

Calories: 333	Fiber: 3g
Fat: 21g	Sugar: 6g
Sodium: 293mg	Protein: 21g
Carbohydrates: 13g	

RICOTTA BERRY TOAST

PREP TIME: 10 MINUTES | COOK TIME: 4 MINUTES | SERVES: 1

 Breakfast for one doesn't have to be boring or monotonous; this colorful, creamy breakfast is one that you'll look forward to eating. Use whatever berries look fresh in your produce department, or you can use chopped stone fruits like peaches, nectarines, or apricots instead.

INGREDIENTS

3 tablespoons whole-milk ricotta cheese

2 teaspoons honey, divided

¼ teaspoon freshly grated lemon zest

1 (½"-thick) slice whole-grain bread

½ teaspoon olive oil

2 tablespoons fresh blueberries

2 tablespoons diced fresh strawberries

⅛ teaspoon ground cinnamon

1. In a small bowl, add ricotta, 1 teaspoon honey, and lemon zest and use a small whisk to whip until mixture is light and fluffy, about 2 minutes. Set aside, or cover and chill overnight.

2. Heat an 8" skillet over medium heat. Brush both sides of bread with olive oil. Grill bread 2–3 minutes per side or until toasted and lightly brown. Transfer bread to a serving plate.

3. To assemble, spread whipped ricotta mixture over toast. Top with mixed berries and drizzle with remaining 1 teaspoon honey. Sprinkle with cinnamon and serve immediately.

PER SERVING

Calories: 230
Fat: 9g
Sodium: 138mg
Carbohydrates: 30g

Fiber: 3g
Sugar: 17g
Protein: 9g

BAKED EGG IN A BELL PEPPER

PREP TIME: 10 MINUTES | COOK TIME: 30 MINUTES | SERVES: 1

 The Mediterranean diet includes lot of vegetables, and here is a way to get a lot of them in at breakfast! Browning mushrooms helps to enhance their naturally meaty flavor, so don't skip this step.

INGREDIENTS

½ medium red bell pepper, seeded and sliced lengthwise

1 teaspoon olive oil

4 button mushrooms, trimmed and sliced

½ clove garlic, peeled and minced

2 tablespoons tomato sauce

1 large egg

1 tablespoon shredded Parmesan cheese

⅛ teaspoon freshly cracked black pepper

1. Preheat oven to 375°F and line a baking sheet with parchment.

2. Place pepper half cut side up on prepared baking sheet. Bake 10–12 minutes or until pepper is just tender. Remove from oven and set aside.

3. In an 8" skillet over medium heat, add olive oil and let it heat briefly. Swirl pan to coat, then add mushrooms, leaving space between each slice, and cook without stirring 3 minutes or until golden brown. Gently stir and continue cooking until mushrooms are soft, about 1 minute. Add garlic and sauté 30 seconds or until fragrant. Stir in tomato sauce and remove from heat.

4. Place mushroom mixture in pepper half, then top with egg, Parmesan, and black pepper.

5. Bake 15–18 minutes or until egg white is set and yolk is set to your preference. Cool 3 minutes before enjoying.

PER SERVING

Calories: 185
Fat: 11g
Sodium: 272mg
Carbohydrates: 11g

Fiber: 3g
Sugar: 7g
Protein: 12g

BERRY AND YOGURT SMOOTHIE

PREP TIME: 5 MINUTES | COOK TIME: 0 MINUTES | SERVES: 1

 This creamy, fruity treat is a perfect breakfast smoothie for one! Using frozen fruit is the key to this frosty smoothie. The oats and almond butter increase the satisfaction factor. Not craving berries? Frozen peaches and mangoes would be an excellent swap here.

INGREDIENTS

½ cup plain low-fat Greek yogurt

½ cup unsweetened almond milk

1 large banana, peeled and cut into 1" chunks and frozen

¾ cup frozen mixed berries

2 tablespoons rolled oats

1 tablespoon honey

1 tablespoon natural almond butter

Add ingredients to a blender in order listed. Purée until smooth, about 1 minute. Serve immediately.

Smoothie Prep

If you are a smoothie lover but not a morning person, it makes sense to prepare some smoothie packs to have stashed in the freezer. Simply measure your frozen fruits, oats, nuts, seeds, or spices into individual containers in the freezer. When you are ready for a smoothie, just add yogurt, liquid, and sweeteners to your blender, then add in your freezer pack and blend.

PER SERVING

Calories: 467	Fiber: 9g
Fat: 13g	Sugar: 47g
Sodium: 128mg	Protein: 18g
Carbohydrates: 77g	

SPANAKOPITA FRITTATA

PREP TIME: 5 MINUTES | COOK TIME: 10 MINUTES | SERVES: 1

 Traditionally, spanakopita is phyllo pastry stuffed with spinach, feta cheese, and fresh herbs and baked until crisp. This version takes the best flavors from the filling and transforms them into an elegant personal-sized frittata. If you prefer, you can swap out the feta for shredded mozzarella or goat cheese.

INGREDIENTS

1 teaspoon olive oil

¼ cup diced yellow onion

1 clove garlic, peeled and minced

1½ cups loosely packed baby spinach, chopped

¼ cup chopped fresh parsley

¼ cup crumbled feta cheese

1 teaspoon dried dill

2 large eggs, beaten

¼ teaspoon freshly cracked black pepper

⅛ teaspoon ground nutmeg

1. Preheat broiler.

2. In an 8" ovenproof skillet over medium heat, add olive oil and let it heat briefly. Swirl pan to coat, then add onion. Cook until onion starts to soften, about 3 minutes. Add garlic and spinach and cook, stirring often, until spinach wilts, about 1 minute.

3. Stir in parsley, feta, and dill and spread mixture into an even layer. Add eggs and gently swirl pan to ensure eggs form an even layer, then sprinkle black pepper and nutmeg over top. Reduce heat to medium-low and cook 3–4 minutes or until bottom of eggs are just set.

4. Transfer pan to oven and broil 3–5 minutes or until top of frittata is set and lightly browned. Remove from oven and cool 3 minutes before serving.

PER SERVING

Calories: 320

Fat: 21g

Sodium: 531mg

Carbohydrates: 11g

Fiber: 3g

Sugar: 4g

Protein: 21g

EGGS FLORENTINE WITH GREEK YOGURT HOLLANDAISE

PREP TIME: 15 MINUTES | COOK TIME: 13 MINUTES | SERVES: 1

 Eggs Florentine is usually served with a butter-based hollandaise sauce that is high in saturated fat, but this version calls for tangy Greek yogurt instead. This sauce can also be used to top grilled or roasted vegetables, or as a dipping sauce for steamed or sautéed shrimp and seafood.

INGREDIENTS

6 cups water

1 teaspoon white vinegar

2 large eggs

1 whole-wheat English muffin

2 teaspoons extra-virgin olive oil, divided

¼ cup plain low-fat Greek yogurt

½ teaspoon lemon juice

½ teaspoon prepared yellow mustard

1 tablespoon chopped fresh chives

1 cup loosely packed baby spinach

4 medium cherry tomatoes, sliced in half

⅛ teaspoon freshly cracked black pepper

1⁄16 teaspoon sea salt

1. In a 2-quart saucepan, add water, making sure to not fill the pot more than ⅔ full. Heat over medium heat until water has small bubbles floating to the top, about 4 minutes. Add vinegar and stir well.

2. Crack eggs one at a time into a heatproof cup. Gently drop eggs into simmering water by placing cup just over top of water and gently tipping cup so egg slides out. (The cup should be heatproof as it will likely touch the simmering water.) Cook 3–4 minutes or until eggs are cooked to your liking. Remove eggs with a slotted spoon, transfer to a plate, and gently pat dry with a paper towel. Set aside.

3. While eggs poach in the pot, heat an 8" skillet over medium heat. Split English muffin with a fork and brush each split side with ½ teaspoon olive oil, then lay oiled sides down in skillet and cook until toasted, about 2–3 minutes. Transfer to a serving plate and set aside.

4. In a small microwave-safe bowl, add Greek yogurt, lemon juice, mustard, and chives. Stir to combine, then microwave on high for 15 seconds. Stir well, then heat in 10-second intervals until sauce is warm, making sure not to let the mixture boil. Cover with foil and set aside.

5. To the same skillet muffin was toasted in over medium heat, add remaining 1 teaspoon olive oil. Add spinach and cook until wilted, about 1 minute. Add tomatoes and cook until tomatoes are softened, about 1 minute more.

6. Divide spinach and tomato mixture between toasted muffin halves. Top each muffin with a poached egg. Stir sauce, then spoon over eggs. Sprinkle tops with black pepper and salt. Serve immediately.

Poaching Eggs in Advance

Fresh eggs can be poached up to three days ahead. Poach your eggs as directed in the recipe but reduce the cooking time by 1 minute. Transfer eggs to ice water to stop cooking. Once they're chilled, about 5 minutes, place eggs in a resealable container filled with fresh water and refrigerate. To serve, place eggs in a hot water bath for 2–3 minutes.

PER SERVING

Calories: 416	Fiber: 6g
Fat: 20g	Sugar: 10g
Sodium: 705mg	Protein: 26g
Carbohydrates: 34g	

BLUEBERRY ALMOND BUTTER SMOOTHIE BOWL

PREP TIME: 5 MINUTES | COOK TIME: 0 MINUTES | SERVES: 1

 Smoothie bowls are a good way to enjoy a breakfast for one—and choosing the toppings is the fun part! This recipe uses fresh blueberries, almonds, and coconut, but you can also add chia, hemp, or other seeds, fresh fruits, granola, or a little bit of chocolate.

INGREDIENTS

1 large banana, peeled, cut into 1" chunks, and frozen

1 cup frozen blueberries

½ cup packed baby spinach

½ cup plain low-fat Greek yogurt

½ cup unsweetened almond milk

2 tablespoons natural almond butter

1 tablespoon honey

¼ cup fresh blueberries

2 tablespoons chopped unsalted roasted almonds

1 tablespoon unsweetened shredded coconut

1. Combine banana, frozen blueberries, spinach, yogurt, almond milk, almond butter, and honey in a blender. Purée until smooth, about 1 minute. Pour mixture into a serving bowl.

2. Top smoothie mixture with fresh blueberries, almonds, and coconut. Serve immediately.

PER SERVING

Calories: 676
Fat: 30g
Sodium: 140mg
Carbohydrates: 90g

Fiber: 15g
Sugar: 56g
Protein: 24g

CHAPTER 3
DIPS AND SNACKS

Spiced Pita Chips 34
White Bean Dip with Garlic
    and Herbs................................ 35
Pinto Bean Dip with Cilantro,
    Cumin, and Lime......................36
Tzatziki Sauce.................................... 37
Baba Ghanoush..................................39
Fresh Tomato Salsa
    (Pico de Gallo) 40
Olive Spread 41
Garlicky Lentil Dip 42
Seasoned Mixed Nuts 43
Mediterranean Deviled Egg.................. 44
Muhammara (Roasted Red
    Pepper Spread)........................46
Baked Vegetable Chips.......................47
Date Nut Energy Bites 48
Mediterranean-Style
    Avocado Dip 49
Veggie Lover's Pita Pizza Bites 51
Crispy Seasoned Chickpeas...................52
Smoked Salmon Spread......................53

It's 3 p.m., your stomach is starting to growl and your brain is getting a little fuzzy. What do you do? Grab a snack, of course! Smart snacking is an excellent way to curb hunger and maintain energy throughout your day. The right snacks can be satisfying and nourishing, and with a little planning, you can have some perfectly portioned snacks ready when you need them most. Snacks should feel special; they should bring you joy and satisfaction as well as provide you with a boost of energy and nutrition.

In this chapter you will find a variety of single-serving snack and dip options sure to satisfy almost any craving. These are snacks perfect for beating the midday slump, enjoying while watching your favorite movie or television show, or savoring while on the go. For those crunchy snack cravings make some Crispy Seasoned Chickpeas or Spiced Pita Chips. Whip up some Garlicky Lentil Dip or Tzatziki Sauce to enjoy with crisp carrots and slices of cucumber. Want some quick energy? Date Nut Energy Bites and Seasoned Mixed Nuts have you covered. So enjoy your snacks knowing they are packed with good-for-you ingredients and portioned just for you!

SPICED PITA CHIPS

PREP TIME: 5 MINUTES | COOK TIME: 15 MINUTES | SERVES: 1

 These small-batch pita chips can be made up to three days ahead and kept in an airtight container. These are wonderful on their own, but can be dipped into any of the dip recipes featured in this chapter.

INGREDIENTS

1 teaspoon olive oil

⅛ teaspoon sea salt

⅛ teaspoon ground cumin

⅛ teaspoon garlic powder

⅛ teaspoon onion powder

1 (2-ounce) whole-wheat pita, cut into 8 wedges

1. Preheat oven to 350°F and line a baking sheet with parchment or a silicone baking mat.

2. In a medium bowl, add olive oil, salt, cumin, garlic powder, and onion powder. Whisk to combine, then add pita pieces and toss until evenly coated.

3. Spread pita wedges on prepared baking sheet. Bake 15–18 minutes, tossing pita wedges every 5 minutes, until pita is golden brown and crisp. Cool to room temperature before serving.

PER SERVING

Calories: 192

Fat: 5g

Sodium: 446mg

Carbohydrates: 32g

Fiber: 4g

Sugar: 0g

Protein: 6g

WHITE BEAN DIP WITH GARLIC AND HERBS

PREP TIME: 5 MINUTES | COOK TIME: 1 MINUTE | SERVES: 1

 White beans have a mild, earthy flavor and are a lovely canvas for other flavors like garlic and herbs. This dip for one is perfect with crisp vegetables, but can also be used with pita chips and whole-grain crackers, or as a spread for wraps.

INGREDIENTS

1 teaspoon olive oil

½ clove garlic, peeled and finely minced

⅓ cup canned cannellini beans, rinsed and drained

1 tablespoon chopped fresh parsley

½ teaspoon chopped fresh rosemary

⅛ teaspoon dried oregano

⅛ teaspoon sea salt

⅛ teaspoon freshly cracked black pepper

1. In an 8" skillet over medium heat, add olive oil and let it heat briefly, then swirl pan to coat. Add garlic and cook 30–45 seconds or until very fragrant. Remove pan from heat and transfer garlic and oil to a small bowl.

2. Add beans to bowl and gently mash with a fork. Add parsley, rosemary, oregano, and salt and mix well to combine. Smooth top and garnish with black pepper. Serve chilled or at room temperature.

Canned Beans

Canned beans are a convenience food that should be in the pantry of anyone pursuing a Mediterranean diet. Beans are an excellent source of plant-based protein, fiber, and other nutrients. The ingredients should be only beans, water, and salt and three and a half ½-cup servings per can.

PER SERVING

Calories: 95

Fat: 4g

Sodium: 350mg

Carbohydrates: 13g

Fiber: 5g

Sugar: 0g

Protein: 4g

PINTO BEAN DIP WITH CILANTRO, CUMIN, AND LIME

PREP TIME: 5 MINUTES | COOK TIME: 2 MINUTES | SERVES: 1

 This creamy dip has a sharp yet earthy flavor that pairs well with celery sticks, whole-grain crackers, or baked tortilla chips. Beans make a tasty and filling snack since they are packed with protein and fiber.

INGREDIENTS

1 teaspoon olive oil

½ clove garlic, peeled and finely minced

1 tablespoon minced yellow onion

⅓ cup canned pinto beans, rinsed and drained

2 teaspoons lime juice

1 tablespoon chopped fresh cilantro

¼ teaspoon ground cumin

⅛ teaspoon sea salt

⅛ teaspoon freshly cracked black pepper

1. In an 8" skillet over medium heat, add olive oil and let it heat briefly, then swirl pan to coat. Add garlic and onion and cook 30–45 seconds or until very fragrant. Reduce heat to low.

2. Add beans to pan and gently mash with back of a wooden spoon or spatula until mostly smooth. Add remaining ingredients and cook, mashing continually, 30 seconds or until beans are very hot and fragrant. Transfer dip to a serving bowl. Serve warm or at room temperature.

PER SERVING

Calories: 114   Fiber: 1g

Fat: 5g   Sugar: 1g

Sodium: 315mg   Protein: 4g

Carbohydrates: 14g

TZATZIKI SAUCE

PREP TIME: 3 HOURS 5 MINUTES | COOK TIME: 0 MINUTES | SERVES: 1

This refreshing dill and cucumber sauce is lovely with vegetables and pita for dipping, but you can also use it as a sauce for roasted fish or as a spread inside whole-grain pita stuffed with chopped crisp lettuce, fresh tomato, and either roasted chicken breast or chickpeas.

INGREDIENTS

6 ounces plain low-fat Greek yogurt

¼ cup grated English cucumber

½ teaspoon grated fresh garlic

1 teaspoon lemon juice

1 teaspoon extra-virgin olive oil

2 teaspoons freeze-dried or dried dill

⅛ teaspoon sea salt

1. Set a strainer over a bowl and line strainer with cheesecloth or two coffee filters. Add yogurt, cover, and refrigerate 2 hours to strain off excess liquid.

2. Place grated cucumber into a lint-free kitchen towel or a few layers of paper towels and squeeze out any excess liquid. Transfer cucumber to a medium bowl and add strained yogurt and remaining ingredients. Mix until smooth. Cover and refrigerate 1 hour before serving.

Strained Yogurt Cheese
Using the same method used in this recipe, you can also make strained yogurt cheese. Set a strainer over a bowl and line the strainer with cheesecloth or two coffee filters. Place 1 cup plain low-fat Greek yogurt into strainer, cover, and chill 8 hours or up to three days depending on the thickness you prefer. Once the yogurt is strained, flavor with herbs and garlic, or a little honey and citrus zest. This will make two servings.

PER SERVING

Calories: 177
Fat: 8g
Sodium: 255mg
Carbohydrates: 10g

Fiber: 0g
Sugar: 7g
Protein: 18g

BABA GHANOUSH

PREP TIME: 10 MINUTES | COOK TIME: 20 MINUTES | SERVES: 1

 Baba ghanoush is made with antioxidant rich eggplant and tahini, which is used to add creaminess to the dip. If you do not have any on hand, you can use plain low-fat Greek yogurt in its place along with an extra ½ teaspoon olive oil for richness.

INGREDIENTS

1 small (about ¾-pound) Italian eggplant

1 tablespoon tahini

2 teaspoons lemon juice

2 teaspoons extra-virgin olive oil

1 clove garlic, peeled and minced

⅛ teaspoon Aleppo pepper

⅛ teaspoon ground cumin

⅛ teaspoon sea salt

⅛ teaspoon freshly cracked black pepper

1. Preheat broiler and line a baking sheet with foil.

2. Place eggplant on prepared baking sheet and prick eggplant three to four times with a fork, then place baking sheet under broiler. Broil 6–8 minutes per side, then rotate eggplant and continue to broil until all sides are charred and eggplant flesh is soft when pierced with a fork, about 20–25 minutes total. Remove from oven, cover eggplant with a layer of foil, and let cool to room temperature.

3. Cut cooled eggplant in half lengthwise. Scoop flesh, discarding skin, into a strainer and gently press flesh with the back of a spoon to remove excess liquid.

4. Place drained eggplant flesh in a medium bowl and add remaining ingredients. Stir with a fork until mixture is creamy. Transfer to a serving bowl and enjoy at room temperature, or cover and refrigerate up to three days. Serve chilled or at room temperature.

PER SERVING

Calories: 256

Fat: 16g

Sodium: 212mg

Carbohydrates: 26g

Fiber: 12g

Sugar: 12g

Protein: 6g

FRESH TOMATO SALSA (PICO DE GALLO)

PREP TIME: 1 HOUR 5 MINUTES | COOK TIME: 0 MINUTES | SERVES: 1

 Salsa recipes typically yield large amounts. But this recipe will make the perfect amount for you to enjoy on your own without a lot of waste. This chunky fresh salsa is best if you can let it stand at room temperature 1–2 hours so the flavors have time to meld together.

INGREDIENTS

1 large ripe plum tomato, stem and seeds removed, chopped (about ½ cup)

1 tablespoon minced red onion

1 teaspoon minced fresh serrano pepper

1 tablespoon chopped fresh cilantro

2 teaspoons lime juice

⅛ teaspoon ground cumin

⅛ teaspoon sea salt

Combine all ingredients in a small bowl. Cover and let stand at room temperature at least 1 hour before serving.

Freezing Fresh Herbs
Instead of tossing out unused fresh herbs, freeze them! Chop herbs finely and put them into an ice cube tray. Add enough water to just cover and freeze solid. You can toss the herb cubes directly into soups and stews, or thaw the herbs, discarding the water, before adding to your recipe.

PER SERVING

Calories: 23
Fat: 0g
Sodium: 199mg
Carbohydrates: 6g

Fiber: 2g
Sugar: 3g
Protein: 1g

OLIVE SPREAD

PREP TIME: 1 HOUR 5 MINUTES | COOK TIME: 0 MINUTES | SERVES: 1

 Jarred olive tapenade is perfect when you are cooking for one because it saves you from having to buy three or more kinds of olives for this dish. This Olive Spread can be used on sandwiches, as a marinade along with olive oil and lemon zest for fish, or in pasta along with olive oil and a little Parmesan cheese for a burst of salty flavor.

INGREDIENTS

¼ cup plain low-fat Greek yogurt

2 tablespoons jarred olive tapenade

1 tablespoon finely chopped green onion (green part only)

1 tablespoon pimentos, rinsed and drained

1 tablespoon chopped fresh parsley

½ teaspoon fresh lemon juice

⅛ teaspoon freshly cracked black pepper

Combine all ingredients in a small bowl. Mix well, then cover and refrigerate 1 hour before serving.

PER SERVING

Calories: 126   Fiber: 3g
Fat: 9g   Sugar: 3g
Sodium: 281mg   Protein: 6g
Carbohydrates: 6g

GARLICKY LENTIL DIP

PREP TIME: 5 MINUTES | COOK TIME: 0 MINUTES | SERVES: 1

 Lentils are rich in fiber, which can help lower cholesterol and keep you full longer. If you don't want to break out the food processor, you can leave this dip chunky by mashing the lentils and roasted red pepper with a fork. This dip is exceptionally good with sliced cucumber and red bell pepper slices for dipping.

INGREDIENTS

¼ cup canned lentils, rinsed and drained

2 tablespoons chopped jarred roasted red pepper

2 teaspoons tahini

½ teaspoon freshly grated garlic

2 teaspoons lemon juice

⅛ teaspoon ground cumin

⅛ teaspoon onion powder

1 teaspoon extra-virgin olive oil

⅛ teaspoon smoked paprika

1. In a food processor or blender, add lentils, roasted red pepper, tahini, garlic, and lemon juice. Pulse until mixture is smooth, about eight to ten pulses. If mixture is too thick, add warm water 1 teaspoon at a time until mixture loosens.

2. Add cumin and onion powder and pulse two to three times to mix. Transfer mixture to a serving bowl. Drizzle top with olive oil and sprinkle with paprika. Serve immediately, or cover and refrigerate for up to three days. Serve at room temperature.

PER SERVING

Calories: 185   Fiber: 4g
Fat: 9g   Sugar: 0g
Sodium: 399mg   Protein: 5g
Carbohydrates: 21g

SEASONED MIXED NUTS

PREP TIME: 5 MINUTES | COOK TIME: 10 MINUTES | SERVES: 1

 To buy nuts in a smaller quantity or make your own custom mix of nuts, buy raw nuts in your natural food store in the bulk section. Raw nuts keep for up to three months at room temperature or up to a year in the freezer.

INGREDIENTS

¼ teaspoon Italian seasoning

⅛ teaspoon smoked paprika

⅛ teaspoon garlic powder

⅛ teaspoon freshly cracked black pepper

½ teaspoon olive oil

¼ teaspoon honey

¼ cup unsalted raw mixed nuts

1. Preheat oven to 325°F and line a small baking sheet with parchment or a silicone baking mat.

2. In a small bowl, combine Italian seasoning, paprika, garlic powder, and black pepper. With the back of a spoon crush spices until they form a chunky powder. Add olive oil, honey, and nuts. Toss to evenly coat.

3. Spread nuts on prepared baking sheet and bake 10–12 minutes, stirring nuts every 3 minutes, until nuts are warm and spices are toasted. Serve warm.

PER SERVING

Calories: 228

Fat: 19g

Sodium: 4mg

Carbohydrates: 11g

Fiber: 3g

Sugar: 1g

Protein: 6g

MEDITERRANEAN DEVILED EGG

PREP TIME: 1 HOUR 5 MINUTES | COOK TIME: 0 MINUTES | SERVES: 1

 You don't have to boil a whole dozen to enjoy deviled eggs—you can easily make a perfectly portioned snack for yourself with just one egg! If you have olives on hand, you can add 1 teaspoon minced olives to the filling for these eggs. If you do not have olive oil mayonnaise, you can use plain low-fat Greek yogurt instead.

INGREDIENTS

1 large hard-boiled egg, sliced in half

1 teaspoon olive oil mayonnaise

¼ teaspoon Dijon mustard

¼ teaspoon freeze-dried or dried dill

⅛ teaspoon freshly cracked black pepper

1. In a small bowl, add yolk from hard-boiled egg, mayonnaise, and mustard. Mash with a fork until yolk mixture is smooth.

2. Stir in dill and spoon mixture back into egg white halves. Sprinkle black pepper over top. Chill 1 hour before enjoying.

PER SERVING

Calories: 95
Fat: 6g
Sodium: 128mg
Carbohydrates: 1g
Fiber: 0g
Sugar: 1g
Protein: 6g

MUHAMMARA (ROASTED RED PEPPER SPREAD)

PREP TIME: 10 MINUTES | COOK TIME: 5 MINUTES | SERVES: 1

Muhammara is a boldly colored and flavored red pepper and walnut spread from Syria, but also enjoyed in Turkey and across the Mediterranean. It is wonderful on warm pita or with fresh vegetables. Traditionally, this dish is made with pomegranate molasses; if you happen to have that ingredient, feel free to use it instead of the honey in this recipe.

INGREDIENTS

1 teaspoon extra-virgin olive oil

¼ cup unsalted dry roasted walnuts

1 clove garlic, peeled and lightly crushed

½ cup chopped jarred roasted red peppers

1 teaspoon tahini

½ teaspoon lemon juice

½ teaspoon Aleppo pepper

1 teaspoon honey

1 teaspoon tomato paste

⅛ teaspoon smoked paprika

1. In an 8" skillet over medium heat, add olive oil, walnuts, and garlic. Cook, stirring constantly, until nuts are toasted and garlic is lightly brown and fragrant, about 5 minutes. Remove pan from heat and cool walnut mixture to room temperature.

2. Add walnut mixture to a food processor, making sure to scrape in any olive oil in pan, and add remaining ingredients. Pulse ten times, then scrape bowl with a spatula and pulse another five to eight times or until mixture forms a thick paste. Transfer to a bowl and serve.

PER SERVING

Calories: 309	Fiber: 4g
Fat: 26g	Sugar: 9g
Sodium: 84mg	Protein: 7g
Carbohydrates: 17g	

BAKED VEGETABLE CHIPS

PREP TIME: 35 MINUTES | COOK TIME: 55 MINUTES | SERVES: 1

 Vegetable chips are a heathy choice for when you have a crispy chip craving, adding more nutrition to your snack. These are great with some of the creamy dips in this chapter like Baba Ghanoush, White Bean Dip with Garlic and Herbs, or Fresh Tomato Salsa (Pico de Gallo). This recipe works well with yellow squash and beets too.

INGREDIENTS

2 medium zucchini, sliced into ⅛"-thick rounds

1 teaspoon sea salt

1 tablespoon olive oil

1. Preheat oven to 250°F and line a baking sheet with parchment or a silicone baking mat.

2. Place a colander in a medium bowl, then place vegetable slices in colander and sprinkle with salt, gently tossing to evenly distribute salt. Let stand 30 minutes to draw off excess moisture. Rinse vegetables under cool water and then with a paper towel or a lint-free kitchen towel, dry vegetable slices and transfer to a medium bowl. Add olive oil and toss to evenly coat.

3. Lay vegetable slices on prepared baking sheet in a single layer. Bake 40 minutes, then rotate pan and bake an additional 15–20 minutes or until chips are crisp and browned. If any chips are crisp or are starting to darken ahead of time, remove them and resume baking. Cool chips completely before enjoying.

What about Root Vegetable Chips?

For vegetables with lower water content, you can skip the salting step. Coat ⅛"-thick slices in olive oil, sprinkle with ¼ teaspoon sea salt, and bake 30 minutes or until crisp, rotating pan after 15 minutes. For a single serving of chips, use one large sweet potato, rutabaga, turnip, or taro.

PER SERVING

Calories: 185

Fat: 14g

Sodium: 187mg

Carbohydrates: 12g

Fiber: 4g

Sugar: 10g

Protein: 5g

DATE NUT ENERGY BITES

PREP TIME: 15 MINUTES | COOK TIME: 0 MINUTES | SERVES: 1

 These energy bites are perfect when you want to make yourself a simple, quick snack. Soaking the dates in hot water before chopping will make them softer and easier to form into a paste. If walnuts aren't to your liking, you could also use pecans or almonds in this recipe.

INGREDIENTS

4 pitted dates

¼ cup hot water

1 tablespoon rolled oats

1 tablespoon natural almond butter

⅛ teaspoon ground cinnamon

1 tablespoon chopped unsalted dry roasted walnuts

2 tablespoons unsweetened flaked coconut

1. In a small bowl, add dates and hot water. Let stand 10 minutes, then drain and pat dates to dry.

2. Finely chop dates until they form a rough paste. Transfer to a small bowl and add oats, almond butter, cinnamon, and walnuts. Mix to combine.

3. Dampen hands with water and form mixture into three equal balls. Roll balls in coconut. Enjoy immediately or refrigerate until ready to eat.

PER SERVING

Calories: 306	Fiber: 7g
Fat: 19g	Sugar: 19g
Sodium: 0mg	Protein: 6g
Carbohydrates: 33g	

MEDITERRANEAN-STYLE AVOCADO DIP

PREP TIME: 5 MINUTES | COOK TIME: 0 MINUTES | SERVES: 1

 While avocados are not a traditional part of the Mediterranean diet, they are certainly a welcome addition since they are full of healthy fats, fiber, and oleic acid, which has been shown to reduce inflammation and may lower cholesterol. Enjoy this dip with warm, soft pita or baked chips for a satisfying snack.

INGREDIENTS

½ cup chopped ripe avocado

¼ cup diced Roma tomato

2 tablespoons minced red onion

2 tablespoons crumbled feta cheese, divided

½ teaspoon lime juice

¼ teaspoon ground cumin

⅛ teaspoon dried oregano

½ teaspoon extra-virgin olive oil

1. In a small bowl, add avocado and mash with a fork. Add tomato, red onion, 1 tablespoon feta, lime juice, cumin, and oregano and fold to mix.

2. Top with remaining 1 tablespoon feta and drizzle with olive oil. Serve immediately, or cover and chill up to one day. Serve chilled or at room temperature.

PER SERVING

Calories: 278

Fat: 22g

Sodium: 183mg

Carbohydrates: 15g

Fiber: 9g

Sugar: 3g

Protein: 6g

VEGGIE LOVER'S PITA PIZZA BITES

PREP TIME: 10 MINUTES | COOK TIME: 11 MINUTES | SERVES: 1

 Pizza is delicious but often covered in unhealthy sodium- and saturated fat–laden toppings. These pita pizza bites covered in fresh, healthy vegetables make a wonderful snack for one anytime a pizza craving strikes.

INGREDIENTS

4 (2½") whole-wheat pita (or 1 (8") whole-wheat pita cut into 4 wedges)

2 teaspoons tomato paste

1 tablespoon water

⅛ teaspoon Italian seasoning

2 tablespoons part-skim mozzarella cheese

1 tablespoon minced red onion

1 tablespoon finely chopped red bell pepper

1 tablespoon chopped black olives

2 medium cherry tomatoes, chopped

1 Preheat oven to 400°F and line a small baking sheet with parchment.

2 Place pita bread on prepared baking sheet and bake 3 minutes or until warm.

3 While pita bakes, in a small bowl, mix tomato paste with water until smooth. Add in Italian seasoning and mix well.

4 Once pita has baked, remove it from oven. Spread tomato paste mixture over tops, then divide remaining ingredients over pitas. Return to oven and bake 8–10 minutes or until cheese is melted and pizzas are bubbling. Cool 1 minute before enjoying.

PER SERVING

Calories: 368

Fat: 6g

Sodium: 726mg

Carbohydrates: 68g

Fiber: 10g

Sugar: 4g

Protein: 15g

CRISPY SEASONED CHICKPEAS

PREP TIME: 5 MINUTES | COOK TIME: 25 MINUTES | SERVES: 1

 Crispy chickpeas are a healthy snack to reach for to crush those crunchy snack cravings. You can use almost any seasoning blend you like, so if you have a particular seasoning you prefer, just swap in a slightly heaped ¼ teaspoonful in place of the seasonings listed here.

INGREDIENTS

½ cup canned chickpeas, rinsed, drained, and patted dry

1 teaspoon extra-virgin olive oil

⅛ teaspoon ground cumin

⅛ teaspoon smoked paprika

⅛ teaspoon freshly cracked black pepper

⅛ teaspoon sea salt

1. Preheat oven to 425°F and line a medium baking sheet with parchment.

2. In a small bowl, add chickpeas and olive oil. Toss to coat, then add cumin, paprika, black pepper, and salt. Toss until chickpeas are evenly coated in spices.

3. Spread chickpeas in an even layer on prepared baking sheet. Roast 25–30 minutes, shaking tray every 10 minutes to ensure even cooking, until chickpeas are brown and crispy.

4. Cool chickpeas completely on pan, about 20 minutes, before enjoying.

Storing Chickpeas

Leftover chickpeas can be drained, dried, and stored in an airtight container for up to three days in the refrigerator. For longer storage, they can be frozen up to six months. Chickpeas can be used in many types of recipes, including soups, salads, dips, and smoothies.

PER SERVING

Calories: 144

Fat: 6g

Sodium: 356mg

Carbohydrates: 18g

Fiber: 5g

Sugar: 3g

Protein: 5g

SMOKED SALMON SPREAD

PREP TIME: 1 HOUR 10 MINUTES | COOK TIME: 0 MINUTES | SERVES: 1

 Whether spread on a toasted whole-grain bagel, dolloped onto cucumber slices, or enjoyed with your favorite crackers, this Smoked Salmon Spread will make your snack time for one feel sophisticated. You can use either hot or cold smoked salmon for this recipe.

INGREDIENTS

1 ounce smoked salmon, finely chopped (about 3 tablespoons)

2 tablespoons plain low-fat Greek yogurt

1 tablespoon finely chopped red bell pepper

¼ teaspoon freshly grated lemon zest

½ teaspoon fresh lemon juice

2 teaspoons chopped fresh chives

1 teaspoon freeze-dried dill

⅛ teaspoon freshly cracked black pepper

1. In a small bowl, add salmon and yogurt. Stir gently to mix, then add bell pepper, lemon zest, lemon juice, chives, and dill. Stir well to combine.

2. Cover and refrigerate 1 hour or up to three days. To serve, garnish with black pepper.

Smoked Salmon
Smoked salmon is great to keep on hand to add protein and healthy fat to your meals. Cold smoked salmon is brined and then exposed to smoke no hotter than 80°F up to 15 hours. Hot smoked salmon is cooked at around 140°F 2–3 hours and has a flaky texture when cut.

PER SERVING

Calories: 58
Fat: 2g
Sodium: 201mg
Carbohydrates: 3g

Fiber: 1g
Sugar: 2g
Protein: 8g

CHAPTER 4
SALADS AND SOUPS

Brown Rice Salad with Zucchini
and Tomato 55
Wild Rice and Mushroom Soup............. 56
Brown Rice and Chickpea Salad........... 57
Fruit and Nut Brown Rice Salad 58
Brown Rice Bowl with Fried
Halloumi and Mint Dressing 60
Farro Salad with Tomatoes
and Olives 61
Potato and Spinach Soup....................... 62
Three-Bean Salad 63
Italian Mixed Green Salad...................... 65
Roasted Carrot Tahini Bisque................ 66
Israeli Couscous with Red Pepper
and Goat Cheese 67
Mushroom Barley Soup 68
Vegetable Barley Soup 69
Tomato Basil Soup 70
Mediterranean Couscous Salad............. 72
Minestrone Soup 73
Vegan Avgolemono................................. 74

Soups and salads are popular lunch and dinner fare because they are filling, offer a wide variety of flavors, and can usually be made ahead of time. Many salad and soup recipes make eight to twelve servings, and if you are cooking for one that means a lot of monotony. Here you will find a wide variety of soups and salads that are portioned for one so you can enjoy more variety in your diet!

In this chapter you will find recipes for well-balanced, filling soups and hearty salads that you can prepare a few days ahead of time. You can add these to your lunch bag, or enjoy these on a busy night when you do not want to cook. If you want something fresh and hearty, look no further than Brown Rice Salad with Zucchini and Tomato or Three-Bean Salad. Sophisticated soup offerings include Vegan Avgolemono (Greek Lemon Chicken Soup) and Roasted Carrot Tahini Bisque. No matter what you pick, you will never be bored with soups and salads made for one!

BROWN RICE SALAD WITH ZUCCHINI AND TOMATO

PREP TIME: 25 MINUTES | COOK TIME: 40 MINUTES | SERVES: 1

 Brown rice is slightly chewy and gives this salad a hearty, satisfying texture and nutty flavor. You can use instant brown rice if you plan to enjoy it the same day, but if you are preparing it in advance you will want to use regular brown rice.

INGREDIENTS

¼ cup medium-grain brown rice, rinsed and drained

½ cup water

1 teaspoon olive oil

⅛ teaspoon sea salt

1 medium plum tomato, stem and seeds removed, chopped

½ medium zucchini, chopped

2 tablespoons diced red onion

2 teaspoons balsamic vinegar

2 teaspoons extra-virgin olive oil

½ teaspoon Dijon mustard

¼ teaspoon Italian seasoning

1. In a 1-quart saucepan with a lid, add rice, water, olive oil, and salt. Cover pot and place over medium heat until mixture comes to a boil. Reduce heat to low and cook 30–35 minutes or until liquid is fully absorbed and rice is tender. Remove pot from heat and let stand covered 10 minutes, then uncover and fluff rice. Transfer rice to a medium bowl and cool to room temperature, about 20 minutes.

2. To cooled rice add remaining ingredients and toss gently to evenly coat. Enjoy immediately, or cover and refrigerate up to five days.

Brown Rice versus White Rice
Brown rice is an easy and tasty choice if you want to add whole grains to your diet. Brown rice has not had the bran or germ removed, so it has more fiber and is a whole grain. White rice is just the starchy inside, which is the least nutritious part.

PER SERVING

Calories: 335
Fat: 15g
Sodium: 269mg
Carbohydrates: 45g

Fiber: 3g
Sugar: 6g
Protein: 6g

WILD RICE AND MUSHROOM SOUP

PREP TIME: 10 MINUTES | COOK TIME: 39 MINUTES | SERVES: 1

 Despite its name, wild rice is actually the seed of a variety of grass that grows near lakes and streams. The flavor is grassy and earthy, and the texture is slightly chewy. It is a healthy choice on the Mediterranean diet because it is high in protein, fiber, and lysine, which is good for collagen production.

INGREDIENTS

2 teaspoons olive oil

2 tablespoons minced yellow onion

½ small carrot, peeled and minced

½ medium stalk celery, minced

½ cup chopped button mushrooms

½ clove garlic, peeled and minced

1⅓ cups low-sodium vegetable broth

3 tablespoons wild rice

½ bay leaf

¼ teaspoon dried oregano

¼ teaspoon dried fennel

1 tablespoon tahini

⅛ teaspoon sea salt

⅛ teaspoon freshly cracked black pepper

1. In a 2-quart saucepan over medium heat, add olive oil and swirl pan to coat. Once oil is hot, add onion, carrot, and celery. Sauté until tender, about 5 minutes. Add mushrooms and cook until mushrooms are soft, about 3 minutes. Add garlic and cook until fragrant, about 30 seconds.

2. Stir in broth, scraping any bits from bottom of pot. Add rice, bay leaf, oregano, and fennel and stir well. Bring soup to a boil, then cover pot with a lid, reduce heat to low, and cook until rice is tender, about 30 minutes.

3. Once rice is cooked, remove lid and discard bay leaf. Stir in tahini, salt, and black pepper. Serve immediately, or cover and refrigerate up to three days.

PER SERVING

Calories: 328
Fat: 16g
Sodium: 428mg
Carbohydrates: 39g

Fiber: 7g
Sugar: 8g
Protein: 10g

BROWN RICE AND CHICKPEA SALAD

PREP TIME: 25 MINUTES | COOK TIME: 40 MINUTES | SERVES: 1

 Chickpeas are a versatile and popular ingredient in the Mediterranean where you find it blended into dips and sauces, or tossed into soups and salads to add protein and fiber. This salad combines chickpeas and nutty brown rice for a filling and nutrition-packed meal.

INGREDIENTS

¼ cup medium-grain brown rice, rinsed and drained

½ cup low-sodium vegetable broth

1 teaspoon olive oil

⅛ teaspoon sea salt

⅛ teaspoon saffron threads

¼ cup canned chickpeas, rinsed and drained

2 tablespoons golden raisins

2 tablespoons grated carrot

2 tablespoons finely chopped green bell pepper

1 tablespoon finely minced red onion

1 tablespoon finely chopped cilantro

2 teaspoons extra-virgin olive oil

2 teaspoons lemon juice

1. In a 1-quart saucepan with a lid, add rice, broth, olive oil, salt, and saffron. Cover pot and place over medium heat until mixture comes to a boil. Reduce heat to low and cook 30–35 minutes or until liquid is fully absorbed and rice is tender. Remove pot from heat and let stand covered 10 minutes, then uncover and fluff rice and transfer to a medium bowl and cool to room temperature, about 20 minutes.

2. To cooled rice add remaining ingredients and toss gently to evenly coat. Enjoy immediately, or cover and refrigerate up to five days. Serve at room temperature.

PER SERVING

Calories: 431

Fat: 15g

Sodium: 357mg

Carbohydrates: 69g

Fiber: 6g

Sugar: 18g

Protein: 8g

FRUIT AND NUT BROWN RICE SALAD

PREP TIME: 25 MINUTES | COOK TIME: 40 MINUTES | SERVES: 1

 Rice is a staple of the Mediterranean diet. When buying rice, pick brown rice. It retains more nutrients, phenols, flavonoids, and antioxidants because the bran and germ are not removed.

INGREDIENTS

¼ cup medium-grain brown rice, rinsed and drained

½ cup water

1 teaspoon olive oil

⅛ teaspoon sea salt

3 tablespoons chopped green onion (green part only)

1 dried fig, chopped

1 dried apricot, chopped

1 pitted date, chopped

2 tablespoons chopped toasted walnuts

2 teaspoons extra-virgin olive oil

2 teaspoons fresh orange juice

1. In a 1-quart saucepan with a lid, add rice, water, olive oil, and salt. Cover pot and place over medium heat until mixture comes to a boil. Reduce heat to low and cook 30–35 minutes or until liquid is fully absorbed and rice is tender. Remove pot from heat and let stand covered 10 minutes, then uncover and fluff rice. Transfer to a medium bowl and cool to room temperature, about 20 minutes.

2. To cooled rice add remaining ingredients and toss gently to evenly coat. Enjoy immediately, or cover and refrigerate up to five days.

Storing Dry Fruit

With the small amount called for in this recipe, you may end up with extra dried fruit you need to store. Use plastic or glass containers to store dry fruits. Never use metal, which can discolor the fruit and change the flavor. Store in a cool, dark place like a pantry. For longer storage, you can stash them in the back of your refrigerator. Stored this way, they will have an extra six months of freshness!

PER SERVING

Calories: 495	Fiber: 6g
Fat: 23g	Sugar: 25g
Sodium: 198mg	Protein: 7g
Carbohydrates: 68g	

BROWN RICE BOWL WITH FRIED HALLOUMI AND MINT DRESSING

PREP TIME: 10 MINUTES | COOK TIME: 6 MINUTES | SERVES: 1

 Halloumi cheese, common in Cypriot cuisine, is a semi-firm cheese with a very high melting point. It has a salty, tangy flavor that is enhanced when it is grilled or fried. If you are unable to find it, you can substitute dairy milk–based bread cheese, which is another type of nonmelting cheese.

INGREDIENTS

1 tablespoon extra-virgin olive oil

1 tablespoon lemon juice

1 teaspoon finely chopped mint leaves

1 teaspoon honey

¼ teaspoon Dijon mustard

⅛ teaspoon freshly cracked black pepper

½ cup cooked brown rice

¼ cup diced English cucumber

2 tablespoons finely chopped red onion

4 medium cherry tomatoes, sliced in half

¼ teaspoon olive oil

1 ounce Halloumi cheese, cut into ½" cubes

1 cup packed baby spinach

4 Kalamata olives, pitted and sliced

1 In a small jar with a tight-fitting lid, add extra-virgin olive oil, lemon juice, mint leaves, honey, mustard, and black pepper. Shake vigorously 30 seconds and then set aside.

2 In a medium bowl, add rice, cucumber, red onion, and tomatoes. Shake dressing again and pour over top of bowl. Gently toss to coat. Set aside.

3 In an 8" skillet over medium heat, add olive oil and use a brush to evenly coat pan. Add Halloumi and cook until cubes are golden brown on two sides, about 3 minutes per side.

4 To serve, place spinach in a bowl. Top with rice mixture, fried cheese cubes, and garnish with sliced olives. Enjoy immediately.

Halloumi
Halloumi cheese has a wide range of health benefits along with its delicious flavor. It is a good source of protein, which will help keep you feeling full longer, and a very good source of calcium. It can be a good replacement for meat in salads, sandwiches, and grilled dishes.

PER SERVING

Calories: 421 | Fat: 26g | Sodium: 570mg | Carbohydrates: 38g Fiber: 4g | Sugar: 10g | Protein: 10g

FARRO SALAD WITH TOMATOES AND OLIVES

PREP TIME: 25 MINUTES | COOK TIME: 20 MINUTES | SERVES: 1

 Farro, a chewy type of wheat grain with a nutty flavor, is commonly grown in Italy and can be used for grain-based meals on the Mediterranean diet. It is most often eaten as a side dish, added to soups, or mixed into salads. Consider garnishing your salad with 1 tablespoon crumbled feta and additional chopped parsley.

INGREDIENTS

¼ cup farro, rinsed and drained

½ cup low-sodium vegetable broth

⅓ cup diced plum tomato

¼ cup sliced Kalamata olives

¼ cup chopped red bell pepper

2 tablespoons chopped red onion

1 tablespoon finely chopped Italian parsley

2 teaspoons extra-virgin olive oil

2 teaspoons red wine vinegar

¼ teaspoon Greek seasoning

⅛ teaspoon dried oregano

1. In a 1-quart saucepan with a lid, add farro and broth. Place over medium heat until mixture comes to a boil. Reduce heat to low, cover, and cook 20–25 minutes or until farro is tender. Remove pot from heat and drain off any excess liquid. Fluff with a fork, then cool to room temperature, about 20 minutes.

2. To cooled farro add remaining ingredients and toss gently to evenly coat. Enjoy immediately, or cover and refrigerate up to five days. Serve at room temperature.

PER SERVING

Calories: 509
Fat: 35g
Sodium: 777mg
Carbohydrates: 42g

Fiber: 8g
Sugar: 6g
Protein: 7g

POTATO AND SPINACH SOUP

PREP TIME: 5 MINUTES | COOK TIME: 15 MINUTES | SERVES: 1

 There is nothing like a bowl of warm soup on a chilly day, but why make a whole batch when you only want a single serving! Greek yogurt adds a delicious creamy flavor with a hint of sharpness to this soup. If you are making this ahead of time, wait until you have reheated it to add in the Greek yogurt.

INGREDIENTS

2 teaspoons olive oil

3 tablespoons chopped yellow onion

3 tablespoons chopped carrot

3 tablespoons chopped celery

1 clove garlic, peeled and minced

¼ teaspoon dried oregano

1 small (about 5-ounce) russet potato, peeled and diced

1¼ cups low-sodium vegetable broth

¼ teaspoon sea salt

¼ teaspoon freshly cracked black pepper

1 cup packed baby spinach

1 tablespoon plain low-fat Greek yogurt

1. In a 1-quart saucepan over medium heat, add olive oil. Once hot, add onion, carrot, and celery and cook until tender, about 3 minutes. Add garlic and oregano and cook until fragrant, about 30 seconds.

2. Add potato, broth, salt, and black pepper to pot and stir well. Bring soup to a boil, then reduce heat to medium-low and simmer until potato is tender, about 10 minutes.

3. Add spinach to pot and cook until wilted, about 30 seconds. Remove pot from heat and whisk in Greek yogurt. Serve immediately.

PER SERVING

Calories: 237
Fat: 9g
Sodium: 647mg
Carbohydrates: 34g
Fiber: 7g
Sugar: 9g
Protein: 7g

THREE-BEAN SALAD

PREP TIME: 4 HOURS 5 MINUTES | COOK TIME: 0 MINUTES | SERVES: 1

 This refreshing salad is a great place to use leftover beans, so feel free to make this with any mix of beans you might have. You can also chop leftover vegetables like bell peppers, green beans, or tomatoes you need to use up and toss them in this salad.

INGREDIENTS

¼ cup canned kidney beans, rinsed and drained

¼ cup canned chickpeas, rinsed and drained

¼ cup canned black beans, rinsed and drained

¼ cup finely chopped celery

2 tablespoons finely chopped red onion

1 tablespoon chopped fresh Italian parsley

1 tablespoon red wine vinegar

2 teaspoons extra-virgin olive oil

½ teaspoon honey

¼ teaspoon Italian seasoning

⅛ teaspoon freshly cracked black pepper

Place all ingredients in a medium bowl. Toss to combine thoroughly. Cover and chill 4 hours before enjoying.

Canned Food Safety

Canned foods with no signs of dents, bloating, or rust are safe to eat right away. Once you open them, transfer food to a clean food storage container. Low acid canned foods like beans will need to be consumed within three days of opening, but acidic foods, like tomatoes, most fruits, pickles, and vinegar-packed olives, can be stored in the refrigerator up to seven days.

PER SERVING

Calories: 416
Fat: 27g
Sodium: 320mg
Carbohydrates: 33g

Fiber: 10g
Sugar: 6g
Protein: 10g

ITALIAN MIXED GREEN SALAD

PREP TIME: 5 MINUTES | COOK TIME: 0 MINUTES | SERVES: 1

 This crisp healthy salad with fresh vegetables, seeds, and cheese is wonderful as it is, but you can also add three to four large grilled shrimp, 3 ounces of grilled or roasted chicken breast, or a grilled or roasted salmon filet to the top to make a hearty meal for one.

INGREDIENTS

1 tablespoon extra-virgin olive oil

2 tablespoons red wine vinegar

¼ teaspoon Dijon mustard

2 teaspoons grated Parmesan cheese

¼ teaspoon Italian seasoning

3 cups mixed salad greens

6 medium cherry tomatoes, sliced in half

¼ cup English cucumber slices

¼ cup shredded part-skim mozzarella cheese

⅛ cup thinly sliced red onion

2 tablespoons unsalted sunflower seeds

¼ teaspoon freshly cracked black pepper

1. In a small jar with a tight-fitting lid, add olive oil, vinegar, and mustard. Shake mixture thoroughly 20 seconds, then add Parmesan and Italian seasoning and shake 30 seconds.

2. Add remaining ingredients to a medium bowl and toss well to mix. Shake dressing again, then pour over salad and toss again to evenly coat salad. Serve immediately.

PER SERVING

Calories: 342	Fiber: 6g
Fat: 26g	Sugar: 5g
Sodium: 310mg	Protein: 12g
Carbohydrates: 16g	

ROASTED CARROT TAHINI BISQUE

PREP TIME: 10 MINUTES | COOK TIME: 30 MINUTES | SERVES: 1

 Bisque for one? Done! This bisque gets its creamy texture not from butter or cream but from roasted carrots and tahini. Roasting the carrots enhances their sweetness, and the touch of lemon juice at the end keeps the flavor bright and fresh. If you don't have tahini on hand, you can use natural peanut butter.

INGREDIENTS

¾ cup baby carrots, or 1 medium peeled carrot cut into ½" pieces

2 teaspoons olive oil, divided

¼ cup chopped yellow onion

1 clove garlic, peeled and minced

¼ teaspoon ground cumin

⅛ teaspoon dried thyme

1 cup low-sodium vegetable broth

½ cup water

1 tablespoon tahini

¼ teaspoon sea salt

¼ teaspoon freshly cracked black pepper

½ teaspoon fresh lemon juice

1 Preheat oven to 400°F.

2 On a small baking sheet, add carrots and 1 teaspoon olive oil. Toss carrots to evenly coat, then roast 20–25 minutes or until carrots are tender and slightly charred on the bottom.

3 During last 10 minutes of roasting, place a 1-quart saucepan over medium heat and add remaining 1 teaspoon olive oil. Once hot, add onion and cook until translucent, about 3 minutes. Add garlic, cumin, and thyme and cook until fragrant, about 30 seconds.

4 Add broth and water to pot along with roasted carrots. Bring to a boil, then reduce heat to medium-low and simmer 10 minutes.

5 Remove pot from heat and transfer soup to a blender along with tahini, salt, black pepper, and lemon juice. Purée until smooth, about 1 minute. Serve hot.

PER SERVING

Calories: 246

Fat: 16g

Sodium: 609mg

Carbohydrates: 23g

Fiber: 6g

Sugar: 9g

Protein: 5g

ISRAELI COUSCOUS WITH RED PEPPER AND GOAT CHEESE

PREP TIME: 25 MINUTES | COOK TIME: 10 MINUTES | SERVES: 1

 Israeli couscous, also called pearl couscous, is not really couscous but tiny ball-shaped wheat pasta. It has a lightly chewy texture and can be served hot as a side dish with olive oil and lemon, mixed into soups, or used in salads as it is here. Toasting it before cooking adds a nutty flavor.

INGREDIENTS

1 teaspoon olive oil

⅓ cup Israeli couscous

½ cup low-sodium vegetable broth

¼ cup chopped jarred roasted red peppers

2 tablespoons chopped red onion

2 tablespoons chopped fresh Italian parsley

¼ cup chopped English cucumber

2 tablespoons crumbled goat cheese

1 teaspoon lemon juice

⅛ teaspoon garlic powder

⅛ teaspoon freshly cracked black pepper

1. In a 1-quart saucepan over medium heat, add olive oil and let it heat briefly, then swirl pan to coat. Add couscous and stir constantly until couscous is lightly golden brown, about 4 minutes.

2. Add broth and bring to a boil, then reduce heat to low and cover pot with a lid. Simmer 6–8 minutes or until liquid is absorbed and couscous is tender. Transfer cooked couscous to a bowl and fluff with a fork, then cool to room temperature, about 15 minutes.

3. Once couscous is cool, add remaining ingredients and fold to combine. Enjoy immediately, or cover and refrigerate up to three days. Serve at room temperature.

PER SERVING

Calories: 424	Fiber: 4g
Fat: 15g	Sugar: 6g
Sodium: 425mg	Protein: 16g
Carbohydrates: 53g	

MUSHROOM BARLEY SOUP

PREP TIME: 10 MINUTES | COOK TIME: 49 MINUTES | SERVES: 1

 Barley, which is rich in minerals, is usually available in the bulk section of most natural or health food stores, so you can buy a smaller amount for your recipes for one. If you are not able to buy it in bulk, you can store it in your freezer in an airtight container where it will keep fresh up to one year.

INGREDIENTS

2 teaspoons olive oil

2 tablespoons minced yellow onion

⅓ cup minced carrot

⅓ cup minced celery

1 medium plum tomato, seeded and diced

4 ounces sliced button mushrooms

½ clove garlic, peeled and minced

1 cup low-sodium vegetable broth

½ cup water

2 tablespoons pearled barley

⅛ teaspoon sea salt

⅛ teaspoon freshly cracked black pepper

½ teaspoon lemon juice

1 In a 2-quart saucepan over medium heat, add olive oil. Once hot, add onion, carrot, and celery. Sauté until tender, about 5 minutes. Add tomato and mushrooms and cook until mushrooms are soft, about 3 minutes. Add garlic and cook until fragrant, about 30 seconds.

2 Stir in broth and water, scraping any bits from the bottom of pot. Add barley, salt, and black pepper and stir well. Bring soup to a boil, then cover pot with a lid, reduce heat to low, and cook until barley is tender, about 40 minutes.

3 Once barley is cooked, remove lid. Stir in lemon juice and serve immediately, or cover and refrigerate up to three days.

PER SERVING

Calories: 252

Fat: 9g

Sodium: 396mg

Carbohydrates: 37g

Fiber: 9g

Sugar: 10g

Protein: 8g

VEGETABLE BARLEY SOUP

PREP TIME: 10 MINUTES | COOK TIME: 35 MINUTES | SERVES: 1

 Frozen vegetables are great to have on hand when you want to add extra vegetables to soups, stews, and other dishes. Frozen vegetables are a great ingredient when cooking for one because they are picked at the peak of freshness, they retain many of their nutrients, and most importantly they allow you to have a wide variety of vegetables on hand without worry of spoiling.

INGREDIENTS

1 teaspoon olive oil

¼ cup diced celery

¼ cup diced white onion

1 medium Roma tomato, seeds and stem removed, diced

½ clove garlic, peeled and minced

⅛ teaspoon dried thyme

⅛ teaspoon freshly cracked black pepper

½ cup frozen mixed vegetables

2 tablespoons pearled barley

1 bay leaf

1¼ cups low-sodium vegetable broth

1. In a 2-quart saucepan over medium heat, add olive oil. Once oil is hot, add celery and onion. Cook until just tender, about 2 minutes, then add tomato and cook until tomato is soft, about 2 minutes. Add garlic, thyme, and black pepper and cook until fragrant, about 30 seconds.

2. Stir in mixed vegetables, barley, bay leaf, and broth. Increase heat to high and bring soup to a boil, then cover pot with a lid, reduce heat to medium-low, and cook 30–40 minutes or until barley is tender. Discard bay leaf before serving.

PER SERVING

Calories: 246
Fat: 5g
Sodium: 240mg
Carbohydrates: 44g

Fiber: 11g
Sugar: 8g
Protein: 8g

TOMATO BASIL SOUP

PREP TIME: 10 MINUTES | COOK TIME: 29 MINUTES | SERVES: 1

 Canned tomatoes are a powerhouse ingredient to keep in your pantry. Not only are they convenient for quick soups, sauces, and meals, but they are also loaded with a more bioavailable version of the antioxidant lycopene than fresh tomatoes, which has been shown to improve heart health and reduce the risks of certain types of cancer.

INGREDIENTS

2 teaspoons olive oil

¼ cup chopped yellow onion

1 (14.5-ounce) can low-sodium diced tomatoes, drained

1 clove garlic, peeled and minced

1 cup low-sodium vegetable broth

2 sun-dried tomatoes, chopped

¼ teaspoon ground fennel

¼ teaspoon dried oregano

2 fresh basil leaves, chopped

⅛ teaspoon crushed red pepper flakes

2 tablespoons grated Parmesan cheese

1. In a 2-quart saucepan over medium heat, add olive oil. Once hot, add onion and cook until translucent, about 3 minutes. Add diced tomatoes and cook until they are slightly darker in color, about 5 minutes. Add garlic and cook until fragrant, about 30 seconds.

2. Add remaining ingredients except Parmesan and bring mixture to a boil, then reduce heat to medium-low and simmer 20 minutes.

3. Transfer soup to a blender, or use an immersion blender, and purée until smooth. Transfer to a bowl and garnish with Parmesan. Serve hot.

PER SERVING

Calories: 274   Fiber: 6g
Fat: 11g   Sugar: 17g
Sodium: 415mg   Protein: 9g
Carbohydrates: 33g

MEDITERRANEAN COUSCOUS SALAD

PREP TIME: 10 MINUTES | COOK TIME: 5 MINUTES | SERVES: 1

 Couscous is a semolina pasta that cooks by soaking in hot water. It is common in Mediterranean cooking, particularly in North African cuisine, and can be served plain, spiced, or mixed with other ingredients, as in the case of this refreshing salad.

INGREDIENTS

1 tablespoon extra-virgin olive oil

2 teaspoons lemon juice

1 teaspoon red wine vinegar

¼ teaspoon dried oregano

¼ teaspoon dried basil

¼ teaspoon freshly cracked black pepper

⅛ teaspoon sea salt

⅓ cup low-sodium vegetable broth

3 tablespoons couscous

½ cup chopped plum tomato

¼ cup chopped English cucumber

¼ cup canned chickpeas, rinsed and drained

¼ cup chopped fresh Italian parsley

2 tablespoons chopped yellow onion

2 tablespoons sliced Kalamata olives

1. In a small jar with a tight-fitting lid, add olive oil, lemon juice, vinegar, oregano, basil, black pepper, and salt. Shake vigorously 30 seconds and then set aside.

2. In a 1-quart saucepan over medium heat, bring broth to a boil. Stir in couscous, remove pan from heat, cover with a lid, and let stand 5 minutes or until liquid is absorbed. Remove lid and fluff with a fork before transferring to a medium bowl.

3. Add remaining ingredients to bowl. Shake dressing again, add to bowl, then toss so all ingredients are evenly coated. Serve immediately, or cover and refrigerate up to three days. Serve at room temperature.

PER SERVING

Calories: 303 | Fat: 20g | Sodium: 671mg | Carbohydrates: 27g Fiber: 6g | Sugar: 7g | Protein: 6g

MINESTRONE SOUP

PREP TIME: 10 MINUTES | COOK TIME: 19 MINUTES | SERVES: 1

If you are looking for a hearty, healthy bowl of comfort that also serves up plenty of vegetables, then minestrone is the soup for you! If you do not have orzo on hand, you can use any small pasta you like such as small elbows, shells, or ditalini.

INGREDIENTS

2 teaspoons olive oil

3 tablespoons chopped yellow onion

3 tablespoons chopped celery

3 tablespoons chopped carrot

3 tablespoons chopped zucchini

1 cup chopped kale

¼ teaspoon Italian seasoning

⅛ teaspoon garlic powder

⅛ freshly cracked black pepper

½ bay leaf

1 cup low-sodium vegetable broth

½ cup canned diced tomatoes, undrained

2 tablespoons orzo

¼ cup canned great northern beans, rinsed and drained

1. In a 1-quart saucepan over medium heat, add olive oil. Once hot, add onion, celery, and carrot. Sauté until vegetables are tender, about 5 minutes, then add zucchini and cook 1 minute more to soften.

2. Stir in kale and cook until wilted, about 3 minutes. Add Italian seasoning, garlic powder, and black pepper and stir well. Add bay leaf, broth, and tomatoes. Bring mixture to a boil, then stir in orzo and cook, stirring occasionally, 7 minutes or until orzo is tender.

3. Reduce heat to medium-low and add beans. Stir well and let simmer 3 minutes to heat beans. Serve immediately, or cover and refrigerate up to three days.

PER SERVING

Calories: 320
Fat: 10g
Sodium: 462mg
Carbohydrates: 46g

Fiber: 10g
Sugar: 11g
Protein: 11g

VEGAN AVGOLEMONO

PREP TIME: 10 MINUTES | COOK TIME: 16 MINUTES | SERVES: 1

This vegan version of the Greek classic uses tahini in place of eggs to enrich the soup, and replaces shredded chicken with chickpeas to keep it hearty and filling. A touch of light soy sauce is added to give this soup a deeper savory flavor but can be left out if you have an allergy to soy.

INGREDIENTS

1 tablespoon tahini

1 tablespoon fresh lemon juice

½ teaspoon light soy sauce

2 teaspoons olive oil

¼ cup chopped celery

¼ cup chopped carrot

2 tablespoons minced yellow onion

½ clove garlic, peeled and minced

1½ cups low-sodium vegetable broth

3 tablespoons orzo

⅛ teaspoon sea salt

⅛ teaspoon freshly cracked black pepper

⅓ cup canned chickpeas, rinsed and drained

1 tablespoon chopped fresh dill

1 tablespoon chopped fresh Italian parsley

1. In a small bowl, combine tahini, lemon juice, and soy sauce until smooth. Set aside.

2. In a 1-quart saucepan over medium heat, add olive oil. Once hot, add celery, carrot, and onion and cook until tender, about 5 minutes. Add garlic and cook until fragrant, about 30 seconds.

3. Stir in broth and bring to a boil. Add orzo, salt, and black pepper. Cook, stirring often, 8 minutes or until orzo is tender. Stir in chickpeas and heat 2 more minutes.

4. Remove pot from heat and remove ¼ cup liquid from pot. Stir tahini mixture into hot liquid, then stir into soup. Add dill and parsley. Serve immediately.

Adding Umami

Here are a few ways to add savory flavor to your cooking. First, a spritz of lemon juice can help enhance the flavors of your food. Second, adding ¼ teaspoon white miso paste to soups, sauces, and dressings will add a richer flavor. And ¼ teaspoon light soy sauce can add a salty edge.

PER SERVING

Calories: 407 | Fat: 17g | Sodium: 712mg | Carbohydrates: 53g Fiber: 9g | Sugar: 11g | Protein: 13g

CHAPTER 5

SIDE DISHES

Brown Rice and Vegetables with
Red Pepper Dressing 76

Lemon Garlic Rice Pilaf 77

Basil Pesto Rice with Olives and
Goat Cheese 78

Herbed Orzo 79

Green Beans with Potatoes
and Tomatoes......................................81

Creamy Mushroom Risotto 82

Creamy Cucumbers with
Red Onion and Dill 83

Baked Lemon Parmesan Asparagus 84

Roasted Broccoli with Feta....................85

Spiced Corn on the Cob 86

Creamy Cheese Polenta 88

Garlic Cauliflower Purée........................89

Lemon Parmesan Risotto...................... 90

Cilantro Lime Rice 91

Citrus Mashed Sweet Potatoes 93

Herb Vinaigrette Potato Salad..............94

Miso Green Beans with Almonds..........95

Olive Oil Mashed Potatoes................... 96

Side dishes are sometimes an afterthought when meal planning, but the not-so-humble side dish is an important part of your meals. It is the place where you can add in some extra nutrition and add flavors to complement your main dish. Traditional recipes for side dishes make more servings than the solo cook needs, but this chapter solves that problem by creating flavorful side dishes that pair well with a variety of main dishes from meat and seafood to pasta and grains. The right side dish takes a good meal and makes it great!

When picking side dishes think of flavors and textures that complement one another. For a rich main dish like Balsamic-Glazed Pork (see Chapter 10), think of a sweet yet tangy side like Citrus Mashed Sweet Potatoes or Herb Vinaigrette Potato Salad. Craving comfort food like Zucchini Lasagna (see Chapter 7)? Pair your hearty main dish with a side of Miso Green Beans with Almonds or Lemon Garlic Rice Pilaf. When you want something lighter for dinner like Lemon Salmon with Dill (see Chapter 8), try Spiced Corn on the Cob for an equally light and refreshing side. With the addition of easy and delicious side dishes made for one, your lunches and dinners are that much better!

BROWN RICE AND VEGETABLES WITH RED PEPPER DRESSING

PREP TIME: 10 MINUTES | COOK TIME: 40 MINUTES | SERVES: 1

 Frozen vegetables make this dish easy to prepare and perfect for a single serving. Use your favorite mix of frozen vegetables, vegetables for stir-fry, or a mix of frozen riced vegetables like cauliflower, broccoli, and carrots.

INGREDIENTS

¼ cup chopped jarred roasted red peppers

1 tablespoon extra-virgin olive oil

1 teaspoon red wine vinegar

¼ teaspoon honey

⅛ teaspoon garlic powder

¼ teaspoon sea salt, divided

⅛ teaspoon freshly cracked black pepper

¼ cup medium-grain brown rice, rinsed and drained

½ cup plus 2 teaspoons water, divided

1 teaspoon olive oil

⅓ cup frozen mixed vegetables including peas, corn, and diced carrot and onion

1. In a blender, add roasted red peppers, extra-virgin olive oil, vinegar, honey, garlic powder, ⅛ teaspoon salt, and black pepper. Purée mixture until smooth. Set aside.

2. In a 1-quart saucepan with a lid, add rice, ½ cup water, olive oil, and remaining ⅛ teaspoon salt. Cover pot and place over medium heat until mixture comes to a boil. Reduce heat to low and cook 30–35 minutes or until liquid is fully absorbed and rice is tender.

3. While rice is cooking, prepare mixed vegetables. In a small microwave-safe bowl, add frozen mixed vegetables and remaining 2 teaspoons water. Microwave 2 minutes or until vegetables are steaming.

4. Once rice is cooked, fluff it with a fork and top with vegetables. Let stand covered 10 minutes, then uncover and fluff a second time to incorporate vegetables. Transfer to a plate and spoon red pepper dressing over top. Serve hot.

PER SERVING

Calories: 389	Fiber: 4g
Fat: 19g	Sugar: 4g
Sodium: 614mg	Protein: 6g
Carbohydrates: 48g	

LEMON GARLIC RICE PILAF

PREP TIME: 5 MINUTES | COOK TIME: 45 MINUTES | SERVES: 1

 Lemon and garlic work together in this dish to make a refreshing side for one. This flavor combination is particularly good with lighter main dishes like seafood, fish, or grilled foods. Fresh lemon zest adds a lot of zing, so don't leave it out!

INGREDIENTS

1 teaspoon olive oil

2 tablespoons chopped yellow onion

½ clove garlic, peeled and minced

1 teaspoon freshly grated lemon zest

¼ teaspoon Italian seasoning

¼ cup medium-grain brown rice, rinsed and drained

½ cup low-sodium vegetable broth

2 teaspoons lemon juice

⅛ teaspoon sea salt

1. In a 1-quart saucepan over medium heat, add olive oil. Once hot, add onion and cook until just tender, about 1 minute. Add garlic, lemon zest, and Italian seasoning and cook until very fragrant, about 30 seconds. Add rice and cook, stirring constantly, until rice is very lightly toasted, about 3 minutes.

2. Add remaining ingredients, stir well, and cover pot. When mixture comes to a boil, reduce heat to low and cook 30–35 minutes or until liquid is fully absorbed and rice is tender. Remove from heat and let stand covered 10 minutes, then uncover, fluff rice, and transfer to a plate. Serve hot.

Aromatic Shortcut

If you do not want to keep cloves of fresh garlic on hand, you can use refrigerated garlic purée in a tube. It can be found in most produce departments and generally comes in two varieties: chunky and smooth. These tubes last for weeks when refrigerated; 1 teaspoon equals 1 clove of garlic.

PER SERVING

Calories: 232

Fat: 6g

Sodium: 266mg

Carbohydrates: 42g

Fiber: 3g

Sugar: 3g

Protein: 4g

BASIL PESTO RICE WITH OLIVES AND GOAT CHEESE

PREP TIME: 10 MINUTES | COOK TIME: 40 MINUTES | SERVES: 1

 Ready-made pesto is a time-saver when cooking for one, and it's an easy way to jazz up vegetables, pasta, marinades, salad dressings, and dips. Refrigerated pesto, often sold in the deli section of the grocery store, will have the best flavor, and leftovers last seven to ten days in the refrigerator.

INGREDIENTS

¼ cup medium-grain brown rice, rinsed and drained

½ cup low-sodium vegetable broth

⅛ teaspoon sea salt

1 tablespoon basil pesto

2 tablespoons sliced Kalamata olives

1 tablespoon crumbled goat cheese

1 basil leaf, finely chopped

⅛ teaspoon freshly cracked black pepper

1. In a 1-quart saucepan, add rice, broth, and salt. Cover pot and place over medium heat until mixture comes to a boil. Reduce heat to low and cook 30–35 minutes or until liquid is fully absorbed and rice is tender. Remove pot from heat and let stand covered 10 minutes, then uncover and fluff rice.

2. Add pesto and fold until rice is evenly coated. Stir in olives, then transfer to a serving plate and garnish with goat cheese, basil, and black pepper. Serve hot.

Small-Batch Fresh Pesto

If you prefer to make your own pesto, place 1 cup fresh basil leaves, 1 clove garlic, 1 tablespoon pine nuts, and 2 teaspoons fresh lemon juice in a food processor. Pulse to chop basil, then set to process and slowly drizzle in 2 tablespoons extra-virgin olive oil. Once a smooth paste forms, add 3 tablespoons Parmesan cheese and pulse to combine. This yields six servings.

PER SERVING

Calories: 357
Fat: 18g
Sodium: 817mg
Carbohydrates: 40g

Fiber: 2g
Sugar: 2g
Protein: 9g

HERBED ORZO

PREP TIME: 10 MINUTES | COOK TIME: 8 MINUTES | SERVES: 1

 Orzo is a rice-shaped pasta that comes in plain and tricolored varieties; use the type you like best here. It is excellent in salads and soups, and it can also help bulk up dishes such as chicken salad and tuna salad so you can reduce the amount of meat used.

INGREDIENTS

1 cup low-sodium chicken stock

¼ cup orzo

⅛ teaspoon sea salt

2 teaspoons chopped fresh parsley

2 teaspoons chopped fresh dill

1 teaspoon olive oil

½ teaspoon fresh lemon juice

2 tablespoons grated Parmesan cheese

⅛ teaspoon freshly cracked black pepper

1. In a 1-quart saucepan, add stock. Cover pot and place over medium heat. When stock begins to boil, add orzo and salt and cook until orzo is tender, about 8–10 minutes. Drain and return orzo to pot.

2. Add parsley, dill, olive oil, and lemon juice to orzo and fold to combine. Transfer to a serving plate and garnish with Parmesan and black pepper. Serve hot.

PER SERVING

Calories: 228
Fat: 7g
Sodium: 555mg
Carbohydrates: 31g

Fiber: 2g
Sugar: 1g
Protein: 9g

GREEN BEANS WITH POTATOES AND TOMATOES

PREP TIME: 10 MINUTES | COOK TIME: 10 MINUTES | SERVES: 1

 Simple yet hearty, this side dish is great to enjoy along with roast chicken or steamed seafood dishes. If you are not a fan of new potatoes, you can use tri-color baby potatoes. Just cut them in half before cooking rather than in quarters.

INGREDIENTS

1 cup water

1 medium (about 4-ounce) new potato, quartered

½ cup (about 2 ounces) fresh green beans, trimmed

1 medium plum tomato, seeded and chopped

2 teaspoons extra-virgin olive oil

1 teaspoon red wine vinegar

¼ teaspoon Dijon mustard

⅛ teaspoon smoked paprika

⅛ teaspoon freshly cracked black pepper

1. In a 2-quart saucepan fitted with a steamer basket, add water. Cover pot with a lid and place over medium heat until water is boiling.

2. Open lid and add potato to basket. Cover and steam 5 minutes. Remove lid and add green beans and tomato to basket. Cover and steam 5–7 minutes or until potato pieces are fork-tender and green beans are tender outside yet crisp in the very center.

3. While vegetables steam, make dressing. In a small bowl, add olive oil, vinegar, mustard, paprika, and black pepper. Whisk to combine. When vegetables are finished steaming, transfer vegetables and dressing to a bowl and gently toss to coat. Serve hot.

PER SERVING

Calories: 321
Fat: 9g
Sodium: 53mg
Carbohydrates: 56g

Fiber: 7g
Sugar: 4g
Protein: 7g

CREAMY MUSHROOM RISOTTO

PREP TIME: 15 MINUTES | COOK TIME: 48 MINUTES | SERVES: 1

If you want to pump up the mushroom flavor in this risotto, replace the vegetable broth with mushroom broth. Feel free to use any mushroom varieties you like here.

INGREDIENTS

¼ cup short-grain brown rice, rinsed and drained

1¼ cups low-sodium vegetable broth, divided

1 teaspoon olive oil

½ cup chopped fresh baby bella mushrooms

1 small shallot, peeled and minced

½ clove garlic, peeled and minced

2 teaspoons freeze-dried chives

2 tablespoons dry white wine

⅛ teaspoon freshly cracked black pepper

3 tablespoons grated Parmesan cheese, divided

½ teaspoon lemon juice

PER SERVING

Calories: 332
Fat: 9g
Sodium: 450mg
Carbohydrates: 50g

Fiber: 4g
Sugar: 6g
Protein: 11g

1. In a 1-quart saucepan with a lid, add rice and ½ cup broth. Bring to a boil over high heat, then reduce heat to low, cover, and cook 25 minutes or until rice is just starting to become tender but is still firm in the center. Turn off heat, remove lid, fluff with a fork, and set aside.

2. Heat remaining ¾ cup broth in a microwave-safe bowl in microwave on high 45 seconds or until steaming hot. Set aside.

3. In an 8" skillet over medium heat, add olive oil. Once hot, add mushrooms and cook until soft, about 5 minutes. Add shallot and cook 30 seconds or until translucent. Add garlic, chives, and parcooked rice and toss to coat rice evenly with oil.

4. Add wine and cook, stirring constantly, until wine is absorbed, about 1 minute.

5. Add ¼ cup warm broth to pan at a time, stirring until each addition of broth is almost completely absorbed, about 5–6 minutes per addition. After last addition is just absorbed, test rice. It should be chewy but tender. If rice is too firm, add water 2 tablespoons at a time, making sure each addition is absorbed, until rice is cooked to your liking. Remove pan from heat.

6. Stir in black pepper, 2 tablespoons Parmesan, and lemon juice and stir until cheese is melted.

7. Transfer risotto to a serving plate and top with remaining 1 tablespoon Parmesan. Serve immediately.

CREAMY CUCUMBERS WITH RED ONION AND DILL

PREP TIME: 1 HOUR 15 MINUTES | COOK TIME: 0 MINUTES | SERVES: 1

 This salad is a refreshing addition to any meal for one! It pairs superbly with grilled foods, roasted dishes, and sandwiches. This side dish improves with time, so make it a day or two ahead for the best flavor.

INGREDIENTS

1 cup peeled and thinly sliced cucumber

¼ cup thinly sliced red onion

½ teaspoon sea salt

2 tablespoons plain low-fat Greek yogurt

½ teaspoon lemon juice

¼ teaspoon white vinegar

¼ teaspoon freeze-dried dill

⅛ teaspoon freshly cracked black pepper

⅛ teaspoon granulated sugar

1. In a colander over a bowl, combine cucumber, red onion, and salt. Toss so cucumber and onion are evenly coated in salt and let stand 10 minutes. After 10 minutes, rinse cucumber and onion slices under cool water, then place between layers of clean paper towels or lint-free kitchen towels and press out excess water.

2. While cucumber and onion drain, make dressing. In a small bowl, add yogurt, lemon juice, vinegar, dill, black pepper, and sugar. Stir well to combine.

3. Transfer cucumber and onion to dressing and gently toss to coat. Cover and refrigerate 1 hour or up to five days before serving. Enjoy chilled.

PER SERVING

Calories: 54
Fat: 1g
Sodium: 90mg
Carbohydrates: 10g

Fiber: 1g
Sugar: 5g
Protein: 4g

BAKED LEMON PARMESAN ASPARAGUS

PREP TIME: 10 MINUTES │ COOK TIME: 10 MINUTES │ SERVES: 1

 Most fresh asparagus is sold in 1-pound bunches, so leftover stems can be placed in a wide-mouthed jar with about ½" of water. Cover loosely with plastic wrap and store in the refrigerator. Change the water every two days. This method can preserve asparagus up to ten days.

INGREDIENTS

¼ pound asparagus, trimmed

2 teaspoons olive oil

1 teaspoon freshly grated lemon zest

½ clove garlic, peeled and minced

¼ teaspoon freshly cracked black pepper

2 tablespoons shredded Parmesan cheese

1. Preheat oven to 400°F and line a small baking sheet with foil.

2. Place asparagus on prepared baking sheet in a single layer. Add olive oil, lemon zest, garlic, and black pepper and toss to coat asparagus evenly. Spread into a single layer again and sprinkle Parmesan over top.

3. Bake 10 minutes or until asparagus is tender-crisp. Serve immediately.

PER SERVING

Calories: 141

Fat: 12g

Sodium: 170mg

Carbohydrates: 5g

Fiber: 2g

Sugar: 2g

Protein: 6g

ROASTED BROCCOLI WITH FETA

PREP TIME: 5 MINUTES | COOK TIME: 15 MINUTES | SERVES: 1

 This version of cheesy broccoli swaps cheese sauce for feta, a staple of the Mediterranean diet. To add even more flavor the broccoli is roasted with plenty of earthy spices. If you want, you can roast the broccoli ahead of time, cool it, and then store covered in the refrigerator up to three days. Simply add the lemon and feta when you reheat it.

INGREDIENTS

1 cup broccoli florets

2 teaspoons extra-virgin olive oil

⅛ teaspoon freshly cracked black pepper

⅛ teaspoon crushed red pepper flakes

⅛ teaspoon garlic powder

⅛ teaspoon onion powder

⅛ teaspoon ground cumin

⅛ teaspoon sea salt

1 lemon wedge

2 tablespoons crumbled feta cheese

1. Preheat oven to 425°F and line a baking sheet with foil.

2. Place broccoli on prepared baking sheet and drizzle with olive oil. Sprinkle with black pepper, red pepper flakes, garlic powder, onion powder, cumin, and salt. Gently toss to evenly coat broccoli.

3. Bake 15–20 minutes, flipping broccoli halfway through cooking, until broccoli is slightly charred and stems are tender. Remove from oven and spritz with lemon wedge.

4. Transfer broccoli to a serving plate and top with feta. Serve immediately.

PER SERVING

Calories: 161
Fat: 13g
Sodium: 396mg
Carbohydrates: 8g

Fiber: 3g
Sugar: 2g
Protein: 5g

SPICED CORN ON THE COB

PREP TIME: 10 MINUTES | COOK TIME: 20 MINUTES | SERVES: 1

 This side for one can be cooked even faster on the grill! Heat your grill to medium heat and place the foil-wrapped corn directly on the grate. Cook 4–5 minutes per side or until the corn is tender. If you want you can remove the foil for the last few minutes to add grill marks.

INGREDIENTS

1 teaspoon extra-virgin olive oil

⅛ teaspoon smoked paprika

⅛ teaspoon chili powder

⅛ teaspoon ground cumin

⅛ teaspoon onion powder

⅛ teaspoon sea salt

1 medium ear corn, shucked

1. Preheat oven to 400°F.

2. In a small bowl, combine olive oil, paprika, chili powder, cumin, onion powder, and salt. Mix to form a paste.

3. Spread paste evenly over corn, wrap in foil, and bake 20 minutes or until corn kernels are tender. Serve hot.

Selecting Fresh Corn

Fresh corn is in season in North America from late spring through summer. Corn should have a crisp green husk that is tight against the cob, and bright, even-colored kernels. The corn silk sticking out of the top of the husks should be golden and soft, not brown, dry, or sticky.

PER SERVING

Calories: 128

Fat: 6g

Sodium: 219mg

Carbohydrates: 20g

Fiber: 2g

Sugar: 6g

Protein: 4g

CREAMY CHEESE POLENTA

PREP TIME: 5 MINUTES | COOK TIME: 15 MINUTES | SERVES: 1

 Polenta is perfect served with sautéed mushrooms or enjoyed with tomato-rich main dishes. You can substitute the Parmesan with any smooth, strong cheese. Cheddar cheese is a popular addition, but you can also use goat cheese, smoked mozzarella, or pepper jack cheese.

INGREDIENTS

½ cup low-sodium vegetable broth

½ cup 1% milk

¼ teaspoon freshly cracked black pepper

⅛ teaspoon onion powder

⅛ teaspoon garlic powder

⅛ teaspoon sea salt

¼ cup polenta

2 tablespoons grated Parmesan cheese

1. In a 1-quart saucepan over medium heat, add broth, milk, black pepper, onion powder, garlic powder, and salt and bring to a boil. Reduce heat to medium-low and slowly whisk in polenta. Cook, stirring often, until polenta is thick and creamy, about 15 minutes.

2. Remove polenta from heat and immediately stir in Parmesan. Serve hot.

Creamier Polenta

If you want a creamier polenta, put the dry polenta into a food processor and give it six to eight 1-second pulses. Check for any large lumps by rubbing it through your fingers. Refining the polenta will cause it to cook more quickly, so keep an eye on it while cooking.

PER SERVING

Calories: 216

Fat: 4g

Sodium: 508mg

Carbohydrates: 34g

Fiber: 3g

Sugar: 8g

Protein: 10g

GARLIC CAULIFLOWER PURÉE

PREP TIME: 5 MINUTES | COOK TIME: 5 MINUTES | SERVES: 1

 Using frozen riced cauliflower is a great shortcut when cooking for one, but it can be a little watery, so dry-frying it first will help reduce the water content for a more satisfying purée. Be sure to add the broth a little at a time to control the texture of the purée. If you add too much, you can always return it to your skillet and cook it down again.

INGREDIENTS

¾ cup frozen riced cauliflower, thawed

3 tablespoons low-sodium vegetable broth

1 teaspoon extra-virgin olive oil

¼ teaspoon freshly cracked black pepper

⅛ teaspoon onion powder

⅛ teaspoon garlic powder

⅛ teaspoon sea salt

1 tablespoon grated Parmesan cheese

1. In an 8" skillet over medium heat, add cauliflower. Cook, stirring often, until cauliflower is dry and lightly golden around the edges, about 5 minutes.

2. Remove from heat and transfer cauliflower to a food processor along with 1 tablespoon broth and olive oil. Pulse, adding additional broth 1 teaspoon at a time, until mixture is thick and smooth to your liking. Add black pepper, onion powder, garlic powder, and salt and pulse to combine.

3. Transfer cauliflower to a serving plate and top with Parmesan. Serve immediately.

PER SERVING

Calories: 81

Fat: 6g

Sodium: 326mg

Carbohydrates: 5g

Fiber: 2g

Sugar: 2g

Protein: 3g

LEMON PARMESAN RISOTTO

PREP TIME: 15 MINUTES | COOK TIME: 43 MINUTES | SERVES: 1

 Arborio rice is the traditional rice for risotto, but this version uses short-grain brown rice, which is less refined, richer in fiber and nutrients, and a better choice on the Mediterranean diet.

INGREDIENTS

¼ cup short-grain brown rice, rinsed and drained

1¼ cups low-sodium vegetable broth, divided

1 teaspoon olive oil

1 small shallot, peeled and minced

1 clove garlic, peeled and minced

2 teaspoons freshly grated lemon zest

¼ teaspoon Italian seasoning

2 tablespoons dry white wine

⅛ teaspoon freshly cracked black pepper

3 tablespoons grated Parmesan cheese, divided

1 teaspoon lemon juice

¼ teaspoon dried parsley

1. In a 1-quart saucepan over high heat, add rice and ½ cup broth. Bring to a boil, then reduce heat to low, cover, and cook 25 minutes or until rice is just starting to become tender. Turn off heat, remove lid, fluff with a fork, and set aside.

2. Heat remaining ¾ cup broth in a microwave-safe bowl in microwave on high 45 seconds or until steaming hot. Set aside.

3. In an 8" skillet over medium heat, add olive oil. Once hot, add shallot and cook 30 seconds. Add garlic, lemon zest, Italian seasoning, and parcooked rice and toss to coat rice evenly in oil.

4. Add wine, stirring constantly until wine is absorbed, about 1 minute.

5. Add ¼ cup warm broth to pan at a time, stirring until each addition of broth is almost completely absorbed, about 5–6 minutes per addition. After last addition is just absorbed, test rice. It should be chewy but tender. If rice is too firm, add water 2 tablespoons at a time, making sure each addition is absorbed, until rice is cooked to your liking. Remove pan from heat.

6. Stir in black pepper, 2 tablespoons Parmesan, and lemon juice and stir until cheese is melted.

7. Transfer risotto to a serving plate and top with remaining 1 tablespoon Parmesan and parsley. Serve immediately.

PER SERVING

Calories: 327	Fiber: 4g
Fat: 9g	Sugar: 6g
Sodium: 448mg	Protein: 10g
Carbohydrates: 49g	

CILANTRO LIME RICE

PREP TIME: 10 MINUTES | COOK TIME: 40 MINUTES | SERVES: 1

Cilantro and lime are flavor partners that balance each other so well. This rice goes well with bean dishes, such as Black Bean Sliders (see Chapter 7), and is the perfect Mediterranean diet grain side dish for fish and seafood meals. You can also wrap this in a whole grain tortilla with some low-fat refried beans for a quick burrito!

INGREDIENTS

¼ cup medium-grain brown rice, rinsed and drained

½ cup water

2 tablespoons finely chopped cilantro, divided

1 teaspoon olive oil

½ teaspoon freshly grated lime zest

⅛ teaspoon garlic powder

⅛ teaspoon sea salt

1 lime wedge

1. In a 1-quart saucepan over medium heat, add rice, water, 1 tablespoon cilantro, olive oil, lime zest, garlic powder, and salt. Cover pot and heat until mixture comes to a boil. Reduce heat to low and cook 30–35 minutes or until liquid is fully absorbed and rice is tender. Remove from heat and let stand covered 10 minutes.

2. Uncover rice and fluff. Transfer to a plate and garnish with remaining 1 tablespoon cilantro and a spritz from lime wedge. Serve hot.

PER SERVING

Calories: 211
Fat: 6g
Sodium: 196mg
Carbohydrates: 37g

Fiber: 2g
Sugar: 0g
Protein: 4g

CITRUS MASHED SWEET POTATOES

PREP TIME: 10 MINUTES | COOK TIME: 10 MINUTES | SERVES: 1

 Sweet potatoes are a popular ingredient in the Mediterranean diet and are excellent sources of beta carotene, fiber, and antioxidants. This means regular consumption of sweet potatoes may help with eye health, healthy digestion, and immunity. This side dish is delicious with pork, chicken, or grilled shrimp.

INGREDIENTS

1 (6-ounce) sweet potato, peeled and cut into ½" pieces

2 tablespoons orange juice

2 teaspoons extra-virgin olive oil

¼ teaspoon freshly grated orange zest

⅛ teaspoon ground cinnamon

⅛ teaspoon ground ginger

⅛ teaspoon freshly cracked black pepper

1. Place sweet potato pieces in a 1-quart saucepan and add water to just cover. Place pot over high heat and bring to a boil, then reduce heat to medium and cook until fork-tender, about 10 minutes. Drain and return to pot.

2. Add remaining ingredients to pot and mash with a potato masher or hand mixer until mixture is smooth, about 30 seconds. If mixture is too thick, add warm water 1 teaspoon at a time until your preferred consistency is reached. Serve hot.

PER SERVING

Calories: 206
Fat: 9g
Sodium: 40mg
Carbohydrates: 31g

Fiber: 4g
Sugar: 11g
Protein: 2g

HERB VINAIGRETTE POTATO SALAD

PREP TIME: 10 MINUTES | COOK TIME: 10 MINUTES | SERVES: 1

 Potatoes are a great cooking for one staple because you can buy one or two at a time, they are naturally portioned, and they keep for weeks if stored in a cool, dry, and dark place in your kitchen. Here, the humble potato is elevated with a tangy herb vinaigrette for a refreshing side!

INGREDIENTS

1 (6-ounce) Yukon Gold potato, peeled and cut into ½" pieces

2 teaspoons extra-virgin olive oil

2 teaspoons red wine vinegar

1 teaspoon Dijon mustard

1 teaspoon fresh lemon juice

1 tablespoon chopped chives, fresh or freeze-dried

1 tablespoon chopped dill, fresh or freeze-dried

¼ teaspoon sea salt

¼ teaspoon freshly cracked black pepper

1. Place potato pieces in a 1-quart saucepan and add water to just cover. Place over high heat and bring to a boil, then reduce heat to medium and cook until fork-tender, about 10 minutes. Drain, then rinse with cold water to stop cooking. Set aside.

2. In a medium bowl, add remaining ingredients and whisk to combine. Add potato pieces and fold to mix. Enjoy immediately, or cover and refrigerate up to five days.

PER SERVING

Calories: 235

Fat: 9g

Sodium: 523mg

Carbohydrates: 35g

Fiber: 3g

Sugar: 2g

Protein: 3g

MISO GREEN BEANS WITH ALMONDS

PREP TIME: 10 MINUTES | COOK TIME: 6 MINUTES | SERVES: 1

 Miso paste is often sold in the produce section or where vegetarian and vegan food items are sold. It keeps up to three months in the refrigerator if you press waxed paper or plastic wrap against the top of the miso to keep it from drying out. It is a good addition to soups, dressings, and marinades.

INGREDIENTS

6 ounces fresh green beans, trimmed

½ teaspoon white miso

1 teaspoon lemon juice

1 teaspoon tahini

1 teaspoon water

¼ teaspoon honey

¼ teaspoon freshly cracked black pepper

2 teaspoons extra-virgin olive oil

1 tablespoon minced shallot

½ clove garlic, peeled and minced

2 tablespoons slivered almonds

1. Place green beans in an 8" skillet and add water to just cover. Place over high heat and bring to a boil, then reduce heat to medium and cook until green beans are tender-crisp, about 4 minutes. Drain green beans and rinse with cold water to stop cooking. Set aside.

2. In a small bowl add miso, lemon juice, tahini, water, honey, and black pepper and stir to combine.

3. Return skillet to medium heat. Add olive oil and swirl to coat pan. Once hot, add green beans, shallot, garlic, almonds, and miso dressing. Cook, tossing constantly, until green beans are hot and evenly coated in dressing, about 2 minutes. Serve hot.

PER SERVING

Calories: 256
Fat: 18g
Sodium: 119mg
Carbohydrates: 21g

Fiber: 7g
Sugar: 8g
Protein: 7g

OLIVE OIL MASHED POTATOES

PREP TIME: 10 MINUTES | COOK TIME: 10 MINUTES | SERVES: 1

 These mashed potatoes are lighter in texture and flavor than traditional dairy-laden mashed potatoes. Feel free to use any fresh herbs you have on hand in these potatoes. A few teaspoons of chopped chives, dill, rosemary, or parsley would be lovely here.

INGREDIENTS

1 (6-ounce) russet potato, peeled and cut into ½" pieces

2 tablespoons low-sodium vegetable broth

2 teaspoons extra-virgin olive oil

¼ teaspoon freshly cracked black pepper

⅛ teaspoon garlic powder

⅛ teaspoon dried thyme

⅛ teaspoon sea salt

1. Place potato in a 1-quart saucepan and add water to just cover. Place over high heat and bring to a boil, then reduce heat to medium and cook until fork-tender, about 10 minutes. Drain and return potato pieces to pot.

2. Add remaining ingredients to pot and mash with a potato masher or hand mixer until mixture is smooth. If it's too thick, add more broth 1 teaspoon at a time until your preferred consistency is reached. Serve hot.

PER SERVING

Calories: 226
Fat: 9g
Sodium: 220mg
Carbohydrates: 35g
Fiber: 3g
Sugar: 2g
Protein: 3g

CHAPTER 6

PASTA DISHES

Fettuccine with Greek Yogurt
  Alfredo Sauce 98
Spicy Mushroom Penne........................99
Rotini with Roasted Vegetable
  Tomato Sauce 100
Olive Oil Pasta with Marinated
  Artichokes and Spinach...................101
Orzo and Mozzarella–Stuffed
  Tomato 102
Fettuccine with Crab
  and Lemon 104
Spanakopita-Stuffed Shells 105
Pasta Primavera 107
Bow Tie Pesto Pasta 108
Creamy Pasta with Chickpeas.............109
Angel Hair Pasta with Shrimp
  and Lemon 110
Rotini with Charred Tomatoes
  and Mozzarella.........................111
Lasagna Rolls.........................112
Baked Ziti 114
Spaghetti with Meat Sauce.................. 115
Macaroni and Cheese.........................116

Pasta is perhaps one of the best foods to keep on hand when cooking for one and for the Mediterranean diet. Dry pasta has an incredibly long shelf life, so you can buy a variety of shapes to keep in your pantry for easy, comforting meals just about any time. Some good shapes to have handy include elbows, penne, orzo, spaghetti, fettuccine, rotini, and bow ties. Pasta is easy to portion too. It's best to transfer dry pasta from an open box or bag to an airtight container or bag to keep it fresh for as long as possible.

This chapter will explore lots of fun ways to enjoy pasta as a main meal. There are pasta meals with plenty of fresh vegetables and healthy fats for balanced, filling meals, and lightened-up twists on classic comfort dishes. Looking for a quick and easy weekday meal? Try the Spicy Mushroom Penne or Fettuccine with Crab and Lemon. Looking to get ahead for the week with some meal prep? Why not make up some comforting baked pasta dishes like Baked Ziti and Spanakopita-Stuffed Shells? Theses perfectly portioned pasta meals are sure to become everyday favorites!

FETTUCCINE WITH GREEK YOGURT ALFREDO SAUCE

PREP TIME: 10 MINUTES | COOK TIME: 10 MINUTES | SERVES: 1

 Alfredo sauce is traditionally made with lots of butter and heavy cream, which are packed with saturated fat. This version, which includes some sautéed vegetables for extra nutrition, uses low-fat Greek yogurt in place of the regular dairy for a lighter, brighter yet totally satisfying version of the classic.

INGREDIENTS

⅓ cup plain low-fat Greek yogurt

3 tablespoons grated Parmesan cheese

1 teaspoon extra-virgin olive oil

½ teaspoon lemon juice

⅛ teaspoon garlic powder

⅛ teaspoon freshly cracked black pepper

2 ounces fettuccine pasta

½ teaspoon sea salt

2 teaspoons olive oil

⅓ cup chopped zucchini

¼ cup chopped yellow squash

¼ cup chopped red bell pepper

¼ teaspoon Italian seasoning

1. In a blender, add yogurt, Parmesan, extra-virgin olive oil, lemon juice, garlic powder, and black pepper. Pulse five times, then purée until smooth, about 30 seconds. Set aside.

2. In a 2-quart saucepan over high heat, add water to fill pot ¾ full. Once water begins to boil, add pasta and salt. Cook, stirring occasionally, until pasta is al dente, about 10 minutes.

3. While pasta is cooking, prepare vegetables. In a 10" skillet over medium heat, add olive oil. Once hot, add zucchini, squash, bell pepper, and Italian seasoning. Cook until vegetables are tender, about 8 minutes. Remove from heat and set aside. Allow pan to cool until vegetables are no longer sizzling.

4. When pasta is finished cooking, drain well and add to pan with vegetables. Stir to combine, then transfer to a serving plate. Pour prepared sauce over pasta and, with tongs, toss pasta and vegetables until evenly coated. Serve immediately.

PER SERVING

Calories: 479	Fiber: 4g
Fat: 19g	Sugar: 7g
Sodium: 482mg	Protein: 21g
Carbohydrates: 53g	

SPICY MUSHROOM PENNE

PREP TIME: 10 MINUTES | COOK TIME: 20 MINUTES | SERVES: 1

 Crushed red pepper flakes give this savory pasta for one a spicy kick. If you enjoy your food extra spicy, feel free to add some Calabrian chilis on top!

INGREDIENTS

2 ounces penne pasta

½ teaspoon sea salt

2 teaspoons olive oil

¾ cup sliced button mushrooms

2 tablespoons finely chopped yellow onion

½ clove garlic, peeled and minced

1 cup lightly packed baby spinach

¼ teaspoon crushed red pepper flakes

2 tablespoons grated Parmesan cheese, divided

1 tablespoon finely chopped fresh parsley

1. In a 2-quart saucepan over high heat, add water to fill pot ¾ full. Once water begins to boil, add pasta and salt. Cook, stirring occasionally, until pasta is just al dente, about 8 minutes. Reserve ½ cup pasta water, then drain pasta and set aside.

2. In an 8" skillet over medium heat, add olive oil. Once hot, add mushrooms and onion. Cook until mushrooms are tender and golden around edges, about 8 minutes. Add garlic, spinach, and red pepper flakes and cook until spinach is wilted, about 2 minutes.

3. Stir in cooked pasta, then add reserved pasta water and cook, stirring constantly, until mixture is thickened, about 2 minutes. Remove skillet from heat and stir in 1 tablespoon Parmesan.

4. Transfer to a plate and garnish with parsley and remaining 1 tablespoon Parmesan. Serve immediately.

Storing Mushrooms
To get the longest shelf life from your mushrooms, you should remove mushrooms from their store packaging, wrap them lightly in paper towels, and place them into a paper bag or an open resealable bag. This will help wick away moisture, which will keep them fresh days longer.

PER SERVING

Calories: 368

Fat: 12g

Sodium: 390mg

Carbohydrates: 50g

Fiber: 4g

Sugar: 3g

Protein: 14g

ROTINI WITH ROASTED VEGETABLE TOMATO SAUCE

PREP TIME: 20 MINUTES | COOK TIME: 41 MINUTES | SERVES: 1

Cooking for one doesn't mean you have to eat boring, packaged meals. This pasta sauce is packed with vegetables and has a robust roasted flavor. Rosemary and thyme are called for here, but you can also add dried basil, dried oregano, or ground fennel if you like. You can prepare the sauce for this dish up to three days ahead of time and keep it refrigerated until ready to use.

INGREDIENTS

½ cup roughly chopped zucchini

½ cup roughly chopped red bell pepper

¼ cup roughly chopped yellow onion

2 medium plum tomatoes, seeded, cut into 1" pieces

1 clove garlic, peeled

1 teaspoon fresh rosemary

2 teaspoons olive oil

¼ teaspoon dried thyme

2 ounces rotini pasta

½ teaspoon sea salt

1. Preheat oven to 450°F and line a baking sheet with foil.

2. To prepared baking sheet add zucchini, bell pepper, onion, tomatoes, garlic, and rosemary. Drizzle with olive oil and toss to coat evenly.

3. Bake 20 minutes, then add thyme and stir well. Bake an additional 10–15 minutes or until vegetables are very tender and lightly charred. Remove from oven and cool 10 minutes.

4. Once cool, place vegetables into a blender or food processor and purée until smooth.

5. In a 2-quart saucepan over high heat, add water to fill pot ¾ full. Once water begins to boil, add pasta and salt. Cook, stirring occasionally, until pasta is just al dente, about 8 minutes. Reserve ½ cup pasta water, then drain pasta and return to pot.

6. Add sauce to pot with pasta and return to medium heat. Cook, stirring constantly, until sauce is bubbling, about 3 minutes. If sauce seems too thick, add reserved pasta water a few teaspoons at a time until thickness is to your liking. Serve immediately.

PER SERVING

Calories: 373

Fat: 10g

Sodium: 196mg

Carbohydrates: 59g

Fiber: 7g

Sugar: 10g

Protein: 11g

OLIVE OIL PASTA WITH MARINATED ARTICHOKES AND SPINACH

PREP TIME: 5 MINUTES | COOK TIME: 10 MINUTES | SERVES: 1

 You can usually find 6-ounce jars of marinated artichoke hearts where they sell olives and pickles. They keep up to a month after opening and can be added to salads or a variety of pasta dishes. They are also delicious as a snack! Look for the type marinated in oil for the best flavor.

INGREDIENTS

2 ounces spaghetti pasta

½ teaspoon sea salt

1 tablespoon olive oil

1 clove garlic, peeled and minced

⅛ teaspoon crushed red pepper flakes

3 marinated artichoke hearts, chopped

1 cup lightly packed baby spinach

1 teaspoon freshly grated lemon zest

1 tablespoon grated Parmesan cheese, divided

1. In a 2-quart saucepan over high heat, add water to fill pot ¾ full. Once water begins to boil, add pasta and salt. Cook, stirring occasionally, until pasta is just al dente, about 8 minutes. Reserve ¼ cup pasta water, then drain. Set aside.

2. In an 8" skillet over medium heat, add olive oil. Once hot, add garlic and red pepper flakes. Cook 1 minute or until garlic is very fragrant and lightly golden around the edges. Add pasta, 2 tablespoons reserved pasta water, artichoke hearts, spinach, and lemon zest. Cook 1 minute or until spinach is wilted and artichokes are hot. Add additional pasta water 1 tablespoon at a time if pasta seems dry. Add ½ tablespoon Parmesan and toss to evenly coat.

3. Transfer to a serving plate and garnish with remaining Parmesan. Serve immediately.

PER SERVING

Calories: 391

Fat: 16g

Sodium: 626mg

Carbohydrates: 49g

Fiber: 5g

Sugar: 1g

Protein: 12g

ORZO AND MOZZARELLA-STUFFED TOMATO

PREP TIME: 10 MINUTES | COOK TIME: 23 MINUTES | SERVES: 1

 This stuffed tomato makes a filling and delicious meal for one. Beefsteak tomatoes are a large variety of tomato that have a higher flesh to pulp ratio compared to other tomato varieties. If you can't find a beefsteak tomato, you can use two smaller vine or plum tomatoes.

INGREDIENTS

1 cup water

¼ teaspoon sea salt

2 tablespoons orzo pasta

1 large beefsteak tomato

¼ cup shredded part-skim mozzarella cheese

½ clove garlic, peeled and minced

½ teaspoon Italian seasoning

½ teaspoon olive oil

1. In a 1-quart saucepan over medium heat, add water and salt and bring to a boil. Add orzo and cook until al dente, about 8 minutes. Drain and rinse with cool water to stop cooking. Set aside.

2. Preheat oven to 350°F and line a small baking sheet with foil.

3. Cut top off tomato and scoop out pulp. Discard top, seeds, and core. Roughly chop pulp with a knife and place it in a small bowl. Mix in cooked orzo, mozzarella, garlic, and Italian seasoning.

4. Stuff mixture into tomato and place on prepared baking sheet. Drizzle olive oil over top. Bake 15–20 minutes or until tomato is tender and filling is hot. Cool 5 minutes before serving.

Measuring Pasta Without a Scale
If you do not have a kitchen scale, you can use the following guide to measure out your dry pastas. For long pasta like spaghetti, measure out enough pasta to equal the diameter of a quarter (.75 inches or 19 mm). Smaller dry pastas like macaroni, rotini, and bow tie equal about ½ cup.

PER SERVING

Calories: 193
Fat: 7g
Sodium: 213mg
Carbohydrates: 25g

Fiber: 3g
Sugar: 6g
Protein: 9g

FETTUCCINE WITH CRAB AND LEMON

PREP TIME: 10 MINUTES | COOK TIME: 12 MINUTES | SERVES: 1

 Just because you are cooking for one doesn't mean you can't enjoy delicacies like crabmeat. With a bright white wine and lemon sauce, this pasta is refreshing and loaded with luscious lump crab! And don't worry if you have leftover crab. It won't go to waste; simply use it to make Baked Crab Cakes (see Chapter 8) for dinner the next day!

INGREDIENTS

2 ounces fettuccine pasta

½ teaspoon sea salt

1 teaspoon olive oil

½ clove garlic, peeled and minced

½ teaspoon freshly grated lemon zest

¼ teaspoon Italian seasoning

2 tablespoons white wine

1 tablespoon lemon juice

6 medium cherry tomatoes, sliced in half

¼ teaspoon freshly cracked black pepper

¼ cup lump crabmeat

2 teaspoons chopped fresh parsley

1. In a 2-quart saucepan over high heat, add water to fill pot ¾ full. Once water begins to boil, add pasta and salt. Cook, stirring occasionally, until pasta is just al dente, about 8 minutes. Reserve ¼ cup pasta water, then drain. Set aside.

2. In an 8" skillet over medium heat, add olive oil. Once hot, add garlic, lemon zest, and Italian seasoning. Cook until very fragrant, about 1 minute. Add wine and lemon juice and cook until reduced by half, about 1 minute.

3. Add tomatoes and black pepper and cook until tomatoes start to soften, about 1 minute, then add pasta and 2 tablespoons pasta water. Toss pasta in mixture, adding additional water if pasta is too dry.

4. Add crabmeat and cook 30 seconds to heat through. Transfer to a serving plate and garnish with parsley. Serve immediately.

PER SERVING

Calories: 319
Fat: 6g
Sodium: 379mg
Carbohydrates: 49g

Fiber: 4g
Sugar: 4g
Protein: 15g

SPANAKOPITA-STUFFED SHELLS

PREP TIME: 15 MINUTES | COOK TIME: 38 MINUTES | SERVES: 1

 Jumbo pasta shells are a fantastic addition to a solo cook's pantry. They can be stuffed with all manner of fillings, they are easy to portion for one, and they are incredibly fun to eat! These shells are filled with the best part of the spanakopita— the filling!

INGREDIENTS

½ cup marinara sauce

5 jumbo size pasta shells (about 2 ounces)

½ teaspoon sea salt

2 teaspoons olive oil

2 tablespoons chopped yellow onion

2 cups lightly packed baby spinach

½ clove garlic, peeled and minced

2 tablespoons chopped green onion (green part only)

1 tablespoon freeze-dried dill

½ teaspoon freshly grated lemon zest

2 tablespoons chopped fresh parsley

¼ cup part-skim ricotta cheese

2 tablespoons crumbled feta cheese

2 tablespoons part-skim mozzarella cheese

1. Preheat oven to 350°F and lightly spray a 6" baking dish with nonstick cooking spray. Spread marinara sauce in bottom of prepared dish. Set aside.

2. In a 2-quart saucepan over high heat, add water to fill pot ¾ full. Once water begins to boil, add pasta and salt. Cook, stirring occasionally, until pasta is just al dente, about 9 minutes. Drain and set aside.

3. In an 8" skillet over medium heat, add olive oil. Once hot, add yellow onion and cook until just tender, about 1 minute. Add spinach and cook until completely wilted, about 2 minutes. Add garlic and cook until fragrant, about 30 seconds. Remove from heat and stir in green onion, dill, lemon zest, and parsley.

4. Transfer spinach mixture to a medium bowl. Add ricotta and feta and stir well to combine. Spoon mixture into shells and place into prepared pan (with spinach filling sides up). Sprinkle with mozzarella.

5. Bake 25–30 minutes or until sauce is bubbling and cheese is melted and starting to brown. Cool 5 minutes before enjoying.

PER SERVING

Calories: 556 | Fat: 21g | Sodium: 1,093mg | Carbohydrates: 64g Fiber: 7g | Sugar: 11g | Protein: 25g

PASTA PRIMAVERA

PREP TIME: 10 MINUTES | COOK TIME: 20 MINUTES | SERVES: 1

 This healthy dish combines pasta and fresh vegetables in a light wine sauce. Bright and clean tasting, this dish is perfect for any season. You can make this dish ahead of time, just keep the pasta and sauce separate while reheating, then plate as directed.

INGREDIENTS

2 ounces penne pasta

½ teaspoon salt

2 teaspoons olive oil

½ cup chopped broccoli florets

¼ cup chopped zucchini

¼ cup chopped yellow squash

2 sun-dried tomatoes, chopped

½ clove garlic, peeled and minced

2 tablespoons white wine

⅛ teaspoon sea salt

⅛ teaspoon freshly cracked black pepper

1 basil leaf, chopped

1. In a 2-quart saucepan over high heat, add water to fill pot ¾ full. Once water begins to boil, add pasta and salt. Cook, stirring occasionally, until pasta is just al dente, about 8 minutes. Drain and transfer pasta to a serving plate.

2. Return pot to medium heat and add olive oil. Once hot, add broccoli, zucchini, and squash and cook until just tender, about 5 minutes. Add sun-dried tomatoes and cook until soft and tender, about 5 minutes. Add garlic and cook until fragrant, about 1 minute.

3. Add wine, salt, and black pepper and toss to combine, then let wine reduce by half, about 1 minute.

4. Pour vegetables and sauce over pasta. Garnish with basil. Serve immediately.

Cooking Without Wine

If you prefer not to cook with alcohol, you can use the following ideas for replacing wine in your cooking. Instead of white wine, use a low-sodium vegetable or chicken broth. For red wine, use a mushroom broth or tomato juice. These substitutions have loads of flavor and will still enhance your dish.

PER SERVING

Calories: 337　　　Fiber: 5g

Fat: 10g　　　　　Sugar: 5g

Sodium: 404mg　　Protein: 11g

Carbohydrates: 51g

BOW TIE PESTO PASTA

PREP TIME: 10 MINUTES | COOK TIME: 16 MINUTES | SERVES: 1

 This dish is a hearty meal for one on its own, but if you'd like, you can toss in some shrimp or a couple ounces of baked or grilled chicken if you have it on hand. This is also a great recipe for using up vegetable scraps so they do not go to waste!

INGREDIENTS

2 ounces bow tie pasta

½ teaspoon salt

2 teaspoons olive oil

¼ cup chopped red bell pepper

¼ cup chopped zucchini

¼ cup chopped yellow squash

5 medium cherry tomatoes, sliced in half

2 tablespoons basil pesto

½ teaspoon fresh lemon juice

⅛ teaspoon freshly cracked black pepper

2 tablespoons grated Parmesan cheese

1. In a 2-quart saucepan over high heat, add water to fill pot ¾ full. Once water begins to boil, add pasta and salt. Cook, stirring occasionally, until pasta is just al dente, about 8 minutes. Drain and set pasta aside.

2. Return pot to medium heat and add olive oil. Once hot, add bell pepper, zucchini, and squash and cook until just tender, about 5 minutes. Add tomatoes and cook until soft and tender, about 3 minutes.

3. Add cooked pasta, pesto, and lemon juice to pot and toss to evenly coat in sauce.

4. Transfer pasta and vegetables to a serving plate. Garnish with black pepper and Parmesan. Enjoy hot.

PER SERVING

Calories: 495

Fat: 24g

Sodium: 650mg

Carbohydrates: 55g

Fiber: 6g

Sugar: 7g

Protein: 14g

CREAMY PASTA WITH CHICKPEAS

PREP TIME: 10 MINUTES | COOK TIME: 14 MINUTES | SERVES: 1

 Chickpeas, a staple of the Mediterranean diet, provide a healthy boost of fiber and protein to this pasta dish. This recipe calls for ditalini, but you can use small elbows or small shells in their place. The Calabrian chilis add heat and a rich tang to the sauce, but you can swap them for ¼ teaspoon crushed red pepper flakes.

INGREDIENTS

2 ounces ditalini pasta

½ teaspoon salt

2 teaspoons olive oil

1 teaspoon chopped fresh rosemary leaves

½ clove garlic, peeled and minced

2 teaspoons tomato paste

2 tablespoons white wine

1 teaspoon chopped Calabrian chilis

½ cup canned chickpeas, rinsed and drained, divided

2 tablespoons grated Parmesan cheese

1. In a 2-quart saucepan over high heat, add water to fill pot ¾ full. Once water begins to boil, add pasta and salt. Cook, stirring occasionally, until pasta is just cooked but still firm, about 7 minutes. Reserve ½ cup pasta water. Drain and set pasta aside.

2. Return pot to medium-low heat and add olive oil. Once hot, add rosemary and garlic and cook until very fragrant, about 1 minute. Stir in tomato paste and cook until paste is darker in color, about 2 minutes.

3. Stir in wine, chilis, ¼ cup chickpeas, and reserved pasta water. Cook, stirring well to loosen any bits on bottom of pot, about 10 seconds. Transfer mixture to a blender and purée until smooth, then return to pot.

4. Return pot to medium-low heat and add cooked pasta and remaining ¼ cup chickpeas. Cook, stirring constantly, until pasta is thoroughly cooked and mixture is thickened, about 3 minutes. Transfer mixture to a serving bowl and garnish with Parmesan. Serve immediately.

PER SERVING

Calories: 465
Fat: 14g
Sodium: 618mg
Carbohydrates: 65g

Fiber: 8g
Sugar: 5g
Protein: 17g

ANGEL HAIR PASTA WITH SHRIMP AND LEMON

PREP TIME: 10 MINUTES | COOK TIME: 10 MINUTES | SERVES: 1

 A simple and easy meal for one, this shrimp pasta is dressed in a light lemon wine sauce and comes together in minutes. Stocking frozen shrimp is a brilliant way to have seafood on hand for easy meals.

INGREDIENTS

2 ounces angel hair pasta

½ teaspoon salt

2 teaspoons olive oil

6 medium shrimp, peeled and deveined, thawed if frozen

½ clove garlic, peeled and minced

2 tablespoons white wine

2 teaspoons lemon juice

2 tablespoons chopped fresh parsley

⅛ teaspoon freshly cracked black pepper

1. In a 2-quart saucepan over high heat, add water to fill pot ¾ full. Once water begins to boil, add pasta and salt. Cook, stirring occasionally, until pasta is just cooked but still firm, about 7 minutes. Reserve ½ cup pasta water. Drain and set pasta aside.

2. Return pot to medium-low heat and add olive oil. Once hot, add shrimp and cook 30 seconds, stirring constantly, then add garlic and cook 30 more seconds. Add wine, lemon juice, and ¼ cup pasta water and stir well.

3. Add cooked pasta and toss to evenly coat with sauce, until shrimp are curled into a C shape and are opaque, about 1 minute. If pasta seems dry, add more pasta water 1 tablespoon at a time until sauce is loosened to your liking.

4. Transfer pasta to a serving bowl and garnish with parsley and black pepper. Serve immediately.

Save Your Scraps

Save your shrimp shells in a zip-top bag in the freezer along with other vegetable scraps. Once you have 2 cups frozen shells, add it to a pot with 1 cup carrot peels, 2 onion skins, ½ cup celery leaves, 2 garlic cloves, and a bay leaf. Cover with cold water and simmer over medium-low heat for 1 hour. Strain and refrigerate or freeze for a rich shrimp broth.

PER SERVING

Calories: 338
Fat: 10g
Sodium: 390mg
Carbohydrates: 45g

Fiber: 3g
Sugar: 1g
Protein: 13g

ROTINI WITH CHARRED TOMATOES AND MOZZARELLA

PREP TIME: 15 MINUTES | COOK TIME: 18 MINUTES | SERVES: 1

 Charring tomatoes brings out their natural sweetness and gives them a slightly smoky flavor that is hard to resist. If you use a larger tomato, such as a plum or vine tomato, use just one and cut it in half before broiling.

INGREDIENTS

8 medium cherry tomatoes

1 teaspoon extra-virgin olive oil

1 teaspoon balsamic vinegar

2 ounces rotini pasta

½ teaspoon salt

2 teaspoons olive oil

1 tablespoon minced yellow onion

½ clove garlic, peeled and minced

⅛ teaspoon crushed red pepper flakes

3 tablespoons grated part-skim mozzarella cheese

2 tablespoons chopped fresh parsley

PER SERVING

Calories: 422
Fat: 17g
Sodium: 303mg
Carbohydrates: 52g

Fiber: 5g
Sugar: 6g
Protein: 14g

1. Preheat broiler and line a small baking sheet with foil.

2. Place tomatoes on prepared baking sheet and broil until skins just start to blister, about 3 minutes. Use tongs to flip tomatoes and return to broiler until second side is just charred and tomatoes are tender, about 3–4 minutes. Transfer tomatoes to a small bowl and add extra-virgin olive oil and balsamic vinegar. Stir to coat and set aside.

3. In a 2-quart saucepan over high heat, add water to fill pot ¾ full. Once water begins to boil, add pasta and salt. Cook, stirring occasionally, until pasta is just cooked but still firm, about 7 minutes. Reserve ¼ cup pasta water. Drain and set pasta aside.

4. Return pot to medium-low heat and add olive oil. Once hot, add onion and cook until just translucent, about 1 minute, then add garlic and cook 30 seconds. Add charred tomatoes along with any juices in bowl and red pepper flakes. Stir, lightly crushing tomatoes with the back of a spatula to form a chunky sauce, about 20 seconds. If sauce seems dry, add reserved pasta water 1 tablespoon at a time until sauce is loosed to your liking.

5. Add cooked pasta to pot and toss to evenly coat with sauce, until pasta is fully cooked, about 2 minutes.

6. Transfer pasta to a serving bowl and garnish with mozzarella and parsley. Serve immediately.

LASAGNA ROLLS

PREP TIME: 20 MINUTES | COOK TIME: 52 MINUTES | SERVES: 1

 Lasagna Rolls are the perfect way to enjoy a single serving of lasagna without having heaps of leftovers. This recipe can be made ahead. Just prepare up to the point of baking and then refrigerate. When you are ready to eat, just slide the dish in the oven and cook as directed.

INGREDIENTS

2 dry lasagna noodles

½ teaspoon salt

2 teaspoons olive oil

3 tablespoons chopped yellow onion

¼ cup sliced button mushrooms

½ clove garlic, peeled and minced

1½ cups lightly packed baby spinach

¼ cup part-skim ricotta cheese

2 tablespoons shredded part-skim mozzarella cheese

¼ teaspoon Italian seasoning

½ cup marinara sauce, divided

2 tablespoons grated Parmesan cheese

PER SERVING

Calories: 473

Fat: 16g

Sodium: 982mg

Carbohydrates: 61g

Fiber: 7g

Sugar: 10g

Protein: 19g

1. Preheat oven to 375°F and lightly spray a 6" casserole dish with nonstick cooking spray.

2. In a 2-quart saucepan over high heat, add water to fill pot ¾ full. Once water begins to boil, add pasta and salt. Cook, stirring occasionally, until pasta is soft enough to bend easily but not cooked through, about 10 minutes. Drain and set pasta aside.

3. Return pot to medium heat and add olive oil. Once hot, add onion and cook until just tender, about 2 minutes. Add mushrooms and cook until mushrooms are soft, about 2 minutes. Add garlic and spinach and cook until spinach is thoroughly wilted, about 3 minutes. Remove from heat and transfer to a medium bowl to cool, about 5 minutes.

4. To cooled spinach mixture add ricotta, mozzarella, and Italian seasoning. Mix well. Lay cooked lasagna noodles on a cutting board and divide filling between noodles. Spread filling over length of each noodle, then roll into a jelly roll shape.

5. To prepared pan add ¼ cup marinara sauce and spread evenly. Place rolls seam side down in pan. Spoon remaining ¼ cup sauce over top of rolls. Cover dish tightly with foil and bake 25 minutes.

6. Remove foil and top rolls with Parmesan and return to oven uncovered for 10–15 minutes or until Parmesan is melted and rolls are heated through. Cool 5 minutes before serving.

BAKED ZITI

PREP TIME: 10 MINUTES | COOK TIME: 34 MINUTES | SERVES: 1

 Ziti is a tube-shaped pasta that is originally from Campagna, Italy. If you can't find it, you can use penne or another smaller tube-shaped pasta. You can easily make this ahead by covering the assembled dish and refrigerating up to three days.

INGREDIENTS

2 ounces ziti pasta

½ teaspoon salt

2 teaspoons olive oil

2 tablespoons chopped yellow onion

½ clove garlic, peeled and minced

1 basil leaf, minced

¼ teaspoon Italian seasoning

½ cup marinara sauce

2 tablespoons part-skim ricotta cheese

2 tablespoons shredded part-skim mozzarella cheese

2 teaspoons chopped fresh parsley

1. Preheat oven to 375°F and lightly spray a 6" casserole dish with nonstick cooking spray.

2. In a 2-quart saucepan over high heat, add water to fill pot ¾ full. Once water begins to boil, add pasta and salt. Cook, stirring occasionally, until pasta is soft enough to bend easily but not cooked through, about 8 minutes. Drain and set pasta aside.

3. Return pot to medium heat and add olive oil. Once hot, add onion and cook until just tender, about 2 minutes. Add garlic, basil, and Italian seasoning and cook until very fragrant, about 30 seconds. Add marinara sauce and stir well. Bring to a simmer, then reduce heat to low and cook 3 minutes. Remove from heat.

4. Spread ¼ cup marinara mixture in prepared dish. With a spoon, add two mounds of ricotta. Stir pasta into remaining marinara mixture and then add to dish. Top with mozzarella.

5. Bake 20 minutes or until pasta is bubbling all over and cheese is melted and starting to brown. Cool 5 minutes before garnishing with parsley and serving.

PER SERVING

Calories: 446	Fiber: 5g
Fat: 15g	Sugar: 9g
Sodium: 840mg	Protein: 16g
Carbohydrates: 58g	

SPAGHETTI WITH MEAT SAUCE

PREP TIME: 10 MINUTES | COOK TIME: 24 MINUTES | SERVES: 1

 A little lean meat goes a long way in this sauce. You will also use some finely chopped vegetables to help round out the sauce and to add some extra nutrition. Serve this with a slice of toasted Italian bread and a crisp salad!

INGREDIENTS

2 ounces spaghetti pasta

½ teaspoon salt

2 ounces 90/10 ground beef

¼ cup finely chopped button mushrooms

2 tablespoons finely chopped yellow onion

1 tablespoon finely grated carrot

½ clove garlic, peeled and minced

1 tablespoon tomato paste

1 tablespoon red wine

¼ teaspoon ground fennel

¼ teaspoon Italian seasoning

⅛ teaspoon dried oregano

1 tablespoon grated Parmesan cheese

1. In a 2-quart saucepan over high heat, add water to fill pot ¾ full. Once water begins to boil, add pasta and salt. Cook, stirring occasionally, until pasta is just cooked but still firm, about 7 minutes. Reserve ½ cup pasta water. Drain and set pasta aside.

2. Return pot to medium-low heat and add beef. Crumble beef and cook until browned, about 5 minutes. Add mushrooms, onion, and carrot and cook until vegetables start to soften, about 3 minutes. Add garlic and cook until fragrant, about 30 seconds.

3. Add tomato paste and cook until paste is darker in color, about 3 minutes, then add wine and scrape pan to loosen any bits stuck to the bottom. Stir in pasta water, fennel, Italian seasoning, and oregano. Bring mixture to a boil, then reduce heat to low and simmer 5 minutes.

4. Transfer pasta to a serving bowl and spoon sauce over top. Garnish with Parmesan. Serve immediately.

PER SERVING

Calories: 359

Fat: 6g

Sodium: 434mg

Carbohydrates: 51g

Fiber: 4g

Sugar: 4g

Protein: 22g

MACARONI AND CHEESE

PREP TIME: 10 MINUTES | COOK TIME: 19 MINUTES | SERVES: 1

 Riced sweet potato and cauliflower blend is available in most frozen vegetable sections, and here it helps take any guilt out of a bowl of comforting macaroni and cheese. If you are unable to find this blend, use 2 tablespoons riced cauliflower and 2 tablespoons finely grated sweet potato.

INGREDIENTS

2 ounces elbow pasta

½ teaspoon salt

2 teaspoons olive oil

¼ cup frozen riced cauliflower and sweet potato blend

½ clove garlic, peeled and minced

¼ teaspoon Dijon mustard

⅛ teaspoon onion powder

1 teaspoon all-purpose flour

½ cup 1% milk

3 tablespoons grated part-skim mozzarella cheese

1 tablespoon grated Parmesan cheese

1. In a 2-quart saucepan over high heat, add water to fill pot ¾ full. Once water begins to boil, add pasta and salt. Cook, stirring occasionally, until pasta is al dente, about 9 minutes. Drain and set pasta aside.

2. Return pot to medium heat and add olive oil. Once hot, add riced cauliflower and sweet potato and cook until tender, about 3 minutes. Add garlic and cook until very fragrant, about 1 minute. Add mustard and onion powder and stir to mix.

3. Sprinkle flour over vegetable mixture and cook 1 minute, then slowly stir in milk. Cook until milk is simmering and has thickened to coat the back of a spoon, about 3 minutes. With an immersion blender, purée sauce until smooth, about 1 minute.

4. Reduce heat to low and stir in mozzarella and Parmesan until melted, about 30 seconds, then fold in pasta. Serve immediately.

PER SERVING

Calories: 456   Fiber: 3g

Fat: 15g   Sugar: 8g

Sodium: 469mg   Protein: 19g

Carbohydrates: 59g

CHAPTER 7
VEGETARIAN MAIN DISHES

White Beans with Garlic and
Fresh Tomatoes 118

Black Bean Sliders 119

Zucchini Lasagna 120

Lentil Balls 121

Black Bean Tostadas with
Corn and Tomato 123

Kale and Lentil Stew 124

White Bean Cassoulet 125

Three-Bean Vegetarian Chili 126

Cauliflower Steak with Balsamic
Glaze 127

Spinach and Artichoke–Stuffed
Mushroom 128

Mediterranean Twice-Baked
Potato 130

Polenta Cakes with Fresh Tomato
Sauce 132

Lentil Curry with Spinach
and Tomato 133

Tofu and Chickpea–
Stuffed Pepper 134

Mediterranean Stuffed Tomato 135

Seasoned Tofu Gyro 137

Lentils with Tomato,
Artichoke, and Feta 138

Lentil and Zucchini Boats 139

Baked Spaghetti Nests with
Mozzarella 140

Reducing animal protein consumption comes with a slew of benefits for your health. Eating more plant-based meals can help reduce inflammation, lower bad cholesterol, reduce risk of heart disease and type 2 diabetes, and increase energy and stamina. When you're cooking for one, it can often feel like a salad or frozen meal is the easiest way to go. With a variety of different vegetables, legumes and lentils, fruits, nuts, and seeds, you can create a variety of satisfying, healthful, and delicious single-serving meals.

This chapter contains tasty, easy, and nutritionally vibrant main meals that avoid animal proteins and, in some cases, all animal-based ingredients entirely. They were developed to feed one along with a side dish, a cup of soup, or a salad. Hearty and healthy Mediterranean Twice-Baked Potato or Lentil and Zucchini Boats are a meal prepper's dream! Craving something a bit more elegant? White Bean Cassoulet or Polenta Cakes with Fresh Tomato Sauce should fit the bill. If it is comfort food you crave, try Zucchini Lasagna or Three-Bean Vegetarian Chili. This chapter is packed with recipes for any day of the week and any occasion, so treat yourself with recipes designed just for you!

WHITE BEANS WITH GARLIC AND FRESH TOMATOES

PREP TIME: 5 MINUTES | COOK TIME: 11 MINUTES | SERVES: 1

Beans are a Mediterranean diet friendly plant-based protein and add nutrition to your meals. If you want to make this dish a little creamy, use the back of a spoon to crush ¼ of the beans while they simmer, then stir them into the sauce. The beans will thicken the sauce and add a creamy texture without cream or butter.

INGREDIENTS

2 teaspoons olive oil

2 tablespoons minced carrot

2 tablespoons minced yellow onion

2 tablespoons minced celery

6 medium cherry tomatoes, sliced in half

½ clove garlic, peeled and minced

⅛ teaspoon dried thyme

⅛ teaspoon smoked paprika

⅛ teaspoon Aleppo pepper

½ cup canned cannellini beans, rinsed and drained

⅓ cup low-sodium vegetable broth

½ teaspoon lemon juice

1 tablespoon grated vegetarian Parmesan cheese

2 teaspoons finely chopped fresh parsley

1. In an 8" skillet over medium heat, add olive oil. Once hot, add carrot, onion, and celery and cook until soft, about 3 minutes. Add tomatoes and cook until tender, about 2 minutes. Add garlic, thyme, paprika, and Aleppo pepper and cook until fragrant, about 1 minute.

2. Stir in cannellini beans, broth, and lemon juice and cook until beans are hot and tomatoes have started to break down slightly, about 5 minutes.

3. Transfer to a serving plate and garnish with Parmesan and parsley. Serve immediately.

Save Time at the Salad Bar

If your grocery store has a salad bar, you can use it to save time at home. You may be able to buy chopped onion, carrot, celery, and other ingredients. You can also often find marinated artichokes, olives, and cheeses. Use the salad bar to buy small amounts of these prepared ingredients on busy days.

PER SERVING

Calories: 230 | Fat: 11g | Sodium: 445mg | Carbohydrates: 31g Fiber: 10g | Sugar: 6g | Protein: 8g

BLACK BEAN SLIDERS

PREP TIME: 10 MINUTES | COOK TIME: 12 MINUTES | SERVES: 1

 These sliders make a fun lunch or dinner for one, and can be made into a larger single patty to be enjoyed on a regular-sized whole-wheat hamburger bun. If you want a quick burger sauce, mix 1 tablespoon Greek yogurt with 1 teaspoon salsa and spread on top buns.

INGREDIENTS

2 teaspoons olive oil, divided

¼ cup finely chopped red bell pepper

2 tablespoons minced yellow onion

1 tablespoon finely chopped fresh cilantro

½ clove garlic, peeled and minced

¼ teaspoon ground cumin

¼ teaspoon chili powder

½ cup low-sodium canned black beans, rinsed and drained

¼ cup water

¼ cup dry whole-wheat bread crumbs

2 whole-wheat slider buns

2 leaves butter lettuce

2 (¼"-thick) slices plum tomato

1. In a 1-quart saucepan over medium heat, add 1 teaspoon olive oil. Once hot, add bell pepper and onion. Cook until tender, about 2 minutes. Add cilantro, garlic, cumin, and chili powder and cook until fragrant, about 30 seconds. Stir in black beans and water. Simmer, stirring often, until all liquid is almost evaporated, about 3 minutes.

2. Remove pot from heat and gently mash beans with the back of a spoon until a chunky mixture forms. Stir in bread crumbs and divide mixture into two patties.

3. In an 8" skillet over medium heat, add remaining 1 teaspoon olive oil and let it heat briefly, then swirl pan to coat. Add patties and cook 3 minutes per side or until patties are crisp. Remove from heat.

4. To assemble, split slider buns. Place patties on bottom bun and top with lettuce leaves folded to fit patty and a tomato slice. Cover with top of bun. Enjoy immediately.

PER SERVING

Calories: 498
Fat: 14g
Sodium: 897mg
Carbohydrates: 75g
Fiber: 9g
Sugar: 12g
Protein: 22g

ZUCCHINI LASAGNA

PREP TIME: 40 MINUTES | COOK TIME: 30 MINUTES | SERVES: 1

 This recipe replaces the traditional pasta sheets with ribbons of zucchini for a hearty vegetarian dish for one that packs in flavor and nutrition. Do not skip salting and draining the zucchini since it draws out a lot of excess moisture. If you skip this step, you will have a soupy result.

INGREDIENTS

1 medium zucchini, ends trimmed

½ teaspoon sea salt

¼ cup part-skim ricotta cheese

1 tablespoon finely chopped fresh parsley

½ teaspoon Italian seasoning

2 tablespoons shredded part-skim mozzarella cheese

½ cup marinara sauce

1 tablespoon grated vegetarian Parmesan cheese

1. With a mandoline slicer or sharp chef's knife slice zucchini into thin ribbons. Place onto layers of paper towels and sprinkle both sides with salt. Let stand 30 minutes to draw off excess liquid. Rinse zucchini under cool water, then place on clean, dry paper towels and press to remove additional moisture. Set aside.

2. Preheat oven to 375°F and spray a 6" casserole dish with nonstick cooking spray.

3. In a small bowl, combine ricotta, parsley, Italian seasoning, and mozzarella.

4. To prepared pan add ¼ cup marinara sauce. Top with ⅓ of zucchini ribbons, and ½ of cheese mixture. Repeat layers, ending with marinara. Sprinkle top with Parmesan.

5. Bake 30–35 minutes or until lasagna is hot and bubbling all over. Cool 5 minutes before serving.

PER SERVING

Calories: 245

Fat: 10g

Sodium: 1,002mg

Carbohydrates: 23g

Fiber: 4g

Sugar: 13g

Protein: 14g

LENTIL BALLS

PREP TIME: 10 MINUTES | COOK TIME: 34 MINUTES | SERVES: 1

 If you are not able to find fine-cut bulgur wheat, you can replace it with ¼ cup almond meal and 1 teaspoon flaxseed meal. This will add the nutty flavor and provide the binding of the bulgur wheat, as well as make the dish gluten-free and add a little extra healthy fat!

INGREDIENTS

1 tablespoon olive oil

¼ cup minced white onion

1 teaspoon tomato paste

⅛ teaspoon smoked paprika

⅛ teaspoon ground cumin

⅛ teaspoon cardamom

⅛ teaspoon allspice

¼ cup dry red lentils, rinsed and drained

1 cup water

¼ cup fine-cut bulgur wheat

2 tablespoons thinly sliced green onion (green part only)

3 leaves butter lettuce, torn in half

1 lemon wedge

1. In a medium saucepan over medium heat, add olive oil. Once hot, add white onion and cook 1 minute, then add tomato paste and cook until tomato paste is darker in color and onion is very tender, about 4 minutes. Add paprika, cumin, cardamom, and allspice and cook until very fragrant, about 1 minute.

2. Stir in lentils, ensuring they are evenly coated in spices, then stir in water, scraping bottom of pot to release any bits.

3. Bring lentil mixture to a boil, then reduce heat to low, cover with a lid, and cook until lentils are starting to fall apart, about 8 minutes. Remove from heat and stir in bulgur wheat. Cover again and let sit 20 minutes or until all liquid is absorbed and bulgur wheat is tender.

4. Stir in green onion and mix well. Form mixture into six balls. Serve on lettuce with a spritz from lemon wedge. Serve warm or at room temperature.

PER SERVING

Calories: 435	Fiber: 11g
Fat: 15g	Sugar: 3g
Sodium: 53mg	Protein: 17g
Carbohydrates: 64g	

BLACK BEAN TOSTADAS WITH CORN AND TOMATO

PREP TIME: 10 MINUTES | COOK TIME: 16 MINUTES | SERVES: 1

 These tostadas swap the usual ground beef for spiced black beans, creamy avocado, and a spritz of sharp lime—making a perfect vegetarian dish for one! If you have a little low-fat sour cream, feel free to add a teaspoon or two to the top of these tostadas.

INGREDIENTS

2 (6") corn tortillas

2 teaspoons olive oil, divided

2 tablespoons minced yellow onion

¼ teaspoon chili powder

⅛ teaspoon ground cumin

½ clove garlic, peeled and minced

½ cup canned black beans, rinsed and drained

¼ cup frozen corn kernels

¼ cup diced plum tomato

¼ cup chopped avocado

1 tablespoon finely chopped cilantro

1 lime wedge

1. Preheat oven to 400°F and lightly spray a small baking sheet with nonstick cooking spray.

2. Place tortillas on prepared baking sheet and lightly brush both sides of tortillas with ½ teaspoon olive oil. Bake 5 minutes. Flip and bake another 5–8 minutes or until tortillas are crisp and golden brown. Remove from oven and cool while you prepare remaining ingredients.

3. In an 8" skillet over medium heat, add remaining olive oil. Once hot, add onion and cook until just tender, about 1 minute. Add chili powder and cumin and cook 30 seconds, then add garlic and cook until very fragrant, about 30 seconds.

4. Stir in black beans, corn, and tomato and cook until beans are hot and corn is cooked through, about 3 minutes.

5. Divide black bean mixture between prepared tortillas. Garnish with avocado, cilantro, and spritzes of lime wedge. Serve immediately.

PER SERVING

Calories: 437
Fat: 19g
Sodium: 318mg
Carbohydrates: 58g

Fiber: 17g
Sugar: 4g
Protein: 13g

KALE AND LENTIL STEW

PREP TIME: 10 MINUTES | COOK TIME: 38 MINUTES | SERVES: 1

 This stew makes a complete meal for one in one pot, so cleanup is a breeze. If you have it on hand, about ⅓ cup chopped potato (russet or Yukon Gold) would be wonderful to add during the last 15 minutes of cooking time to make this even more filling.

INGREDIENTS

1 tablespoon olive oil

¼ cup chopped white onion

¼ cup chopped carrot

¼ cup chopped celery

½ cup chopped kale

½ clove garlic, peeled and minced

⅛ teaspoon smoked paprika

⅛ teaspoon dried thyme

¼ cup dry green lentils, rinsed and drained

1 cup low-sodium vegetable broth

½ bay leaf

½ teaspoon lemon juice

1. In a medium pot over medium heat, add olive oil. Once hot, add onion, carrot, and celery and cook until tender, about 5 minutes. Add kale and cook until thoroughly wilted, about 2 minutes. Add garlic, paprika, and thyme and cook until fragrant, about 30 seconds.

2. Add lentils to pot and stir to combine. Stir in broth and bay leaf. Bring mixture to a boil, then reduce heat to medium-low, cover pot, and simmer 30 minutes or until lentils are tender.

3. Remove lid and discard bay leaf. Stir in lemon juice, then remove pot from heat and let cool 3 minutes before serving hot.

Swapping Lentils

You can use any lentils you like for your cooking, but be aware some are sturdier after cooking than others. Green lentils tend to keep their shape and are a little chewier, but red and yellow lentils tend to fall apart after cooking, creating a creamier, smoother finished dish.

PER SERVING

Calories: 345
Fat: 14g
Sodium: 188mg
Carbohydrates: 44g
Fiber: 9g
Sugar: 8g
Protein: 14g

WHITE BEAN CASSOULET

PREP TIME: 10 MINUTES | COOK TIME: 26 MINUTES | SERVES: 1

 This French dish is typically slow-cooked all day with some sort of meat such as chicken or sausage. This version leaves out the chicken and sausage but packs in all the flavor, and makes just enough for one to enjoy. Add a bit of crusty bread for mopping up the savory juices.

INGREDIENTS

1 tablespoon olive oil

¼ cup chopped white onion

¼ cup chopped carrot

¼ cup chopped celery

½ cup chopped zucchini

½ clove garlic, peeled and minced

½ cup canned diced tomatoes, drained, juice reserved

⅓ cup tomato juice from canned tomatoes

⅛ teaspoon ground fennel

⅛ teaspoon freshly cracked black pepper

1 cup low-sodium vegetable broth

½ sprig fresh rosemary

½ bay leaf

½ cup canned cannellini beans, rinsed and drained

1. In a medium pot over medium heat, add olive oil. Once hot, add onion, carrot, and celery and cook until tender, about 5 minutes. Add zucchini and garlic and cook until garlic is fragrant, about 30 seconds.

2. Add diced tomato, tomato juice, fennel, and black pepper and stir well, scraping any bits stuck to the bottom of pot. Add broth, rosemary, and bay leaf and stir well. Bring mixture to a boil, then reduce heat to medium-low, stir in beans, and let simmer 20 minutes or until liquid has reduced by half. Remove bay leaf and serve hot.

PER SERVING

Calories: 284	Fiber: 12g
Fat: 13g	Sugar: 10g
Sodium: 563mg	Protein: 9g
Carbohydrates: 36g	

THREE-BEAN VEGETARIAN CHILI

PREP TIME: 10 MINUTES | COOK TIME: 25 MINUTES | SERVES: 1

 This bean chili is hearty and warming, and it has lots of flavor without the saturated fat and excess servings. Most grocery stores will sell a canned mix of beans, such as pinto beans, black beans, and kidney beans, but if you can't find that, black beans would be a good substitute.

INGREDIENTS

1 tablespoon olive oil

¼ cup chopped white onion

¼ cup chopped red bell pepper

¼ cup chopped celery

½ cup canned diced tomatoes, drained, juice reserved

⅓ cup tomato juice from canned tomatoes

1 cup low-sodium vegetable broth

½ cup water

½ cup canned three-bean blend, rinsed and drained

1 teaspoon chili powder

¼ teaspoon garlic powder

⅛ teaspoon smoked paprika

⅛ teaspoon ground cumin

⅛ teaspoon freshly cracked black pepper

1. In a medium pot over medium heat, add olive oil. Once hot, add onion, bell pepper, and celery and cook until tender, about 5 minutes.

2. Add remaining ingredients and stir well. Bring mixture to a boil, then reduce heat to medium-low and simmer 20–25 minutes or until chili is thickened to your preference. Serve hot.

PER SERVING

Calories: 330   Fiber: 11g
Fat: 15g   Sugar: 11g
Sodium: 736mg   Protein: 11g
Carbohydrates: 40g

CAULIFLOWER STEAK WITH BALSAMIC GLAZE

PREP TIME: 5 MINUTES | COOK TIME: 9 MINUTES | SERVES: 1

 This main dish would be excellent paired with creamy Olive Oil Mashed Potatoes (see Chapter 5). Most well-stocked produce departments sell ready-cut cauliflower steaks, but if yours does not, simply cut a 1" slice from the center of a head of cauliflower at the thickest part.

INGREDIENTS

1 (1"-thick) cauliflower steak (about 6 ounces)

1 teaspoon olive oil

¼ teaspoon Italian seasoning

⅛ teaspoon garlic powder

⅛ teaspoon smoked paprika

⅛ teaspoon freshly cracked black pepper

2 tablespoons balsamic vinegar

1 teaspoon honey

1. Brush both sides of cauliflower steak with olive oil. Sprinkle Italian seasoning, garlic powder, paprika, and black pepper evenly on both sides. Set aside.

2. Heat an 8" skillet over medium heat. Once hot, add cauliflower steak. Cook 4 minutes, then carefully flip and cook 4–5 minutes more or until steak is browned on both sides and tender throughout. Transfer to a plate and lightly cover with foil.

3. To same skillet add balsamic vinegar and honey. Cook, scraping any bits from the bottom of skillet, until mixture is reduced by half, about 30–40 seconds. Remove from heat and drizzle over cauliflower steak. Serve hot.

Balsamic Vinegar

Here are some tips for buying balsamic vinegar. Look at the ingredients first. The first ingredient should be cooked grape must and then wine vinegar. This will have good flavor and is good for cooking. If the only ingredient is cooked grape must, you should only use it as a dressing or condiment and never heat it.

PER SERVING

Calories: 130

Fat: 5g

Sodium: 58mg

Carbohydrates: 20g

Fiber: 4g

Sugar: 14g

Protein: 4g

SPINACH AND ARTICHOKE–STUFFED MUSHROOM

PREP TIME: 5 MINUTES | COOK TIME: 14 MINUTES | SERVES: 1

 If you do not have feta cheese on hand, you could also use goat cheese or mozzarella. Large portobello mushroom caps are often sold in packs of two, so use one for this recipe and use the other for Spicy Mushroom Penne (see Chapter 6) or Beef and Mushroom Stroganoff (see Chapter 10).

INGREDIENTS

1 large portobello mushroom cap, gills removed

2 teaspoons olive oil, divided

2 tablespoons minced yellow onion

2 cups lightly packed baby spinach, chopped

4 marinated artichoke hearts, patted dry and chopped

½ clove garlic, peeled and minced

⅛ teaspoon Aleppo pepper

2 tablespoons crumbled feta cheese

1. Preheat broiler. Line a small baking sheet with foil and lightly spray with nonstick cooking spray.

2. Lightly brush mushroom with ½ teaspoon olive oil. Place on prepared sheet and broil 3–4 minutes per side or until mushroom is tender. Remove from oven and set aside.

3. In an 8" skillet over medium heat, add remaining 1½ teaspoons olive oil. Add onion and cook until tender, about 2 minutes. Add spinach and cook until completely wilted, about 2 minutes. Add artichoke hearts, garlic, and Aleppo pepper and cook until mixture is hot, about 2 minutes. Remove from heat and stir in feta.

4. Drain any liquids off baking sheet and place mushroom cap top side down. Spoon filling into mushroom cap and broil 2–3 minutes or until filling is golden brown on top. Serve hot.

Make It an Appetizer
You can make this large stuffed mushroom using baby bella mushrooms caps if you like. Use six large mushroom caps; remove stems and gills. Do not broil—instead, stuff them raw and bake at 375°F for 20 minutes or until mushroom caps are tender.

PER SERVING

Calories: 199	Fiber: 5g
Fat: 14g	Sugar: 4g
Sodium: 665mg	Protein: 9g
Carbohydrates: 13g	

MEDITERRANEAN TWICE-BAKED POTATO

PREP TIME: 30 MINUTES | COOK TIME: 55 MINUTES | SERVES: 1

 This twice-baked potato is packed with vegetables, tangy feta, and creamy Greek yogurt. It is the perfect cooking for one dinner when you want something comforting and hearty, and makes a great meal prep too. Once stuffed, cover and refrigerate until ready to bake a second time, adding an additional 5 minutes to the cooking time.

INGREDIENTS

1 medium (about 7-ounce) russet potato

2 teaspoons olive oil, divided

¼ teaspoon sea salt

¼ cup chopped red bell pepper

2 tablespoons chopped yellow onion

¼ cup chopped broccoli florets

1 cup loosely packed baby spinach, chopped

1 tablespoon water

¼ teaspoon garlic powder

¼ teaspoon Italian seasoning

¼ cup plain low-fat Greek yogurt

¼ cup crumbled feta cheese

¼ teaspoon freshly cracked black pepper

1 green onion (green part only), chopped

1. Preheat oven to 425°F.

2. Pierce potato three to four times on both sides with a paring knife. Rub 1 teaspoon olive oil into skin of potato and sprinkle all sides with salt. Place potato directly on oven rack and bake 35–45 minutes or until a fork pierces the flesh all the way to center of potato easily. Remove from oven and cool 20 minutes.

3. While potato bakes, prepare vegetables for filling. In an 8" skillet over medium heat, add remaining 1 teaspoon olive oil. Once hot, add bell pepper and onion and cook until tender, about 3 minutes. Add broccoli and cook 3 minutes, then add spinach and cook until just wilted, about 1 minute. Add water, cover pan with a lid, and let stand 4 minutes or until broccoli is very tender. Remove lid and add garlic powder and Italian seasoning and mix well. Transfer to a medium bowl to cool.

4. Reduce oven to 375°F and line a small baking sheet with foil.

5. Once potato has cooled, carefully slice off top quarter of potato lengthwise. Carefully scoop potato flesh into bowl with cooked vegetables. Discard potato skin from top of potato. To bowl add Greek yogurt, feta, and black pepper. Mix well, then fold in green onion.

6. Spoon mixture back into potato skin and bake 20 minutes or until filling is hot and top of potato is lightly brown. Cool 5 minutes before eating.

PER SERVING

Calories: 410	Fiber: 7g
Fat: 18g	Sugar: 9g
Sodium: 805mg	Protein: 18g
Carbohydrates: 46g	

POLENTA CAKES WITH FRESH TOMATO SAUCE

PREP TIME: 2 HOURS 15 MINUTES | COOK TIME: 25 MINUTES | SERVES: 1

Polenta is perfect for solo cooks who want to add a little variety to their plates because you can cook as much or as little as you like.

INGREDIENTS

½ cup low-sodium vegetable broth

¼ cup polenta

⅛ teaspoon sea salt

⅛ teaspoon onion powder

⅛ teaspoon garlic powder

2 tablespoons grated vegetarian Parmesan cheese

2 teaspoons olive oil, divided

2 medium plum tomatoes, seeded and chopped (about 1 cup)

2 tablespoons finely chopped yellow onion

½ clove garlic, peeled and minced

1 teaspoon tomato paste

¼ teaspoon Italian seasoning

⅛ teaspoon ground fennel

1 teaspoon chopped fresh parsley

PER SERVING

Calories: 327	Fiber: 4g
Fat: 12g	Sugar: 6g
Sodium: 598mg	Protein: 5g
Carbohydrates: 49g	

1. Spray a 6" casserole dish with nonstick cooking spray. Set aside.

2. In a 1-quart saucepan over medium heat, add broth. Once it comes to a boil, reduce heat to medium-low and whisk in polenta, salt, onion powder, and garlic powder. Cook, stirring constantly, until polenta is very thick like mashed potatoes, about 3–4 minutes. Turn off heat and stir in Parmesan. Spread polenta evenly in prepared dish, cover, and refrigerate at least 2 hours or overnight.

3. While polenta cools, prepare sauce. In a 1-quart saucepan over medium heat, add 1 teaspoon olive oil. Once hot, add tomatoes and cook, stirring often, about 5 minutes. Add onion and cook until onion is very tender, about 5 minutes. Stir in garlic, tomato paste, Italian seasoning, and fennel and cook about 1 minute. Reduce heat to low and simmer until sauce resembles pancake batter, thick but still pourable, about 5–10 minutes.

4. Once polenta is cooled, cut into four squares. In an 8" skillet over medium heat, add remaining 1 teaspoon olive oil and let it heat briefly, then swirl pan to coat. Add polenta cakes and cook 3–4 minutes per side or until golden brown and crisp on both sides.

5. Transfer cakes to a serving plate and cover with sauce and parsley. Serve.

LENTIL CURRY WITH SPINACH AND TOMATO

PREP TIME: 10 MINUTES | COOK TIME: 27 MINUTES | SERVES: 1

 If you love aromatic curry dishes and want a one pot meal, then you are going to love this lentil curry made with spinach and tomato. Enjoy this with toasted naan or pita bread for dipping. If you have chopped kale on hand, you can use it in place of the spinach.

INGREDIENTS

2 teaspoons olive oil

¼ cup finely chopped yellow onion

½ clove garlic, peeled and minced

¼ cup dry yellow lentils, rinsed and drained

1 cup low-sodium vegetable broth

¼ teaspoon curry powder

¼ teaspoon ground cumin

⅛ teaspoon ground turmeric

1 plum tomato, seeded and chopped (about ½ cup)

2 cups lightly packed baby spinach, chopped

1. In a 2-quart saucepan over medium heat, add olive oil. Once hot, add onion and cook until just tender, about 1 minute. Add garlic and cook until fragrant, about 30 seconds. Stir in lentils and mix well. Add broth, curry powder, cumin, and turmeric and stir well. Bring to a boil, then reduce heat to low, cover, and cook 20 minutes or until lentils are tender and starting to fall apart.

2. Uncover and add tomato and spinach. Stir well, cover, and cook 5 minutes or until spinach is wilted and tomato pieces are soft. Transfer to a serving bowl. Enjoy immediately, or cover and refrigerate up to three days.

PER SERVING

Calories: 313
Fat: 10g
Sodium: 194mg
Carbohydrates: 44g

Fiber: 9g
Sugar: 8g
Protein: 16g

TOFU AND CHICKPEA–STUFFED PEPPER

PREP TIME: 15 MINUTES | COOK TIME: 45 MINUTES | SERVES: 1

 Tofu makes an excellent and healthful replacement for beef in this Mediterranean-inspired stuffed bell pepper recipe. You can prepare this to the point of baking, cover, and refrigerate up to five days. When you are ready, just add an additional 5 minutes to the baking time.

INGREDIENTS

1 medium red bell pepper, sliced in half, stem and seeds removed

2 teaspoons olive oil, divided

2 tablespoons finely chopped yellow onion

¼ cup crumbled firm tofu

½ teaspoon Greek seasoning

½ clove garlic, peeled and minced

¼ cup canned chickpeas, rinsed and drained

4 medium cherry tomatoes, cut into quarters

4 Kalamata olives, pitted and chopped

¼ cup tomato sauce

2 tablespoons crumbled feta cheese

1. Preheat oven to 350°F and line a small baking sheet with foil.

2. Brush bell pepper halves on both sides with ½ teaspoon olive oil. Place cut side up on baking sheet and set aside.

3. In an 8" skillet over medium heat, add remaining olive oil. Once hot, add onion and cook until tender, about 2 minutes. Add tofu and Greek seasoning and cook 1 minute to heat through, then add garlic and cook until very fragrant, about 30 seconds.

4. Add chickpeas, tomatoes, and olives and mix well. Cook 1 minute more or until chickpeas are hot and then remove from heat. Stir in tomato sauce, then divide mixture between bell pepper halves.

5. Cover baking sheet with foil and bake 30 minutes. Remove foil, crumble feta over top of bell pepper halves, and bake 10–15 minutes more, or until bell pepper is tender and filling is hot. Remove from oven and cool 3 minutes before serving.

PER SERVING

Calories: 357
Fat: 21g
Sodium: 1,202mg
Carbohydrates: 31g

Fiber: 8g
Sugar: 16g
Protein: 14g

MEDITERRANEAN STUFFED TOMATO

PREP TIME: 10 MINUTES | COOK TIME: 30 MINUTES | SERVES: 1

 A stuffed tomato makes a delicious main dish for one, and would be perfect paired with Creamy Mushroom Risotto or Lemon Garlic Rice Pilaf (see Chapter 5). You can make these up to the point of baking and then cover and refrigerate until ready to bake. They can be made up to three days ahead of time.

INGREDIENTS

1 tablespoon plus 1 teaspoon couscous

¼ cup boiling water

1 medium beefsteak tomato

2 tablespoons chopped baby spinach

1 tablespoon minced white onion

1 tablespoon chopped jarred roasted red pepper

2 Kalamata olives, pitted and minced

2 tablespoons crumbled feta cheese

¼ teaspoon Greek seasoning

1 teaspoon olive oil

1. Preheat oven to 350°F and line a small baking sheet with foil.

2. In a small bowl, add couscous and boiling water. Stir, then cover and let stand 10 minutes. When time is up, drain off any excess liquid.

3. Slice top off tomato and scoop out pulp with a spoon. Discard seeds and core. Chop pulp and transfer to a medium bowl and stir in couscous, spinach, onion, roasted red pepper, olives, feta, and Greek seasoning.

4. Spoon mixture into tomato and place tomato top back on. Brush tomato on all sides with olive oil and place on prepared baking sheet.

5. Bake 20–25 minutes or until tomato is tender and filling is hot. Cool 3 minutes before enjoying.

PER SERVING

Calories: 206
Fat: 12g
Sodium: 700mg
Carbohydrates: 18g

Fiber: 2g
Sugar: 5g
Protein: 6g

SEASONED TOFU GYRO

PREP TIME: 1 HOUR 10 MINUTES | COOK TIME: 20 MINUTES | SERVES: 1

 Firm tofu makes an excellent plant-based replacement for meat in this wrap that also features plenty of fresh, crisp vegetables. If you do not have the Tzatziki Sauce from Chapter 3, you can mix 2 tablespoons plain low-fat Greek yogurt with ¼ teaspoon dill for a similar flavor.

INGREDIENTS

3 ounces firm tofu, cut into ½" strips

2 teaspoons olive oil

½ clove garlic, peeled and minced

¼ teaspoon dried oregano

¼ teaspoon ground cumin

⅛ teaspoon dried thyme

⅛ teaspoon freshly cracked black pepper

1 (6") whole-wheat pita

2 tablespoons Tzatziki Sauce (see Chapter 3)

¼ cup shredded iceberg lettuce

2 tablespoons diced English cucumber

2 tablespoons diced plum tomato

1 tablespoon chopped red onion

1. Place tofu strips on a tray lined with paper towels. Top with a layer of paper towels and press gently to release any excess moisture.

2. In a medium bowl, add tofu, olive oil, garlic, oregano, cumin, thyme, and black pepper. Gently toss to coat tofu strips evenly. Cover and refrigerate 1 hour.

3. Preheat oven to 425°F and line a small baking sheet with parchment or a silicone baking mat.

4. Spread tofu mixture evenly on prepared baking sheet. Bake 20–25 minutes or until tofu is browned around edges and hot. During the final 3 minutes of cooking, add pita to oven rack to warm.

5. To serve, place warm pita on a serving plate. Spread with Tzatziki Sauce, then top with lettuce, cucumber, tomato, and red onion. Add tofu strips, fold pita in half, and enjoy.

PER SERVING

Calories: 352	Fiber: 7g
Fat: 15g	Sugar: 4g
Sodium: 339mg	Protein: 17g
Carbohydrates: 42g	

LENTILS WITH TOMATO, ARTICHOKE, AND FETA

PREP TIME: 5 MINUTES | COOK TIME: 17 MINUTES | SERVES: 1

This dish is a complete one pot meal, takes less than 20 minutes to cook, and offers a lovely array of colors and flavors. If you have any leafy green vegetables, such as baby spinach or kale, you can chop up 1 cup and stir that in with the other ingredients.

INGREDIENTS

2 teaspoons olive oil

¼ cup finely chopped white onion

½ clove garlic, peeled and minced

¼ cup dry red lentils, rinsed and drained

1 cup low-sodium vegetable broth

6 medium cherry tomatoes, quartered

2 tablespoons chopped marinated artichoke hearts

¼ cup chopped English cucumber

2 tablespoons crumbled feta cheese

1 teaspoon balsamic vinegar

⅛ teaspoon freshly cracked black pepper

1. In a 1-quart saucepan over medium heat, add olive oil. Once hot, add onion and cook until just tender, about 1 minute. Add garlic and cook until fragrant, about 30 seconds. Stir in lentils and mix well. Add broth and stir well. Bring to a boil, then reduce heat to low, cover and cook 15 minutes or until lentils are tender and starting to fall apart.

2. Uncover and stir in remaining ingredients. Transfer to a serving bowl and enjoy immediately.

Olive Oil versus Extra-Virgin Olive Oil
Extra-virgin olive oil is made from the first cold press of the olives and should be a grassy green color with a peppery flavor. It has a very low smoke point and is best for dressings and garnishes. Regular olive oil is made from the ground pulp of the olives after the first press and is more refined, so it can be heated and used for cooking.

PER SERVING

Calories: 372	Fiber: 9g
Fat: 14g	Sugar: 9g
Sodium: 467mg	Protein: 17g
Carbohydrates: 47g	

LENTIL AND ZUCCHINI BOATS

PREP TIME: 10 MINUTES | COOK TIME: 52 MINUTES | SERVES: 1

 These zucchini boats are a fun way to enjoy your Italian food, and are perfect served with some fresh boiled pasta dressed with a little olive oil. When hollowing out the zucchini, be sure to leave about ¼" of flesh around sides so the boats will retain their shape after baking.

INGREDIENTS

1 teaspoon olive oil

¼ cup finely chopped red onion

½ clove garlic, peeled and minced

⅛ teaspoon crushed red pepper flakes

¼ cup dry red lentils, rinsed and drained

1 cup low-sodium vegetable broth

¼ cup marinara sauce

1 medium zucchini, sliced in half lengthwise

¼ cup shredded part-skim mozzarella cheese

⅛ teaspoon freshly cracked black pepper

1. Preheat oven to 350°F and spray a 6" baking dish long enough to fit a medium zucchini with nonstick cooking spray.

2. In a 1-quart saucepan over medium heat, add olive oil. Once hot, add red onion and cook until just tender, about 1 minute. Add garlic and red pepper flakes. Cook until fragrant, about 30 seconds. Stir in lentils and broth and stir well. Bring to a boil, then reduce heat to low, cover, and cook 20 minutes or until lentils are tender. Remove lid, stir in marinara sauce, and remove pan from heat.

3. Hollow out each zucchini half with a teaspoon. Spoon lentil mixture into each prepared zucchini and place into prepared baking dish. Top with mozzarella.

4. Bake 30–35 minutes or until zucchini is tender and cheese is melted and golden brown. Garnish with black pepper and serve hot.

PER SERVING

Calories: 378
Fat: 10g
Sodium: 581mg
Carbohydrates: 55g

Fiber: 10g
Sugar: 14g
Protein: 21g

BAKED SPAGHETTI NESTS WITH MOZZARELLA

PREP TIME: 20 MINUTES | COOK TIME: 22 MINUTES | SERVES: 1

 These adorable nests of spaghetti are nestled in a bed of sautéed baby spinach and filled with bocconcini, which is a small fresh mozzarella ball. You can substitute the bocconcini with crumbled feta, goat cheese, or shredded mozzarella if you have it on hand.

INGREDIENTS

2 ounces spaghetti pasta

½ teaspoon sea salt

3 tablespoons marinara sauce

2 tablespoons basil pesto

3 fresh bocconcini

⅛ teaspoon freshly cracked black pepper

1 teaspoon olive oil

2 cups lightly packed baby spinach

½ clove garlic, peeled and minced

⅛ teaspoon Italian seasoning

1. In a 2-quart saucepan over high heat, add water to fill pot ¾ full. Once water begins to boil, add pasta and salt. Cook, stirring occasionally, until pasta is al dente, about 10 minutes. Drain and set aside.

2. Preheat oven to 375°F and line a small baking sheet with parchment or a silicone baking mat.

3. In a medium bowl, combine marinara sauce and pesto. Add pasta and toss to thoroughly coat in sauce.

4. Divide pasta into thirds. Twirl pasta into a nest shape and place on prepared baking sheet. Make a hole in center of pasta and place bocconcini. Sprinkle lightly with black pepper.

5. Bake 12–15 minutes or until cheese is melted and pasta is lightly browned around edges.

6. While pasta bakes, prepare spinach. In an 8" skillet over medium heat, add olive oil. Once hot, add spinach and cook until wilted, about 1 minute. Add garlic and Italian seasoning and cook 30 seconds. Remove from heat and set aside.

7. When pasta is ready, place spinach on a plate in a flat circle. Top with spaghetti nests. Enjoy hot.

PER SERVING

Calories: 603
Fat: 30g
Sodium: 908mg
Carbohydrates: 56g

Fiber: 6g
Sugar: 8g
Protein: 24g

CHAPTER 8

SEAFOOD

Linguine with Clams..............................142

Mediterranean Seafood Chowder.......143

Steamed Mussels...................................144

Shrimp Scampi.......................................145

Shrimp Pasta with Basil
and Feta 146

Mussels Saganaki...................................148

Baked Crab Cake...................................149

Lobster Tail with Olive Oil
and Herbs..150

Mustard Herb Whitefish.......................151

Seasoned Steamed Crab Legs 153

Pistachio-Crusted Halibut....................154

Steamed Cod with Capers
and Lemon 155

Tomato-Poached Fish...........................156

Mediterranean Cod...............................157

Lemon Salmon with Dill........................158

Lemon Herb Fish Packet 160

Rosemary Salmon..................................161

Whitefish Stew 162

Fish and seafood are an important part of the Mediterranean diet, and you should aim to have two to three servings per week. Preferred cooking methods include steamed, poached, grilled, in soups or stews, or panfried in olive oil. Deep-fried fish and seafood should be eaten rarely. When shopping for fish and seafood, you can choose to buy just what you need fresh from the seafood counter, you can opt for frozen fish and seafood, or you can choose preserved seafood such as smoked or canned packed in water or olive oil.

This chapter is full of single-serving fish and seafood recipes that will become favorites on your Mediterranean diet journey. How does a dinner of Steamed Cod with Capers and Lemon sound? Perhaps a lunch of Mediterranean Seafood Chowder that can be made ahead to save time? On a busy night Shrimp Pasta with Basil and Feta or Mustard Herb Whitefish means a satisfying and healthful meal is ready in less than 15 minutes. No matter what you choose, you can't go wrong with these perfectly portioned Mediterranean fish and seafood meals.

LINGUINE WITH CLAMS

PREP TIME: 5 MINUTES | COOK TIME: 10 MINUTES | SERVES: 1

 If you are unable to buy fresh clams at your fresh fish counter, you can use canned chopped clams for this recipe. Rinse and drain half of a 6-ounce can and add them in at the end of cooking with the pasta to warm through. Leftover clams are great in seafood chowders.

INGREDIENTS

½ teaspoon sea salt

2 ounces linguine pasta

2 teaspoons olive oil

1 tablespoon minced shallot

1 clove garlic, peeled and minced

⅛ teaspoon crushed red pepper flakes

10 littleneck clams (about ½ pound), scrubbed

¼ cup white wine

½ teaspoon lemon juice

2 teaspoons finely chopped fresh parsley

1. In a 2-quart saucepan over high heat, add water to fill pot ¾ full. Once water begins to boil, add salt and pasta. Cook, stirring occasionally, until pasta is just al dente, about 8 minutes. Reserve ⅓ cup cooking water.

2. While pasta is cooking, prepare the sauce. In an 8" skillet over medium heat, add olive oil. Once hot, add shallot and garlic. Cook until just tender, about 1 minute. Add red pepper flakes and cook until fragrant, about 30 seconds.

3. Add clams, wine, lemon juice, and parsley. Bring to a simmer and cover with a lid. Cook 6–8 minutes or until clams are open. Discard any unopened clams.

4. When pasta is finished cooking, drain and add directly to skillet along with reserved cooking water. Cook, tossing constantly, until the sauce reduces and pasta finishes cooking, about 2 minutes. Serve immediately.

PER SERVING

Calories: 405
Fat: 10g
Sodium: 726mg
Carbohydrates: 50g

Fiber: 3g
Sugar: 2g
Protein: 22g

MEDITERRANEAN SEAFOOD CHOWDER

PREP TIME: 10 MINUTES | COOK TIME: 43 MINUTES | SERVES: 1

 You can use any mix of seafood you happen to have on hand in this chowder, making it the perfect place to use up any leftovers and scraps you have from your previous cooking for one meals. If you want this chowder thicker, let it simmer uncovered after the rice has cooked 6–8 minutes before adding seafood.

INGREDIENTS

2 teaspoons olive oil

2 tablespoons minced carrot

2 tablespoons minced yellow onion

2 tablespoons minced celery

2 tablespoons minced green bell pepper

½ clove garlic, peeled and minced

¼ teaspoon seafood seasoning, such as Old Bay

2 tablespoons white wine

¼ cup canned diced tomatoes, drained, juice reserved

½ cup reserved tomato juice

½ cup seafood stock

2 tablespoons long-grain brown rice

2 ounces medium shrimp, peeled and deveined

½ cup cubed fresh cod fillet

1 teaspoon chopped fresh parsley

1. In a 2-quart saucepan over medium heat, add olive oil. Once hot, add carrot, onion, celery, and bell pepper. Cook, stirring often, until vegetables are tender, about 3 minutes. Add garlic and seafood seasoning and cook until fragrant, about 30 seconds.

2. Add wine and scrape any bits from the bottom of pot, then add diced tomatoes, tomato juice, seafood stock, and rice. Bring to a boil, then reduce heat to medium-low, and cover with lid. Cook 35–40 minutes or until rice is tender.

3. Once rice is cooked, remove lid and increase heat to high to bring mixture to a boil. Add shrimp and cod and cook 4–5 minutes or until fish and shrimp are cooked through. Serve immediately with parsley for garnish.

PER SERVING

Calories: 336 | Fat: 11g | Sodium: 820mg | Carbohydrates: 27g Fiber: 3g | Sugar: 4g | Protein: 29g

STEAMED MUSSELS

PREP TIME: 5 MINUTES | COOK TIME: 8 MINUTES | SERVES: 1

 Frozen mussels, which are partially cooked, are great for the solo chef because you can cook exactly what you need without fear of their spoiling. You should thaw frozen mussels in an airtight container in the refrigerator overnight. If you're using fresh mussels, increase cooking time to 8 minutes.

INGREDIENTS

2 teaspoons olive oil

2 tablespoons minced shallot

2 tablespoons minced celery

½ clove garlic, peeled and minced

¼ teaspoon seafood seasoning, such as Old Bay

¼ cup white wine

½ cup seafood stock

½ pound frozen cleaned mussels, thawed

1 teaspoon chopped fresh parsley

1 lemon wedge

1. Place a 2-quart saucepan that fits a steaming basket and has a lid over medium heat. Once pot is hot, add olive oil, shallot, and celery. Cook, stirring often, until vegetables are tender, about 2 minutes. Add garlic and seafood seasoning and cook until fragrant, about 30 seconds.

2. Add wine and seafood stock and stir well. Carefully place steaming basket into pot, cover with lid, and bring to a boil.

3. Once boiling, add mussels and cover with lid. Steam until all mussels are opened, about 5 minutes. Discard any mussels that did not open. Transfer mussels to a serving bowl and pour liquid over top. Garnish with parsley and the juice from lemon wedge.

Preparing Fresh Mussels

If you are cooking fresh mussels, you will want to prepare them properly for cooking. First, soak them in clean water for 20 minutes. Next, remove the beard if it is attached. Finally, scrub the shells to remove any dirt, discard any cracked mussels, and rinse in clean water. You are now ready to cook!

PER SERVING

Calories: 322

Fat: 15g

Sodium: 875mg

Carbohydrates: 5g

Fiber: 1g

Sugar: 2g

Protein: 36g

SHRIMP SCAMPI

PREP TIME: 10 MINUTES | COOK TIME: 3 MINUTES | SERVES: 1

 A little salted butter gives this shrimp classic it's signature flavor, but you can forego the butter in favor of regular olive oil if you prefer. If you only use olive oil, be sure to add ⅛ teaspoon sea salt to enhance the flavor at the end of cooking.

INGREDIENTS

1 tablespoon olive oil

2 teaspoons salted butter

1 tablespoon minced shallot

1 clove garlic, peeled and minced

¼ teaspoon freshly cracked black pepper

2 tablespoons white wine

2 tablespoons low-sodium chicken stock

8 large tail-on shrimp

1 teaspoon lemon juice

1 teaspoon chopped fresh parsley

1. In an 8" skillet over medium heat, add olive oil and butter. Once butter is melted and oil is hot, add shallot, garlic, and black pepper and cook 30 seconds. Stir in wine and stock and stir well. Bring to a boil and add shrimp. Cook until shrimp are pink, opaque, and curled into a C shape, about 2–3 minutes.

2. Once shrimp are cooked, add lemon juice and stir to mix. Transfer shrimp to a serving plate and garnish with parsley. Serve immediately.

PER SERVING

Calories: 264

Fat: 21g

Sodium: 453mg

Carbohydrates: 5g

Fiber: 1g

Sugar: 1g

Protein: 9g

SHRIMP PASTA WITH BASIL AND FETA

PREP TIME: 5 MINUTES | COOK TIME: 8 MINUTES | SERVES: 1

This bright, summery shrimp pasta is great served along with a slice of crusty bread for soaking up the sauce. You could have this with Baked Lemon Parmesan Asparagus (see Chapter 5) or a green salad. It's a perfect meal for one because you won't want to share!

INGREDIENTS

½ teaspoon sea salt

2 ounces penne pasta

2 teaspoons olive oil

2 tablespoons minced red bell pepper

6 medium cherry tomatoes, sliced in half

2 tablespoons minced green onion (green part only)

8 large peeled and deveined shrimp

½ clove garlic, peeled and minced

1 teaspoon freshly grated lemon zest

¼ cup white wine

2 teaspoons lemon juice

2 teaspoons finely chopped fresh basil

2 tablespoons crumbled feta cheese

PER SERVING

Calories: 434
Fat: 14g
Sodium: 681mg
Carbohydrates: 52g

Fiber: 5g
Sugar: 6g
Protein: 20g

1. In a 2-quart saucepan over high heat, add water to fill pot ¾ full. Once water begins to boil, add salt and pasta. Cook, stirring occasionally, until pasta is al dente, about 8 minutes.

2. While pasta is cooking, prepare shrimp. In an 8" skillet over medium heat, add olive oil. Once hot, add bell pepper and cook until just tender, about 1 minute. Add tomatoes, green onion, and shrimp. Cook 30 seconds, then add garlic and lemon zest and cook until fragrant, about 30 seconds.

3. Add wine and lemon juice and cook, stirring constantly, until liquid has reduced to about 2 tablespoons, about 3 minutes.

4. When pasta is finished cooking, drain it and add to pan with shrimp. Add basil and feta and toss with tongs until evenly coated. Serve immediately.

Cooking Frozen Shrimp

Frozen shrimp should be thawed before cooking. To safely thaw them, you can place the shrimp in a bowl in the refrigerator overnight to slowly thaw. If you need them for immediate cooking, place them in a bowl under cool, slow running water. Thawed shrimp should never be refrozen.

MUSSELS SAGANAKI

PREP TIME: 10 MINUTES | COOK TIME: 7 MINUTES | SERVES: 1

These Greek-style mussels are cooked in a tomato wine sauce and garnished with fresh basil and tangy feta cheese. Pair this with some crusty bread and a side of Lemon Garlic Rice Pilaf (see Chapter 5) for a solo meal you will want to make again and again!

INGREDIENTS

2 teaspoons olive oil

1 tablespoon minced shallot

½ clove garlic, peeled and minced

⅛ teaspoon crushed red pepper flakes

¼ teaspoon freshly cracked black pepper

¼ teaspoon Greek seasoning

¼ cup white wine

6 medium cherry tomatoes, quartered

1 teaspoon tomato paste

¼ pound frozen cleaned mussels, thawed

1 tablespoon crumbled feta cheese

1 basil leaf, chopped

1 In an 8" skillet over medium heat, add olive oil. Once hot, add shallot, garlic, red pepper flakes, and black pepper and cook 30 seconds. Add Greek seasoning and cook 30 seconds or until fragrant.

2 Add wine and scrape the bottom of pot to release any bits, then add cherry tomatoes and tomato paste and stir well. Add mussels, stir well to combine, then cover with lid and cook until mussels have opened, about 5 minutes.

3 Open lid and discard any mussels that did not open. Transfer to a serving bowl and garnish with feta and basil. Enjoy immediately.

PER SERVING

Calories: 248

Fat: 14g

Sodium: 644mg

Carbohydrates: 9g

Fiber: 2g

Sugar: 5g

Protein: 19g

BAKED CRAB CAKE

PREP TIME: 5 MINUTES | COOK TIME: 27 MINUTES | SERVES: 1

 You can find 6-ounce cans of canned crabmeat along with the tuna and canned meats in most grocery stores. Once drained, the cans yield 4 ounces of meat. You can also use 4 ounces of refrigerated lump crab that comes in an 8-ounce container, and then use the leftover crab on a green salad.

INGREDIENTS

2 tablespoons dry bread crumbs

1 tablespoon finely chopped yellow onion

2 teaspoons finely chopped jarred roasted red pepper

1 tablespoon olive oil mayonnaise

½ teaspoon lemon juice

⅛ teaspoon seafood seasoning, such as Old Bay

1 (6-ounce) can crabmeat, drained well

1. Preheat oven to 375°F and line a small baking sheet with foil and lightly spray with nonstick cooking spray.

2. To a small bowl add bread crumbs, onion, roasted red pepper, mayonnaise, lemon juice, and seafood seasoning and mix well. Add crab and fold to mix. Form mixture into a patty, adding water ¼ teaspoon at a time if mixture is too dry.

3. Place crab cake onto prepared baking sheet and bake 15 minutes, then flip cake and bake 12–15 minutes more or until crab cake is browned well on both sides. Cool 3 minutes before serving.

PER SERVING

Calories: 250
Fat: 7g
Sodium: 1,262mg
Carbohydrates: 12g

Fiber: 1g
Sugar: 2g
Protein: 32g

LOBSTER TAIL WITH OLIVE OIL AND HERBS

PREP TIME: 5 MINUTES | COOK TIME: 8 MINUTES | SERVES: 1

 Lobster tails are easier to prepare than most people think, and they make the perfect luxury dinner for one! To make this lobster tail a complete meal, consider serving it with a side of Herb Vinaigrette Potato Salad or Roasted Broccoli with Feta (see Chapter 5).

INGREDIENTS

1 medium (about 6-ounce) lobster tail

1 teaspoon olive oil

¼ teaspoon Italian seasoning

⅛ teaspoon freshly cracked black pepper

⅛ teaspoon smoked paprika

½ teaspoon lemon juice

1. Preheat broiler and line a baking sheet with foil.

2. Using kitchen shears, cut down the top of lobster shell, stopping at the end of the tail. Carefully open shell and remove lobster meat from tail and place on top of shell. Place on prepared baking sheet.

3. In a small bowl, combine olive oil, Italian seasoning, black pepper, and paprika. Brush mixture over lobster meat.

4. Broil 8–10 minutes or until lobster is opaque in the center and shell is bright red. Serve hot with lemon juice for dipping.

Make It with Shrimp

If you do not like lobster, or if you can't find lobster tails at your market, you can make this with shrimp. Use 4 ounces extra-large shrimp, peeled and deveined. Toss the shrimp in the oil and seasonings, lay in a small ceramic baking dish, and broil 6–8 minutes or until shrimp are opaque and curled into a C.

PER SERVING

Calories: 114	Fiber: 0g
Fat: 5g	Sugar: 0g
Sodium: 413mg	Protein: 16g
Carbohydrates: 1g	

MUSTARD HERB WHITEFISH

PREP TIME: 5 MINUTES | COOK TIME: 13 MINUTES | SERVES: 1

 Freeze-dried herbs make it easy to have flavorful herbs that cook and bake like fresh without worry of them wilting or spoiling before you use them all. This mustard herb glaze is also good on salmon or steelhead trout.

INGREDIENTS

1 teaspoon Dijon mustard

½ teaspoon olive oil

½ teaspoon freeze-dried chopped chives

½ teaspoon freeze-dried dill

⅛ teaspoon garlic powder

⅛ teaspoon freshly cracked black pepper

1 (6-ounce) whitefish fillet

1. Preheat oven to 400°F and line a baking sheet with foil lightly sprayed with nonstick cooking spray.

2. In a small bowl, combine mustard, olive oil, chives, dill, garlic powder, and black pepper. Mix well.

3. Place fillet on prepared baking sheet. Brush evenly with mustard mixture. Bake 13–15 minutes or until fish is opaque and flakes when gently pressed at thickest part with a fork. Serve immediately.

What Is Whitefish?

Generally, whitefish refers to a variety of fish that lives near the seafloor. Pollock, haddock, Atlantic cod, and hake are examples of whitefish. The flesh is pale in color, it is less oily than fish like salmon or herring, and it has a mild flavor. Because it is mild, it benefits from citrus and herbs when cooking to enhance the flavor.

PER SERVING

Calories: 257

Fat: 11g

Sodium: 211mg

Carbohydrates: 1g

Fiber: 0g

Sugar: 0g

Protein: 33g

SEASONED STEAMED CRAB LEGS

PREP TIME: 5 MINUTES | COOK TIME: 12 MINUTES | SERVES: 1

 You can buy fresh crab legs from your seafood counter, which means you can easily purchase just enough for this dish! If you are using precooked crab legs, you can reduce the steaming time to 6 minutes, which is long enough to heat them through without overcooking.

INGREDIENTS

1 teaspoon olive oil

1 clove garlic, peeled and minced

¼ teaspoon seafood seasoning, such as Old Bay

¼ teaspoon freshly cracked black pepper

½ pound raw snow crab legs

2 teaspoons clarified butter or ghee, melted

1 teaspoon lemon juice

1. Place a 2-quart saucepan that fits a steaming basket over medium heat. Add enough water to come just under steaming basket. Cover with lid and let heat.

2. To a small bowl, add olive oil, garlic, seafood seasoning, and black pepper. Mix well, then coat crab legs in seasoning.

3. Once water is boiling, add crab legs to steamer basket. Cover with lid and steam 12–15 minutes or until crab legs are thoroughly cooked and bright red.

4. In a small bowl, mix clarified butter with lemon juice. Serve crab legs hot with butter sauce for dipping.

Garlic Butter Dipping Sauce
Simple lemon butter is delicious with crab, but here's another version you can try. Combine 2 teaspoons clarified butter with ¼ teaspoon lemon juice, ¼ teaspoon fresh minced garlic, and ⅛ teaspoon fresh or dried minced parsley. Heat in the microwave for 15 seconds and serve.

PER SERVING

Calories: 147
Fat: 10g
Sodium: 677mg
Carbohydrates: 0g

Fiber: 0g
Sugar: 0g
Protein: 15g

PISTACHIO-CRUSTED HALIBUT

PREP TIME: 10 MINUTES | COOK TIME: 13 MINUTES | SERVES: 1

 Pistachios are packed with unsaturated fat and fiber, meaning they are a wonderful addition to a heart-healthy diet! You can find shelled unsalted pistachios in the bulk section of most grocery stores or in the produce department with the salad toppings. You could also use unsalted almonds if you like.

INGREDIENTS

1 (6-ounce) halibut fillet

½ teaspoon olive oil mayonnaise

2 tablespoons finely chopped unsalted pistachios

1 tablespoon dry bread crumbs

¼ teaspoon freshly grated lemon zest

⅛ teaspoon freshly cracked black pepper

1. Preheat oven to 425°F and line a baking sheet with foil lightly sprayed with nonstick cooking spray.

2. Place fillet on prepared baking sheet. Brush evenly with mayonnaise.

3. In a small bowl, combine pistachios, bread crumbs, lemon zest, and black pepper. Mix well, then press topping over top of fillet.

4. Bake 13–15 minutes or until fish is opaque and flakes when gently pressed at thickest part with a fork. Serve immediately.

PER SERVING

Calories: 275

Fat: 9g

Sodium: 181mg

Carbohydrates: 10g

Fiber: 2g

Sugar: 2g

Protein: 36g

STEAMED COD WITH CAPERS AND LEMON

PREP TIME: 5 MINUTES | COOK TIME: 7 MINUTES | SERVES: 1

 Steaming is a quick and healthy way to prepare fish, vegetables, and poultry. In this healthy meal for one, cod is seasoned and steamed on a bed of lemons and served with salty capers and lemon juice for extra zing. You can also make this with haddock, flounder, or sea bass.

INGREDIENTS

1 (6-ounce) cod fillet

1 teaspoon olive oil

½ teaspoon freeze-dried dill

⅛ teaspoon garlic powder

⅛ teaspoon onion powder

⅛ teaspoon freshly cracked black pepper

3 (⅛"-thick) fresh lemon slices

½ teaspoon lemon juice

1 teaspoon capers, drained

1. Place a 2-quart saucepan that fits a steaming basket over medium heat. Add enough water to come just under steaming basket. Cover with lid and let heat.

2. Brush cod with olive oil on all sides, then season all sides with dill, garlic powder, onion powder, and black pepper.

3. Once water is boiling, add lemon slices to basket and top with fish fillet. Cover with lid and steam 7–9 minutes or until fish is opaque and flakes when gently pressed in the thickest part with a fork.

4. Remove fish from steamer, discarding lemon slices. Drizzle with fresh lemon juice and garnish with capers before serving.

PER SERVING

Calories: 180

Fat: 5g

Sodium: 158mg

Carbohydrates: 1g

Fiber: 0g

Sugar: 0g

Protein: 31g

TOMATO-POACHED FISH

PREP TIME: 5 MINUTES | COOK TIME: 15 MINUTES | SERVES: 1

 This dish uses the shortcut of jarred marinara sauce to add flavor without needing to buy extra herbs and other ingredients. Look for a jarred sauce that is lower in sodium and contains whole-food ingredients. Jarred sauce keeps for a week in the refrigerator once opened.

INGREDIENTS

⅓ cup marinara sauce

½ teaspoon Italian seasoning

5 pitted Kalamata olives

1 teaspoon capers, drained

2 tablespoons water

1 (6-ounce) cod fillet

½ teaspoon olive oil

⅛ teaspoon freshly cracked black pepper

1. Place a 2-quart saucepan over medium heat and add marinara sauce, Italian seasoning, olives, and capers. Mix well. Stir in water and bring to a simmer, about 5 minutes.

2. Brush cod with olive oil on all sides, then season with black pepper.

3. Once marinara is simmering, nestle fish in center of pot. Cover and cook 10 minutes or until fish is opaque and flakes when gently pressed in the thickest part with a fork.

4. Carefully remove fish from pot and place on a serving plate. Spoon poaching sauce over top. Enjoy immediately.

PER SERVING

Calories: 244

Fat: 9g

Sodium: 813mg

Carbohydrates: 7g

Fiber: 2g

Sugar: 5g

Protein: 32g

MEDITERRANEAN COD

PREP TIME: 5 MINUTES | COOK TIME: 20 MINUTES | SERVES: 1

Topped with layers of briny olives, fresh tomato, and basil, this cod dish is bursting with flavor, and the foil pouch helps keep the flesh tender and moist while cooking. If you want to add more flavor, add a couple of lemon slices under the fish before baking.

INGREDIENTS

1 (6-ounce) cod fillet

1 teaspoon olive oil

¼ teaspoon Greek seasoning

5 Kalamata olives, pitted and chopped

4 medium cherry tomatoes, chopped

1 basil leaf, chopped, divided

⅛ teaspoon freshly cracked black pepper

1. Preheat oven to 375°F and tear off a 10"-long square of foil.

2. Brush cod with olive oil on all sides, then lay on foil square and add Greek seasoning, olives, tomatoes, and half of the basil. Sprinkle top with black pepper. Bring up the sides of the foil and crimp at the top to create a foil packet.

3. Place packet on a small baking sheet and bake 20–25 minutes or until fish is opaque and flakes easily when pressed with a fork in the thickest part.

4. Carefully remove fish from packet and transfer to a serving plate and garnish with remaining basil. Enjoy immediately.

PER SERVING

Calories: 233	Fiber: 1g
Fat: 10g	Sugar: 2g
Sodium: 622mg	Protein: 31g
Carbohydrates: 3g	

LEMON SALMON WITH DILL

PREP TIME: 10 MINUTES | COOK TIME: 15 MINUTES | SERVES: 1

 Baking salmon with lemon slices over top helps prevent the fish from drying out while baking, and infuses the fish with sharp lemon flavor without extra salt or fat. This would be perfect served with an Italian Mixed Green Salad (see Chapter 4), Lemon Garlic Rice Pilaf (see Chapter 5), or Lemon Parmesan Risotto (see Chapter 5).

INGREDIENTS

1 (6-ounce) salmon fillet

1 teaspoon olive oil

⅛ teaspoon sea salt

⅛ teaspoon freshly cracked black pepper

3 (⅛"-thick) slices fresh lemon

2 tablespoons plain low-fat Greek yogurt

¼ teaspoon freeze-dried dill

¼ teaspoon fresh lemon juice

2 dashes hot sauce

1. Preheat oven to 400°F and line a baking sheet with foil lightly sprayed with nonstick cooking spray.

2. Place salmon fillet on prepared baking sheet. Brush flesh with olive oil, then sprinkle with salt and black pepper. Top with lemon slices. Bake 15–17 minutes or until fish is opaque and flakes at the thickest part when pressed with a fork.

3. While fish bakes, combine yogurt, dill, lemon juice, and hot sauce in a small bowl. Mix well.

4. When fish is ready, remove from oven and transfer to a serving plate. Remove lemon slices and discard. Spoon sauce over top of fillet. Serve immediately.

PER SERVING

Calories: 301

Fat: 14g

Sodium: 316mg

Carbohydrates: 1g

Fiber: 0g

Sugar: 1g

Protein: 37g

LEMON HERB FISH PACKET

PREP TIME: 5 MINUTES | COOK TIME: 15 MINUTES | SERVES: 1

 This recipe is the perfect way to use up fresh herbs from your refrigerator, so feel free to add in what you have on hand. You can add a different flavor profile by using fresh limes and cilantro in place of the lemon and herbs.

INGREDIENTS

2 sprigs fresh rosemary

2 sprigs fresh thyme

2 stems fresh oregano

1 (6-ounce) rainbow trout fillet

1 teaspoon olive oil

⅛ teaspoon freshly cracked black pepper

3 (⅛"-thick) slices fresh lemon

1. Preheat oven to 375°F and tear off a 10"-long square of foil. Place rosemary, thyme, and oregano in center of foil.

2. Brush fish with olive oil on all sides, lay on top of herbs, then sprinkle top with black pepper. Top with lemon slices. Bring up the sides of the foil and crimp at the top to create a foil packet.

3. Place packet on a small baking sheet and bake 15–20 minutes or until fish is opaque and flakes easily when pressed with a fork in the thickest part.

4. Carefully remove fish from packet and transfer to a serving plate. Enjoy immediately.

PER SERVING

Calories: 241	Fiber: 0g
Fat: 10g	Sugar: 0g
Sodium: 52mg	Protein: 35g
Carbohydrates: 0g	

ROSEMARY SALMON

PREP TIME: 5 MINUTES | COOK TIME: 5 MINUTES | SERVES: 1

Lemon Garlic Rice Pilaf (see Chapter 5) would make a perfect bed for this easy roasted salmon dish. You can also serve this fish chilled over a green salad for lunch or flaked into the center of an omelet for breakfast.

INGREDIENTS

1 (6-ounce) salmon fillet

1 teaspoon olive oil

½ teaspoon finely chopped fresh rosemary

⅛ teaspoon freshly cracked black pepper

3 (⅛"-thick) slices fresh lemon

1. Preheat broiler and line a small baking sheet with foil lightly sprayed with nonstick cooking spray.

2. Brush fish with olive oil on all sides, then sprinkle top with rosemary and black pepper.

3. Lay lemon slices on top of fish and place on prepared baking sheet. Broil 5–6 minutes or until fish is opaque and flakes easily when pressed with a fork in the thickest part.

4. Transfer fish to a serving plate. Enjoy immediately.

PER SERVING

Calories: 280	Fiber: 0g
Fat: 14g	Sugar: 0g
Sodium: 74mg	Protein: 34g
Carbohydrates: 0g	

WHITEFISH STEW

PREP TIME: 5 MINUTES | COOK TIME: 16 MINUTES | SERVES: 1

 Any non-oily fish will work in this single serving stew, but avoid oily fish like salmon and steelhead trout. You can also add two to three shrimp or a few mussels or clams if you have them handy. The more you add, the more flavor you will have!

INGREDIENTS

1 teaspoon olive oil

2 tablespoons chopped yellow onion

½ clove garlic, peeled and minced

½ teaspoon Italian seasoning

2 tablespoons white wine

⅓ cup canned diced tomatoes, undrained

⅓ cup seafood stock

1 (6-ounce) whitefish fillet, cut into 1" pieces

⅛ teaspoon freshly cracked black pepper

2 dashes hot sauce

1. In a 2-quart saucepan over medium heat, add olive oil and let it heat briefly, then swirl pan to coat. Add onion and cook until tender, about 3 minutes. Add garlic and Italian seasoning and cook until fragrant, about 30 seconds.

2. Add wine and scrape any browned bits from the bottom of pot. Add tomatoes with juice and seafood stock and bring to a boil, about 4 minutes. Once boiling, reduce heat to medium-low and simmer 3 minutes.

3. Add fish and simmer 5–8 minutes or until fish is opaque and flakes easily. Add black pepper and hot sauce and stir to combine. Serve hot.

PER SERVING

Calories: 311
Fat: 13g
Sodium: 391mg
Carbohydrates: 7g

Fiber: 2g
Sugar: 3g
Protein: 35g

CHAPTER 9
POULTRY DISHES

Chicken and Lemon Asparagus............ 164

Chicken and Mushroom Marsala 165

Chicken Cacciatore............................. 166

Chicken with Toasted Orzo 167

Vegetable Bowls with Turkey and
    Hummus 169

Kale and Orzo Chicken 170

Chicken Scallopine............................. 171

Feta and Spinach–Stuffed Chicken
    Breast 172

Turkey Meatballs in Red Pepper
    Sauce 173

Chicken Lettuce Wraps 174

Chicken and Noodles Casserole.......... 176

Balsamic Chicken Thigh with
    Tomato and Basil 177

Mini Turkey Meatloaf........................ 178

Fig-Glazed Chicken Breast................. 179

Turkey Burger 181

Easy Pesto Chicken........................... 182

Wine-Braised Chicken Thigh.............. 183

When meal planning for your week, you will want to include a variety of high-quality protein sources, and poultry like chicken and turkey is the perfect way to add low-fat protein to your weekly meals. Chicken and turkey are readily available year-round in grocery stores, and they are low in fat after you discard the skin. You can easily buy chicken at the meat counter as a single breast or thigh, so they are perfect for those cooking for one, but both chicken and turkey come in bone-in; boneless, skinless; and ground varieties, so you can get exactly what you need. Poultry also freezes well; consider buying a larger pack when it's on sale to save money!

The dishes in this chapter feature poultry, but you will find plenty of vegetables and grains to make the dishes more flavorful. Portioned for one, these also ensure you have a satisfying meal when paired with a fresh salad or a vegetable side dish. Looking for lunch inspiration? Chicken Lettuce Wraps or juicy Turkey Burgers are just the ticket. Chicken and Lemon Asparagus or Chicken and Mushroom Marsala make for an elegant dinner that won't take all night to prepare.

CHICKEN AND LEMON ASPARAGUS

PREP TIME: 10 MINUTES | COOK TIME: 15 MINUTES | SERVES: 1

 This single-skillet meal is refreshing and easy, and perfect for nights when you want a delicious meal without a lot of dishes to clean up later. If asparagus is not in season or available, you can use cut fresh green beans or broccoli florets.

INGREDIENTS

1 (4-ounce) boneless, skinless chicken breast

¼ teaspoon Italian seasoning

⅛ teaspoon freshly cracked black pepper

⅛ teaspoon sea salt

1 teaspoon olive oil, divided

1 teaspoon unsalted butter

2 tablespoons minced yellow onion

½ clove garlic, peeled and minced

⅛ teaspoon crushed red pepper flakes

¼ pound fresh asparagus, trimmed, cut into 1" pieces

¼ cup low-sodium chicken broth

1 tablespoon lemon juice

1 teaspoon Dijon mustard

1 teaspoon chopped fresh parsley

1. With a meat mallet, pound chicken breast until it is ½" thick throughout. Season both sides with Italian seasoning, black pepper, and salt. Set aside.

2. Heat an 8" skillet over medium heat. Once hot, add ½ teaspoon olive oil. Add chicken and cook 4 minutes per side or until chicken is golden on both sides and reaches an internal temperature of 160°F. Remove from pan and set aside.

3. Add remaining ½ teaspoon olive oil and butter. Once butter has melted, add onion and cook 1 minute, then add garlic and red pepper flakes and cook until fragrant, about 30 seconds. Add asparagus and cook 3–4 minutes or until asparagus is just tender.

4. Move asparagus to sides of pan and add broth, lemon juice, and mustard. Mix well, scraping any bits from the bottom of pan. Stir in asparagus and add chicken back to pan. Let simmer 2–3 minutes or until asparagus is cooked to your preference. If sauce is too thick, add water 2 teaspoons at a time until desired consistency is reached.

5. Transfer mixture to a serving plate and garnish with parsley. Enjoy immediately.

PER SERVING

Calories: 242	Fiber: 3g
Fat: 11g	Sugar: 3g
Sodium: 399mg	Protein: 29g
Carbohydrates: 8g	

CHICKEN AND MUSHROOM MARSALA

PREP TIME: 10 MINUTES | COOK TIME: 16 MINUTES | SERVES: 1

 Marsala is a fortified Italian wine frequently used in cooking. If you can't find it you can use Madeira or white wine, or for a nonalcoholic substitute, white grape juice. For the best flavor, avoid wines labeled as cooking wine. They are low quality and loaded with preservatives and sugar.

INGREDIENTS

1 tablespoon all-purpose flour

⅛ teaspoon sea salt

⅛ teaspoon freshly cracked black pepper

1 (4-ounce) boneless, skinless chicken breast

1 teaspoon olive oil

⅓ cup sliced yellow onion

½ cup sliced button mushrooms

½ clove garlic, peeled and minced

⅛ teaspoon dried thyme

⅛ teaspoon dried oregano

2 tablespoons marsala wine

2 tablespoons low-sodium chicken broth

1 teaspoon chopped fresh parsley

PER SERVING

Calories: 259
Fat: 11g
Sodium: 347mg
Carbohydrates: 14g

Fiber: 2g
Sugar: 3g
Protein: 24g

1. Combine flour, salt, and black pepper in a small dish. Dredge chicken breast in flour, shaking to remove excess.

2. In an 8" skillet over medium heat, add olive oil. Once hot, add chicken and cook 4 minutes per side or until chicken is golden brown and reaches an internal temperature of 160°F. Remove chicken from pan and set aside.

3. To same pan add onion and mushrooms. Cook, stirring often, until mushrooms are tender, about 4 minutes. Add garlic, thyme, and oregano and cook until fragrant, about 30 seconds.

4. Stir in wine, scraping any brown bits from the bottom of pan, then add broth and top with chicken breast. Cover skillet and let cook 3 minutes. Transfer chicken to a serving plate and cover with mushrooms and onion. Garnish with parsley and serve immediately.

Chicken Cutlets

Chicken breats can range in weight from 4–8 ounces, so you may need to trim larger breasts to get the right size. They best way to do this is to cut the larger breast into smaller cutlets. Place the chicken breast on a cutting board and carefully slice it in half parallel to the cutting board.

CHICKEN CACCIATORE

PREP TIME: 10 MINUTES | COOK TIME: 26 MINUTES | SERVES: 1

 This personal sized stew has all the flavor and comfort of a full-sized batch. While this calls for a chicken thigh, you can substitute chicken breast if you prefer. This tastes wonderful if you make it a day or two ahead and reheat it so the flavors can develop.

INGREDIENTS

1 tablespoon all-purpose flour

⅛ teaspoon sea salt

⅛ teaspoon freshly cracked black pepper

1 (4-ounce) boneless, skinless chicken thigh, cut into 1" pieces

1 teaspoon olive oil

2 tablespoons diced white onion

2 tablespoons diced carrot

2 tablespoons diced celery

1 large Roma tomato, seeds and stem removed, diced

½ clove garlic, peeled and minced

⅛ teaspoon dried thyme

½ teaspoon tomato paste

2 tablespoons white wine

½ cup low-sodium chicken broth

1 bay leaf

1. In a small bowl, combine flour, salt, and black pepper. Add chicken to bowl and toss to coat.

2. In a 2-quart saucepan over medium heat, add olive oil. Once hot, add chicken and cook until browned on all four sides, about 2 minutes per side. Remove chicken from pot and set aside.

3. To same pot add onion, carrot, and celery. Cook, stirring often, until vegetables are just tender, about 3 minutes. Add diced tomato, garlic, and thyme and cook until garlic is very fragrant, about 1 minute. Add tomato paste and cook 1 minute.

4. Add wine and stir, scraping any bits from the bottom of pot. Add broth and bay leaf and stir well. Bring mixture to a boil, add chicken, reduce heat to medium-low, cover, and simmer 10 minutes. Uncover and continue to simmer until the stew is thickened to your liking, at least 3 minutes. Discard bay leaf before serving.

PER SERVING

Calories: 259

Fat: 10g

Sodium: 376mg

Carbohydrates: 16g

Fiber: 3g

Sugar: 6g

Protein: 23g

CHICKEN WITH TOASTED ORZO

PREP TIME: 10 MINUTES | COOK TIME: 23 MINUTES | SERVES: 1

 This recipe calls for fresh tomato, but if you have leftover canned tomatoes or even a bit of chunky tomato or marinara sauce, you can use any of those instead. Just add ½ cup of drained canned tomatoes, or ⅓ cup of sauce in place of the fresh tomato.

INGREDIENTS

1 (4-ounce) boneless, skinless chicken breast

⅛ teaspoon freshly cracked black pepper

⅛ teaspoon sea salt

1 teaspoon olive oil

1 teaspoon salted butter

3 tablespoons minced yellow onion

½ clove garlic, peeled and minced

⅛ teaspoon ground fennel

1 teaspoon tomato paste

2 ounces orzo pasta

1 medium Roma tomato, seeds and stem removed, diced

½ cup plus 2 tablespoons low-sodium chicken broth

1 teaspoon chopped fresh parsley

1. With a meat mallet, pound chicken breast until it is ½" thick throughout. Season both sides with black pepper and salt. Set aside.

2. In an 8" skillet over medium heat, add olive oil. Once hot, add chicken and cook 4 minutes per side or until chicken is golden on both sides and reaches an internal temperature of 160°F. Remove from pan and set aside.

3. To same skillet add butter. Once melted, add onion and cook 1 minute, then add garlic, fennel, and tomato paste. Cook until garlic is fragrant, about 45 seconds. Add orzo and cook until pasta is lightly golden and coated, about 3 minutes. Add diced tomato and stir well, scraping up any bits from the bottom of skillet.

4. Stir in broth and bring to a boil. Once boiling, reduce heat to medium-low, add chicken to skillet, cover, and simmer 10 minutes or until orzo is tender.

5. Transfer mixture to a serving plate and garnish with parsley. Enjoy immediately.

PER SERVING

Calories: 429
Fat: 12g
Sodium: 400mg
Carbohydrates: 50g

Fiber: 4g
Sugar: 6g
Protein: 34g

VEGETABLE BOWLS WITH TURKEY AND HUMMUS

PREP TIME: 10 MINUTES | COOK TIME: 0 MINUTES | SERVES: 1

 Looking for ways to use up leftover roasted turkey breast? This bowl has you covered, and makes a delicious lunch or dinner anytime. If you have cooked chicken on hand, you can use that instead, or you can use low-sodium turkey lunch meat.

INGREDIENTS

1 teaspoon extra-virgin olive oil

½ teaspoon red wine vinegar

2 cups loosely packed baby spinach

1 cup chopped romaine lettuce

½ cup chopped cooked turkey breast

½ cup chopped English cucumber

½ cup chopped tomato

2 tablespoons sliced Kalamata olives

2 tablespoons finely chopped red onion

2 tablespoons roasted red pepper hummus

2 tablespoons crumbled feta cheese

⅛ teaspoon freshly cracked black pepper

1. In a medium bowl, add olive oil and red wine vinegar. Whisk until combined, then immediately add spinach and lettuce and toss to evenly coat.

2. Top lettuce with turkey, cucumber, tomato, olives, and red onion. Dollop hummus in center of bowl. Garnish with feta and black pepper. Serve immediately.

PER SERVING

Calories: 319

Fat: 17g

Sodium: 783mg

Carbohydrates: 16g

Fiber: 6g

Sugar: 6g

Protein: 28g

KALE AND ORZO CHICKEN

PREP TIME: 10 MINUTES | COOK TIME: 19 MINUTES | SERVES: 1

 Kale is a nutritional powerhouse and is usually available already washed and chopped in most produce departments with the salad mixes. If you are chopping it from a fresh bunch, buy kale that is firm and vibrant, thoroughly wash it to remove any dirt, and cut the leaves from the tough stems before chopping.

INGREDIENTS

1 (4-ounce) boneless, skinless chicken thigh, cut into 1" pieces

⅛ teaspoon freshly cracked black pepper

⅛ teaspoon sea salt

1 teaspoon olive oil

3 tablespoons minced yellow onion

2 tablespoons chopped red bell pepper

2 cups chopped kale

½ clove garlic, peeled and minced

¼ teaspoon Greek seasoning

2 ounces orzo pasta

½ cup plus 2 tablespoons low-sodium chicken broth

1 tablespoon crumbled feta cheese

1. Season chicken cubes with black pepper and salt. Set aside.

2. In an 8" skillet over medium heat, add olive oil. Once hot, add chicken and cook until golden on all sides, about 2 minutes per each of two sides. Remove from pan and set aside.

3. To same skillet add onion and bell pepper. Cook until just tender, about 1 minute. Add kale and cook until kale is completely wilted and starting to soften, about 3 minutes. Add garlic and Greek seasoning and cook until fragrant, about 1 minute.

4. Stir in orzo and broth and bring to a boil. Once boiling, reduce heat to medium-low, add chicken, cover, and simmer 10 minutes or until orzo is tender.

5. Transfer mixture to a serving plate and garnish with feta. Enjoy immediately.

PER SERVING

Calories: 440
Fat: 13g
Sodium: 682mg
Carbohydrates: 50g

Fiber: 4g
Sugar: 5g
Protein: 31g

CHICKEN SCALLOPINE

PREP TIME: 10 MINUTES | COOK TIME: 8 MINUTES | SERVES: 1

Thin chicken cutlets make this dish cook quickly, so you can have dinner ready in a flash! If you can find them in your fresh meat section, you can buy them; otherwise, use the process detailed here. Enjoy this with some spaghetti or fettuccine and a side of steamed vegetables.

INGREDIENTS

1 (4-ounce) boneless, skinless chicken breast

2 tablespoons all-purpose flour

⅛ teaspoon freshly cracked black pepper

⅛ teaspoon sea salt

1 tablespoon olive oil

2 tablespoons white wine

¼ cup low-sodium chicken broth

1 tablespoon lemon juice

1 teaspoon unsalted butter

1 teaspoon capers

1. Slice chicken breast into two cutlets. With a meat mallet, pound each breast until it is ¼" thick throughout. Set aside.

2. In a shallow dish, combine flour, black pepper, and salt. Dredge both sides of chicken in flour mixture. Set aside.

3. Heat an 8" skillet over medium heat. Once hot, add olive oil. Add chicken and cook 3 minutes per side or until chicken is golden on both sides and reaches an internal temperature of 165°F. Remove from pan and place on a serving plate.

4. To same skillet add wine and scrape any browned bits from the bottom of skillet. Add broth and stir well. Bring mixture to a boil and cook until broth has reduced by half, about 1 minute. Add lemon juice, butter, and capers and stir constantly until butter has melted and sauce is glossy, about 30 seconds. Pour sauce over chicken. Enjoy immediately.

Make It with Turkey Breast

You can make most chicken dishes with turkey if you would like to add a little variety to your poultry dishes. From October through January, whole boneless, skinless turkey breasts are more readily available at your butcher's counter. One serving of turkey breast is about 3-ounces, so portion your breast into 3-ounce servings and store them in an airtight bag in the freezer up to three months.

PER SERVING

Calories: 345	Fiber: 1g
Fat: 19g	Sugar: 1g
Sodium: 339mg	Protein: 27g
Carbohydrates: 14g	

FETA AND SPINACH–STUFFED CHICKEN BREAST

PREP TIME: 15 MINUTES | COOK TIME: 28 MINUTES | SERVES: 1

 This recipe calls for panko bread crumbs, but you can use leftover stale bread to make bread crumbs. Add cubes of stale bread to a blender and pulse until it forms coarse bread crumbs. Any sort of bread works for this, but a crusty loaf will have the best texture.

INGREDIENTS

1 (6-ounce) boneless, skinless chicken breast

⅛ teaspoon sea salt

⅛ teaspoon freshly cracked black pepper

⅛ teaspoon Italian seasoning

½ teaspoon olive oil

2 tablespoons finely chopped yellow onion

1 cup loosely packed baby spinach, chopped

1 tablespoon crumbled feta cheese

1 sun-dried tomato, minced

⅛ teaspoon garlic powder

1 tablespoon all-purpose flour

1 large egg, beaten

¼ cup panko bread crumbs

PER SERVING

Calories: 410
Fat: 11g
Sodium: 460mg
Carbohydrates: 31g

Fiber: 2g
Sugar: 3g
Protein: 47g

1. With a sharp knife, cut a deep pocket into the thickest part of the chicken breast, making sure not to cut all the way through the meat. Season chicken with salt, black pepper, and Italian seasoning. Set aside.

2. Preheat oven to 350°F and line a small baking sheet with foil; lightly spray with nonstick cooking spray.

3. In an 8" skillet over medium heat, add olive oil. Once hot, add onion and cook 30 seconds, then add spinach and cook, stirring constantly, until fully wilted and soft, about 2 minutes. Turn off heat and transfer spinach mixture to a small bowl. Cool 5 minutes, then add feta, sun-dried tomato, and garlic powder. Mix well, then stuff mixture into prepared chicken breast.

4. In three shallow dishes, add flour, egg, and bread crumbs. Dredge chicken in flour, dip in egg, then cover in bread crumbs. Place on prepared baking sheet.

5. Bake 25–28 minutes or until chicken is cooked through and the chicken reads 160°F in the thickest part. Cool 3 minutes before serving.

TURKEY MEATBALLS IN RED PEPPER SAUCE

PREP TIME: 1 HOUR 12 MINUTES | COOK TIME: 12 MINUTES | SERVES: 1

 Grated carrot is the trick to keeping these turkey meatballs moist and juicy, and they give you some extra vegetables in your diet! If you love a meatball sub, meatballs with your spaghetti, or want some meatballs to top your Creamy Cheese Polenta (see Chapter 5), then you are in the right place!

INGREDIENTS

5 ounces ground lean turkey

2 tablespoons panko bread crumbs

2 tablespoons finely grated carrot

1 tablespoon grated yellow onion

1 tablespoon finely chopped fresh parsley

¼ teaspoon Italian seasoning

⅛ teaspoon ground fennel

⅛ teaspoon garlic powder

⅛ teaspoon sea salt

⅛ teaspoon freshly cracked black pepper

⅓ cup finely chopped jarred roasted red peppers

1 basil leaf, finely chopped

½ clove garlic, peeled and minced

½ teaspoon lemon juice

½ teaspoon extra-virgin olive oil

1. In a medium bowl, add turkey, bread crumbs, carrot, onion, parsley, Italian seasoning, fennel, garlic powder, salt, and black pepper. Mix until well combined then form into six meatballs. Place on a tray and refrigerate 1 hour or overnight.

2. Preheat oven to 400°F and line a small baking sheet with foil lightly sprayed with nonstick cooking spray.

3. Arrange meatballs on prepared baking sheet and bake 12–15 minutes, turning halfway through cooking, until meatballs reach an internal temperature of 165°F.

4. While meatballs cook, add remaining ingredients to a 1-quart saucepan. With an immersion blender, purée mixture until smooth. Place over medium-low heat and bring to a simmer. Hold until meatballs are ready.

5. Once meatballs are ready, transfer to sauce along with any juices on tray. Stir to ensure meatballs are evenly coated in sauce. Serve hot.

PER SERVING

Calories: 331 | Fat: 14g | Sodium: 594mg | Carbohydrates: 17g Fiber: 1g | Sugar: 5g | Protein: 32g

CHICKEN LETTUCE WRAPS

PREP TIME: 2 HOURS 10 MINUTES | COOK TIME: 25 MINUTES | SERVES: 1

 This meal for one is light, refreshing, and great for lunch or dinner with a cup of soup. You can save time by using cooked and shredded chicken from your grocery store's deli section. Just mix up the marinade in a small bowl and toss 3½ ounces of the cooked chicken in the mixture before enjoying!

INGREDIENTS

1 teaspoon extra-virgin olive oil

¼ teaspoon Dijon mustard

¼ teaspoon ground cumin

⅛ teaspoon onion powder

⅛ teaspoon garlic powder

1 (4-ounce) boneless, skinless chicken breast

3 leaves butter lettuce

2 tablespoons prepared hummus

¼ cup chopped English cucumber

¼ cup chopped plum tomato

2 tablespoons minced red onion

1. In a small resealable bag, add olive oil, mustard, cumin, onion powder, and garlic powder. Squeeze bag to mix, then add chicken breast, press air out of bag, seal, and massage to evenly coat chicken. Refrigerate at least 2 hours or up to 8 hours.

2. Preheat oven to 350°F and line a small baking sheet with foil lightly sprayed with nonstick cooking spray.

3. Place chicken breast on prepared baking sheet and bake 25–30 minutes or until the internal temperature reaches 160°F. Remove from oven and tent chicken with foil. Cool to room temperature, about 20 minutes, then shred chicken into large pieces.

4. Arrange lettuce on a serving plate. Spread each leaf with hummus and top with chicken, cucumber, tomato, and red onion. Roll into small wraps. Serve immediately.

PER SERVING

Calories: 239

Fat: 10g

Sodium: 190mg

Carbohydrates: 10g

Fiber: 3g

Sugar: 3g

Protein: 29g

CHICKEN AND NOODLES CASSEROLE

PREP TIME: 12 MINUTES | COOK TIME: 14 MINUTES | SERVES: 1

 Do you ever want the comfort of a casserole, but you can't stand the thought of cooking a whole one for yourself? This casserole is perfect for those occasions! This recipe also avoids condensed soup, which is packed with salt, so you can feel good about this comforting dish.

INGREDIENTS

1 ounce wide egg noodles

¼ teaspoon sea salt, divided

1 teaspoon olive oil

2 tablespoons chopped yellow onion

2 tablespoons chopped carrot

2 tablespoons chopped celery

½ clove garlic, peeled and minced

¼ teaspoon poultry seasoning

2 teaspoons all-purpose flour

¾ cup low-sodium chicken broth

1 (4-ounce) boneless, skinless chicken breast, cut into 1" pieces

2 tablespoons frozen peas

⅛ teaspoon freshly cracked black pepper

1. In a 2-quart saucepan over high heat, add water to fill pot ¾ full. Once water begins to boil, add noodles and salt. Cook, stirring occasionally, 4 minutes. Drain and set noodles aside.

2. Return pot to heat and add olive oil. Once hot, add onion, carrot, and celery. Cook, stirring constantly, until softened, about 2 minutes. Add garlic and poultry seasoning and cook until fragrant, about 30 seconds. Sprinkle all-purpose flour and cook 1 minute, then slowly stir in broth, making sure no lumps form. Stir in chicken breast and cooked noodles.

3. Bring mixture to a boil, then reduce heat to medium-low and simmer, stirring occasionally, until chicken is cooked to an internal temperature of 160°F and pasta is tender, about 5–6 minutes. Stir in peas and cook 1 minute more. Add black pepper on top before serving hot.

PER SERVING

Calories: 284	Fiber: 3g
Fat: 8g	Sugar: 3g
Sodium: 270mg	Protein: 30g
Carbohydrates: 24g	

BALSAMIC CHICKEN THIGH WITH TOMATO AND BASIL

PREP TIME: 4 HOURS 10 MINUTES | COOK TIME: 11 MINUTES | SERVES: 1

 This marinade works for any cut of chicken, but it can also be used for marinating portobello mushrooms, beef, pork, and fatty fish like salmon. The longer you can let the chicken marinate, the better the flavor will be, so prep this the night before cooking when possible.

INGREDIENTS

2 teaspoons extra-virgin olive oil

½ clove garlic, peeled and minced

1 teaspoon balsamic vinegar

¼ teaspoon Italian seasoning

¼ teaspoon Dijon mustard

⅛ teaspoon onion powder

¼ teaspoon poultry seasoning

1 (4-ounce) boneless, skinless chicken thigh

8 medium cherry tomatoes

⅛ teaspoon freshly cracked black pepper

1 basil leaf, chopped

1. In a small resealable bag, add olive oil, garlic, balsamic vinegar, Italian seasoning, mustard, onion powder, and poultry seasoning. Squeeze bag to mix, then add chicken thigh, press air out of bag, seal, and massage to evenly coat chicken in marinade. Refrigerate at least 4 hours or overnight.

2. Preheat a grill pan to high heat. Once smoking hot, reduce heat to medium. Place chicken on grill pan and grill until chicken is browned and lightly charred, about 4 minutes. Flip and cook on second side until chicken is browned and reaches an internal temperature of 160°F, about 4–6 minutes. Transfer chicken to a serving plate and lightly cover with foil.

3. Add tomatoes to grill pan and cook until tomatoes are tender and slightly charred, about 3 minutes.

4. Arrange tomatoes around chicken and garnish with black pepper and basil. Serve hot.

PER SERVING

Calories: 252	Fiber: 2g
Fat: 15g	Sugar: 4g
Sodium: 99mg	Protein: 21g
Carbohydrates: 7g	

MINI TURKEY MEATLOAF

PREP TIME: 1 HOUR 10 MINUTES | COOK TIME: 40 MINUTES | SERVES: 1

 Barbecue sauce and ketchup mixed together give this meatloaf a zesty kick, but you can use only ketchup if that is all you have. If you do not have a mini-loaf pan, you could also divide this mixture between two muffin cups and make meatloaf muffins; just reduce the cooking time to 25 minutes.

INGREDIENTS

6 ounces ground lean turkey

3 tablespoons panko bread crumbs

2 tablespoons finely grated carrot

2 tablespoons finely chopped yellow onion

1 tablespoon water

2 teaspoons tomato paste

¼ teaspoon smoked paprika

⅛ teaspoon onion powder

⅛ teaspoon garlic powder

⅛ teaspoon sea salt

⅛ teaspoon freshly cracked black pepper

1 tablespoon ketchup

1 tablespoon barbecue sauce

1. In a medium bowl, add turkey, bread crumbs, carrot, onion, water, tomato paste, paprika, onion powder, garlic powder, salt, and black pepper. Mix until well combined, then cover and chill 1 hour.

2. Preheat oven to 350°F and spray a mini-loaf pan with nonstick cooking spray.

3. Press turkey mixture into prepared pan. Bake 20 minutes, then spoon ketchup and barbecue sauce over top of meatloaf and return to oven 20–25 minutes or until meatloaf reaches an internal temperature of 165°F.

4. Remove pan from oven and let stand 10 minutes before serving. Serve hot.

Meatloaf Sandwiches

To make meatloaf sandwiches, make meatloaf as directed and refrigerate until cold. Heat ½ teaspoon olive oil in an 8" skillet over medium heat. Slice meatloaf into six slices and add to hot pan. Cook 2–3 minutes per side or until golden. Serve on your favorite whole-grain bread with ketchup and mustard.

PER SERVING

Calories: 422

Fat: 15g

Sodium: 774mg

Carbohydrates: 33g

Fiber: 2g

Sugar: 13g

Protein: 39g

FIG-GLAZED CHICKEN BREAST

PREP TIME: 10 MINUTES | COOK TIME: 20 MINUTES | SERVES: 1

 Sheet pan meals are great when cooking for one as they reduce cleanup and require little effort for a lot of reward. Fig preserves add earthy sweetness to the chicken, but if they are not available, you can use 1 tablespoon orange marmalade mixed with ¼ teaspoon balsamic vinegar.

INGREDIENTS

1 medium (about 5-ounce) new potato, cut into ¼" slices

¼ cup sliced yellow onion

½ teaspoon olive oil

⅛ teaspoon ground cumin

⅛ teaspoon ground cinnamon

⅛ teaspoon garlic powder

⅛ teaspoon sea salt

1 (4-ounce) boneless, skinless chicken breast

1 tablespoon fig preserves, divided

⅛ teaspoon freshly cracked black pepper

1. Preheat oven to 350°F and line a small baking sheet with foil sprayed with nonstick cooking spray.

2. In a small bowl, combine potato, onion, and olive oil. Toss to coat, then spread potato and onion in a single layer on prepared baking sheet.

3. In a separate small bowl, combine cumin, cinnamon, garlic powder, and salt. Mix and then sprinkle mixture on all sides of chicken breast. Place breast on top of potato and onion pieces.

4. Brush chicken with 1 teaspoon fig preserves. Bake 10 minutes, then brush with remaining 2 teaspoons fig preserves. Return to oven and bake 10–15 minutes or until internal temperature reaches 160°F.

5. Transfer chicken to a plate along with potato and onion. Garnish with black pepper. Serve immediately.

PER SERVING

Calories: 371

Fat: 5g

Sodium: 261mg

Carbohydrates: 54g

Fiber: 5g

Sugar: 13g

Protein: 30g

TURKEY BURGER

PREP TIME: 40 MINUTES | COOK TIME: 8 MINUTES | SERVES: 1

 Most grocery store bakery sections have smaller packages of buns and rolls available, so you do not have to buy a whole eight-pack of buns for one burger. If you can't find a single bun or roll, you can freeze the extra buns. Be sure to separate them into individual buns before freezing so they are easy to access.

INGREDIENTS

4 ounces ground lean turkey

2 tablespoons panko bread crumbs

1 tablespoon grated yellow onion

1 tablespoon ketchup, divided

⅛ teaspoon onion powder

⅛ teaspoon garlic powder

⅛ teaspoon sea salt

⅛ teaspoon freshly cracked black pepper

2 teaspoons olive oil

2 teaspoons olive oil mayonnaise

1 teaspoon Dijon mustard

½ teaspoon dill pickle relish

1 whole-wheat hamburger bun

¼ cup shredded iceberg lettuce

1 (¼"-thick) slice beefsteak tomato

1 tablespoon chopped white onion

1 In a medium bowl, add turkey, bread crumbs, onion, 2 teaspoons ketchup, onion powder, garlic powder, salt, and black pepper. Mix until well combined, then cover and chill 30 minutes.

2 Preheat grill pan over medium heat, then add olive oil and swirl pan to coat.

3 Press turkey mixture into a ½"-thick patty. Cook 4 minutes, then flip and cook 4–5 minutes more or until burger reaches an internal temperature of 165°F.

4 While patty cooks, prepare burger sauce. In a small bowl, combine remaining teaspoon ketchup, mayonnaise, mustard, and relish. Mix well. Spread on top and bottom of bun.

5 When burger is ready, transfer it to bottom bun. Top with lettuce, tomato slice, and onion. Top with top bun. Serve immediately.

PER SERVING

Calories: 543 | Fat: 24g | Sodium: 1,009mg | Carbohydrates: 48g
Fiber: 5g | Sugar: 9g | Protein: 33g

EASY PESTO CHICKEN

PREP TIME: 5 MINUTES | COOK TIME: 20 MINUTES | SERVES: 1

 Dinner for one has never been easier than this three-ingredient chicken. Serve it with some fresh cooked pasta tossed in a little olive oil and lemon or Lemon Garlic Rice Pilaf (see Chapter 5) and some steamed vegetables for a meal you will make again and again.

INGREDIENTS

1 (4-ounce) boneless, skinless chicken breast

1 tablespoon basil pesto

2 tablespoons grated Parmesan cheese

1. Preheat oven to 350°F and line a small baking sheet with foil sprayed with nonstick cooking spray.

2. Place chicken breast on prepared baking sheet. Spread pesto evenly over chicken, then sprinkle with Parmesan, pressing gently to adhere cheese to pesto.

3. Bake 20–25 minutes or until cheese is golden brown and internal temperature reaches 160°F. Cool 3 minutes before serving.

Freezing Pesto

Not sure you will be able to use your pesto up before it expires? Freeze it! Use an ice cube tray and divide the pesto into the tray, then drizzle the tops with enough olive oil to cover them. Freeze overnight and then pop the pesto cubes out of the tray and into an airtight freezer-safe bag or container and freeze until ready to use, up to six months.

PER SERVING

Calories: 226

Fat: 11g

Sodium: 362mg

Carbohydrates: 3g

Fiber: 0g

Sugar: 1g

Protein: 29g

WINE-BRAISED CHICKEN THIGH

PREP TIME: 20 MINUTES | COOK TIME: 44 MINUTES | SERVES: 1

 Braising is an easy way to ensure tender, flavorful chicken. Serve this chicken on a mound of creamy Olive Oil Mashed Potatoes or a bed of Creamy Cheese Polenta (see Chapter 5).

INGREDIENTS

1 (6-ounce) bone-in chicken thigh, skin removed and reserved

⅛ teaspoon sea salt

⅛ teaspoon freshly cracked black pepper

½ cup sliced button mushrooms

3 tablespoons chopped yellow onion

1 clove garlic, peeled and smashed

⅛ teaspoon dried thyme

¼ cup zinfandel wine

½ cup low-sodium chicken stock

PER SERVING

Calories: 298
Fat: 14g
Sodium: 569mg
Carbohydrates: 6g

Fiber: 1g
Sugar: 2g
Protein: 30g

1. In a 1-quart saucepan over medium-low heat, add chicken skin. Cook, turning often, until it renders at least 2 teaspoons fat, about 5 minutes. Remove skin and discard.

2. Season chicken thigh on both sides with salt and black pepper. Add chicken meat side down to pan and cook until golden brown, about 4–5 minutes. Transfer to a plate. Chicken is not cooked at this point, just browned.

3. Add mushrooms to pan and let stand 2 minutes to brown before stirring. Cook, stirring occasionally, until mushrooms are tender, about 5 minutes. Add onion and cook until just tender, 2 minutes. Add garlic and thyme and stir to combine.

4. Add wine, scraping any browned bits from the bottom of pan, and let cook 30 seconds, then add stock and stir well. Place chicken thigh (bone side down) into liquid.

5. Bring mixture to a boil, then reduce heat to low, cover, and cook 20–25 minutes or until chicken reaches an internal temperature of 170°F.

6. Remove chicken from pot and cover with foil. Strain off mushrooms and onions and reserve, discarding garlic. Return liquid to stove over medium heat and bring to a boil. Reduce liquid by half, about 5 minutes.

7. To serve, place mushrooms and onions on a serving plate. Top with chicken and sauce. Serve.

CHAPTER 10
PORK, LAMB, AND BEEF DISHES

Balsamic-Glazed Pork 185

Beef and Vegetable Stew with
    Olives 186

Spaghetti with Meaty Mushroom
    Sauce 188

Beef Stew with Red Wine 189

Minty Lamb Meatballs in Spicy
    Red Pepper Ragu 190

Beef and Mushroom Stroganoff 192

Beefy Stuffed Peppers 193

Beef and Black Bean Enchilada
    Casserole 194

Greek Meatballs 195

Vegetable-Packed Pork
    Meatball Sub 197

Unstuffed Cabbage Rolls in a Bowl 198

Herbed Lamb Chop 199

Minute Steak with Garlic
    and Herbs 200

Lamb Stew for One 201

Pork Medallions with Mustard
    Sauce 202

Phyllo-Wrapped Beef Tenderloin 204

Pork-Stuffed Mushrooms 205

Salisbury Steak 206

Red meats like lamb, beef, and pork are considered occasional foods on the Mediterranean diet, and as such the recipes you use should make them feel like a special occasion. Combined with some delicious vegetables and grains, you can enjoy the recipes in this chapter a few times every month. Your butcher will be your best ally when it comes to beef, pork, and lamb. Their fresh meat counter will have bulk ground beef and pork you can buy in smaller quantities, and they sell single steaks and chops so you don't have to buy more than you need.

This chapter is your source for delicious beef, lamb, and pork dishes that layer flavor and make the most of the ingredients you are using. Craving comfort food after a long week? Unstuffed Cabbage Rolls in a Bowl or Lamb Stew for One are ready in no time. Greek Meatballs and Pork-Stuffed Mushrooms are great when you want something light and delicious. Celebrating something special? Phyllo-Wrapped Beef Tenderloin or Herbed Lamb Chops feel super special but are surprisingly easy. When you want to enjoy that special meal, you can't go wrong with these red meat dishes for one!

BALSAMIC-GLAZED PORK

PREP TIME: 5 MINUTES | COOK TIME: 8 MINUTES | SERVES: 1

 Center cut pork chops are among the leanest cuts of pork, and are a better choice when enjoying a Mediterranean diet. Here the pork is seasoned with Montreal steak seasoning which adds bold, savory flavor without having to pull out multiple jars of spices and herbs.

INGREDIENTS

1 (4-ounce) center cut pork chop, fat trimmed

¼ teaspoon Montreal steak seasoning

1 teaspoon all-purpose flour

1 teaspoon olive oil

2 tablespoons low-sodium vegetable broth

2 teaspoons balsamic vinegar

2 teaspoons honey

1. Season both sides of pork chop with Montreal steak seasoning, then dust both sides with flour.

2. In an 8" skillet over medium heat, add olive oil and let it heat briefly, then swirl pan to coat. Add pork chop and brown well on both sides, about 3–4 minutes per side. Remove from pan and set aside.

3. Add broth and reduce heat to low. Scrape pan to loosen any brown bits stuck to the bottom, then add balsamic vinegar and honey to pan and stir well. Place pork chop back in pan and turn to coat in balsamic mixture. Cook, turning often, until pork is thickly coated in glaze, about 2 minutes and the internal temperature reaches 145°F.

4. Transfer pork chop to a serving plate and let rest 3 minutes before serving.

Steak Seasoning Blend
To make your own seasoning blend, mix 1 tablespoon onion powder, 2 teaspoons smoked paprika, 1 teaspoon dried oregano, 1 teaspoon freshly cracked black pepper, ½ teaspoon sea salt, ¼ teaspoon ground cumin, and ¼ teaspoon packed light brown sugar. Store in an airtight jar up to six months.

PER SERVING

Calories: 303	Fiber: 0g
Fat: 13g	Sugar: 14g
Sodium: 249mg	Protein: 28g
Carbohydrates: 16g	

BEEF AND VEGETABLE STEW WITH OLIVES

PREP TIME: 20 MINUTES | COOK TIME: 1 HOUR 16 MINUTES | SERVES: 1

 The best stew meat should have some marbling, but not be overly fatty or lean. Stew meat freezes well, so break a larger pack into smaller portions and save for another day of stew making!

INGREDIENTS

3 ounces beef stew meat, cut into ½" pieces

1 teaspoon all-purpose flour

¼ teaspoon Montreal steak seasoning

1 teaspoon olive oil

⅓ cup roughly chopped yellow onion

⅓ cup roughly chopped celery

⅓ cup sliced carrot

½ cup sliced button mushrooms

½ clove garlic, peeled and minced

½ teaspoon tomato paste

¼ teaspoon Italian seasoning

⅛ teaspoon dried thyme

3 tablespoons red wine

1 cup low-sodium vegetable broth

½ bay leaf

1 teaspoon balsamic vinegar

1 small (about 4-ounce) russet potato, peeled and chopped

4 large pitted black olives, quartered

2 teaspoons chopped fresh parsley

1. In a 1-quart bowl, add beef, flour, and Montreal steak seasoning. Toss until meat is evenly coated in flour and seasoning.

2. Place a 1-quart Dutch oven or pot over medium heat, add olive oil and let it heat briefly, then swirl to coat pot. Add beef cubes, leaving ½" between pieces, and brown on all sides, about 3 minutes per side. You may need to work in batches. Once browned, transfer to a plate and set aside.

3. To pot, add onion, celery, and carrot. Cook, stirring often, until just tender, about 4 minutes. Add mushrooms and cook until tender, about 3 minutes.

4. Add garlic, tomato paste, Italian seasoning, and thyme and cook until fragrant, about 30 seconds. Stir in wine, scraping any brown bits from the bottom of pot, then add beef with any juices on plate, broth, bay leaf, and balsamic vinegar.

5. Bring mixture to a boil, reduce heat to medium-low, cover with lid, and let simmer 30 minutes. Remove lid and add potato and olives. Cover pot and simmer 20 minutes or until potato and meat are tender and falling apart.

6. Remove from heat and discard bay leaf. Serve stew hot with parsley for garnish.

PER SERVING

Calories: 386	Fiber: 8g
Fat: 9g	Sugar: 11g
Sodium: 580mg	Protein: 21g
Carbohydrates: 54g	

SPAGHETTI WITH MEATY MUSHROOM SAUCE

PREP TIME: 15 MINUTES | COOK TIME: 35 MINUTES | SERVES: 1

 Finely chopped mushrooms have a rich, savory flavor that pairs well with beef, and they can help extend the meat in your recipe so you need less to get the same impact. You can make this up to three days ahead and reheat in the microwave for an easy meal for one when you need it!

INGREDIENTS

1 teaspoon olive oil

2 ounces 90/10 ground beef

4 ounces button mushrooms, trimmed and finely chopped

2 tablespoons chopped yellow onion

2 teaspoons tomato paste

½ clove garlic, peeled and minced

⅛ teaspoon dried thyme

⅛ teaspoon dried oregano

1 medium Roma tomato, seeds and stems removed, chopped

⅓ cup low-sodium chicken broth

½ teaspoon sea salt

2 ounces whole-wheat spaghetti pasta

1 teaspoon chopped fresh parsley

1. Heat a 1-quart saucepan over medium heat. Once hot, add olive oil, then add beef and cook, crumbling well, until browned, about 4 minutes. Add mushrooms and onion and cook, stirring often, until vegetables are very tender, about 5 minutes.

2. Add tomato paste, garlic, thyme, and oregano and cook until fragrant, about 30 seconds, then stir in tomato pieces and cook until they start to break down and are very soft, about 5 minutes. Stir in broth, scraping any bits from bottom of pan. Bring mixture to a boil, then reduce heat to low, cover with a lid, and simmer 20 minutes.

3. While sauce is simmering, cook pasta. In a medium pot over high heat, add water to fill pot ¾ full. Once water begins to boil, add salt and pasta. Cook, stirring occasionally, until pasta is al dente, about 10 minutes. Drain and set aside.

4. After 20 minutes of simmering, remove lid and stir sauce. Add pasta and toss to coat in sauce. Transfer to a serving plate and garnish with parsley. Serve immediately.

PER SERVING

Calories: 352

Fat: 9g

Sodium: 251mg

Carbohydrates: 48g

Fiber: 9g

Sugar: 7g

Protein: 23g

BEEF STEW WITH RED WINE

PREP TIME: 10 MINUTES | COOK TIME: 1 HOUR 10 MINUTES | SERVES: 1

 Beef stew is the perfect cold weather meal. It is hearty, rich in flavor, and really warms you up. The problem is you can have a lot of leftover food with traditional stew recipes. Fortunately, this recipe is perfectly portioned for one! Stew is also perfect meal prep material as the flavors are even better if you let it sit for a day or two!

INGREDIENTS

1 tablespoon all-purpose flour

⅛ teaspoon sea salt

⅛ teaspoon freshly cracked black pepper

3 ounces beef chuck roast, cut into ½" pieces

1 teaspoon olive oil

¼ cup roughly chopped white onion

¼ cup sliced carrot

2 tablespoons diced celery

½ teaspoon tomato paste

½ clove garlic, peeled and minced

⅛ teaspoon Montreal steak seasoning

3 tablespoons red wine

½ cup low-sodium beef broth

1 small (about 4-ounce) russet potato, peeled and chopped

PER SERVING

Calories: 362
Fat: 8g
Sodium: 416mg
Carbohydrates: 40g

Fiber: 4g
Sugar: 5g
Protein: 28g

1. In a small bowl, combine flour, salt, and black pepper. Add beef and toss to coat in flour. Set aside.

2. In a medium pot over medium heat, add olive oil. Once hot, add beef and cook until browned on all four sides, about 4 minutes per side. Remove beef from pot and set aside.

3. Return pot to heat and add onion, carrot, and celery. Cook, stirring often, until vegetables are just tender, about 3 minutes. Add tomato paste, garlic, and Montreal steak seasoning and cook until garlic is very fragrant, about 1 minute.

4. Add wine and stir, scraping any bits from bottom of pot. Add broth and stir well. Bring mixture to a boil, add beef, reduce heat to medium-low, cover, and simmer 30 minutes. Add potato and simmer another 20–25 minutes or until beef is tender and potato pieces are very soft. Serve hot.

Benefits of Wine in a Box

Wine in a box may have a bad reputation, but good-quality wines are available in boxes. The packaging extends the life of the wine once opened so you have longer to drink and cook with it. An opened bottle is often oxidized in a day or two. Boxed wine keeps fresh in the refrigerator up to a month.

MINTY LAMB MEATBALLS IN SPICY RED PEPPER RAGU

PREP TIME: 1 HOUR 15 MINUTES | COOK TIME: 12 MINUTES | SERVES: 1

 Mint and lamb are a classic Mediterranean duo; fresh mint has a sharp flavor that pairs well with the richness of the meat.

INGREDIENTS

5 ounces ground lamb

2 tablespoons panko bread crumbs

2 tablespoons finely minced fresh parsley

1 tablespoon finely minced fresh mint

1 tablespoon grated yellow onion

2 teaspoons 1% milk

¼ teaspoon Montreal steak seasoning

⅛ teaspoon freshly cracked black pepper

1 teaspoon olive oil

2 tablespoons finely chopped yellow onion

2 tablespoons finely chopped celery

2 tablespoons finely chopped carrot

½ clove garlic, peeled and minced

1 jarred roasted red pepper, finely chopped

¼ teaspoon crushed red pepper flakes

½ teaspoon red wine vinegar

1. In a medium bowl, add lamb, bread crumbs, parsley, mint, grated onion, milk, Montreal steak seasoning, and black pepper. Mix until well combined, then form into six meatballs. Place on a tray and refrigerate 1 hour.

2. Preheat oven to 400°F and line a small baking sheet with foil lightly sprayed with nonstick cooking spray.

3. Arrange meatballs on prepared baking sheet and bake 12–15 minutes, turning halfway through cooking, until meatballs reach an internal temperature of 165°F.

4. While meatballs cook, prepare sauce. To a 1-quart saucepan over medium heat add olive oil. Once hot, add chopped onion, celery, and carrot. Cook, stirring frequently, until tender, about 4 minutes. Add garlic and cook until fragrant, about 30 seconds. Add roasted red pepper, red pepper flakes, and vinegar and cook 3 minutes or until everything is tender.

5. Once meatballs are ready, transfer them to sauce along with any juices on tray. Stir to ensure meatballs are evenly coated in sauce. Serve hot.

PER SERVING

Calories: 463 | Fat: 27g | Sodium: 399mg | Carbohydrates: 18g Fiber: 2g | Sugar: 4g | Protein: 33g

BEEF AND MUSHROOM STROGANOFF

PREP TIME: 20 MINUTES | COOK TIME: 1 HOUR 5 MINUTES | SERVES: 1

 Traditional stroganoff is made with a sour cream–based sauce, but this version lightens things up by swapping it for low-fat Greek yogurt. Be sure to remove the pot from the heat before adding the yogurt so the sauce remains smooth.

INGREDIENTS

4 ounces beef stew meat, cut into 1" pieces

2 teaspoons all-purpose flour

½ teaspoon olive oil

¼ cup chopped yellow onion

4 ounces sliced button mushrooms

½ clove garlic, peeled and minced

⅛ teaspoon sea salt

⅛ teaspoon freshly cracked black pepper

¾ cup low-sodium beef broth

1 ounce wide egg noodles

2 tablespoons plain low-fat Greek yogurt

1. In a small bowl, add beef and flour. Toss until beef is evenly coated in flour.

2. In an 8" skillet over medium heat, add olive oil and let it heat briefly, then swirl pan to coat. Add beef cubes and brown well on all sides, about 3 minutes on each of the four sides. Transfer to a plate and reserve.

3. Return skillet to heat and add onion and cook until just tender, about 3 minutes. Add mushrooms and cook until tender, about 4 minutes. Add garlic, salt, and black pepper. Cook until garlic is fragrant, about 30 seconds.

4. Return beef to pot along with any juices on place. Stir in broth and bring to a boil, then reduce heat to medium-low, cover, and simmer 30 minutes.

5. After 30 minutes add egg noodles and stir well. Cook uncovered 15–20 minutes or until beef is tender and noodles are soft. Remove skillet from heat and stir in yogurt. Enjoy immediately.

PER SERVING

Calories: 320	Fiber: 3g
Fat: 8g	Sugar: 6g
Sodium: 334mg	Protein: 30g
Carbohydrates: 34g	

BEEFY STUFFED PEPPERS

PREP TIME: 10 MINUTES | COOK TIME: 39 MINUTES | SERVES: 1

 Lean beef that has 10% fat or less is a better choice when having beef on the Mediterranean diet. These stuffed peppers reheat well in the microwave and can be made up to three days ahead, making them great for lunches at the office or school.

INGREDIENTS

1 teaspoon extra-virgin olive oil

2 tablespoons minced yellow onion

2 cups lightly packed baby spinach, chopped

½ clove garlic, peeled and minced

¼ teaspoon Greek seasoning

3 ounces 90/10 ground beef

1 teaspoon tomato paste

¼ cup chopped Roma tomato

1 medium red bell pepper, sliced in half vertically, stem and seeds removed

2 tablespoons crumbled feta cheese

⅛ teaspoon freshly cracked black pepper

1. Preheat oven to 375°F and lightly spray a 6" baking dish with nonstick cooking spray.

2. In an 8" skillet over medium heat, add olive oil. Once hot, add onion and cook until just tender, about 4 minutes. Add spinach, garlic, and Greek seasoning and cook until spinach is wilted, about 2 minutes. Transfer mixture to a medium bowl and set aside.

3. Return pan to medium heat and add beef. Cook, crumbling well, until thoroughly browned, about 5 minutes. Add tomato paste and chopped tomato and cook until tomato pieces are soft, about 3 minutes. Add spinach mixture back to skillet and mix well. Remove pan from heat.

4. Place pepper halves cut side up in prepared baking dish. Fill with beef mixture and top each with feta and black pepper. Bake 25–30 minutes or until peppers are tender and filling has lightly browned. Cool 3 minutes before serving.

PER SERVING

Calories: 302	Fiber: 5g
Fat: 15g	Sugar: 9g
Sodium: 561mg	Protein: 24g
Carbohydrates: 15g	

BEEF AND BLACK BEAN ENCHILADA CASSEROLE

PREP TIME: 15 MINUTES | COOK TIME: 32 MINUTES | SERVES: 1

 Corn tortillas add fiber and whole grains to this casserole, and they are also a better choice than flour tortillas if you are watching your sugar and saturated fat intake. Leftover corn tortillas can be stored in the refrigerator up to two weeks or frozen up to six months.

INGREDIENTS

2 ounces 90/10 ground beef

¼ teaspoon chili powder

¼ teaspoon ground cumin

⅛ teaspoon garlic powder

⅛ teaspoon onion powder

3 tablespoons minced onion

3 tablespoons chopped red bell pepper

⅓ cup canned black beans, rinsed and drained

¼ cup chopped tomato

¼ cup tomato sauce

2 (6") corn tortillas, cut into 1" strips

3 tablespoons reduced-fat shredded sharp Cheddar cheese

1. Preheat oven to 350°F and lightly spray a 6" casserole dish with nonstick cooking spray.

2. Heat an 8" skillet over medium heat. Once hot, add beef. Cook, crumbling well, until well browned, about 5 minutes. Drain and discard fat. Add chili powder, cumin, garlic powder, and onion powder. Mix until beef is evenly coated in spices.

3. Add onion and bell pepper and cook, stirring constantly, until soft, about 2 minutes.

4. Remove skillet from heat and stir in black beans, chopped tomato, and tomato sauce. Spoon ⅓ of beef mixture into prepared casserole dish. Lay half of tortilla strips over top. Repeat with remaining beef and tortillas, ending with beef. Top with Cheddar.

5. Bake 25–30 minutes or until cheese topping is melted and lightly browned. Cool 5 minutes before enjoying.

PER SERVING

Calories: 413

Fat: 12g

Sodium: 610mg

Carbohydrates: 51g

Fiber: 12g

Sugar: 10g

Protein: 27g

GREEK MEATBALLS

PREP TIME: 1 HOUR 15 MINUTES | COOK TIME: 8 MINUTES | SERVES: 1

 Greek seasoning is a blend of herbs and spices that includes oregano, garlic, dill, marjoram, and cinnamon. Here it is added to a blend of fresh herbs to give these bite-sized meatballs bold flavor. You can make these with 90/10 ground beef if ground lamb is not available.

INGREDIENTS

4 ounces lean ground lamb

3 tablespoons minced yellow onion

2 tablespoons finely grated carrot

3 tablespoons panko bread crumbs

2 tablespoons finely minced fresh parsley

½ teaspoon finely minced fresh dill

½ teaspoon minced fresh mint

2 teaspoons 1% milk

¼ teaspoon Greek seasoning

⅛ teaspoon freshly cracked black pepper

1 teaspoon olive oil

1. In a medium bowl, add lamb, onion, carrot, bread crumbs, parsley, dill, mint, milk, Greek seasoning, and black pepper. Mix until well combined, then form into eight meatballs. Place on a tray and refrigerate 1 hour.

2. In an 8" skillet over medium heat, add olive oil and let it heat briefly, then swirl pan to coat. Add meatballs and brown on all sides, about 2 minutes per side or 8 minutes total. Meatballs are ready when they reach an internal temperature of 160°F. Serve hot.

Freezing Meatballs

The best way to freeze meatballs is to cook them thoroughly, cool, then freeze them on a baking sheet. Once frozen, transfer them to a resealable freezer-safe bag so you can grab just what you need when you want them. Reheat them by adding them directly to simmering sauce, or baking them at 300°F for 25–30 minutes.

PER SERVING

Calories: 378

Fat: 20g

Sodium: 370mg

Carbohydrates: 21g

Fiber: 1g

Sugar: 3g

Protein: 24g

VEGETABLE-PACKED PORK MEATBALL SUB

PREP TIME: 1 HOUR 12 MINUTES | COOK TIME: 18 MINUTES | SERVES: 1

 Grated zucchini and carrot help provide an added boost of nutrition to the meatballs in this tasty sandwich. For even more flavor you can brush the inside of the sandwich roll with ¼ teaspoon olive oil and toast in a pan over medium heat for 3 minutes or until toasted and golden.

INGREDIENTS

4 ounces ground pork

3 tablespoons panko bread crumbs

¼ cup finely grated zucchini

3 tablespoons finely grated carrot

1 tablespoon finely chopped yellow onion

¼ teaspoon Italian seasoning

¼ teaspoon ground fennel

⅛ teaspoon garlic powder

⅛ teaspoon sea salt

⅛ teaspoon freshly cracked black pepper

⅓ cup marinara sauce

1 whole-wheat sandwich roll

¼ cup shredded part-skim mozzarella

PER SERVING

Calories: 495	Fiber: 7g
Fat: 12g	Sugar: 11g
Sodium: 1,160mg	Protein: 39g
Carbohydrates: 56g	

1. In a medium bowl, add pork and bread crumbs. Mix until just combined, then add zucchini, carrot, onion, Italian seasoning, fennel, garlic powder, salt, and black pepper. Mix until well combined, then form into six meatballs. Place on a tray and refrigerate 1 hour or overnight.

2. Preheat oven to 400°F and line a small baking sheet with foil lightly sprayed with nonstick cooking spray.

3. Arrange meatballs on prepared baking sheet and bake 12–15 minutes, turning halfway through cooking, until meatballs reach an internal temperature of 165°F.

4. Once meatballs are ready, transfer to a medium saucepan along with any juices on tray. Stir in marinara sauce and heat over medium heat. Once sauce starts to simmer, about 3 minutes, remove from heat.

5. Preheat broiler. Place sandwich roll on small baking sheet. Fill with meatballs and sauce. Top with mozzarella. Broil 3–5 minutes or until cheese is melted and bubbling and starting to brown. Cool 2 minutes before serving.

UNSTUFFED CABBAGE ROLLS IN A BOWL

PREP TIME: 10 MINUTES | COOK TIME: 32 MINUTES | SERVES: 1

 Cabbage rolls are a little time-consuming to make, but here you get all the same flavors with a lot less effort. You can shred fresh cabbage and carrot if you have them on hand, but here coleslaw mix is used to save time. Serve this over rice or mashed potatoes.

INGREDIENTS

4 ounces 90/10 ground beef

¼ cup chopped yellow onion

½ clove garlic, peeled and minced

1½ cups shredded coleslaw mix

½ cup chopped Roma tomato

3 tablespoons tomato sauce

2 tablespoons water

1. Heat an 8" skillet over medium heat. Once hot, add beef. Cook, crumbling well, until fully browned, about 4 minutes. Drain and discard fat. Add onion to pan and cook until onion is soft, about 3 minutes. Add garlic and coleslaw mix and cool until cabbage is wilted, about 5 minutes.

2. Add chopped tomato, tomato sauce, and water. Stir well, then bring mixture to a boil. Reduce heat to medium-low, cover, and simmer 20 minutes, stirring occasionally. Serve hot.

Coleslaw for One

Whisk together in a medium bowl 1 tablespoon plain low-fat Greek yogurt, ½ teaspoon apple cider vinegar, and ¼ teaspoon honey until smooth. Add ⅛ teaspoon freshly cracked black pepper and sea salt, then fold in 1½ cups coleslaw mix. Refrigerate at least two hours before serving.

PER SERVING

Calories: 290	*Fiber: 6g*
Fat: 9g	*Sugar: 13g*
Sodium: 274mg	*Protein: 27g*
Carbohydrates: 21g	

HERBED LAMB CHOP

PREP TIME: 2 HOURS 10 MINUTES | COOK TIME: 6 MINUTES | SERVES: 1

 Lamb marinated in garlic and herbs creates a bold flavor with minimal effort. Lamb chops are sold in most grocery store butcher departments, and extra chops can be frozen up to three months to enjoy later. Lamb loves mint, so serve this with a little mint jelly if you like.

INGREDIENTS

1 double rib lamb chop (about 5 ounces)

1 teaspoon olive oil

½ clove garlic, peeled and minced

2 teaspoons chopped fresh rosemary

2 teaspoons chopped fresh parsley

⅛ teaspoon sea salt

⅛ teaspoon freshly cracked black pepper

1. Trim any excess fat from lamb chop. Place in a resealable bag and add remaining ingredients. Massage to coat lamb chop in herbs and garlic. Seal and refrigerate at least 2 hours or overnight.

2. Remove lamb chop from refrigerator 30 minutes before cooking. Heat an 8" skillet over medium-high heat. Once hot, add lamb and sear both sides until browned, about 3 minutes per side. If you prefer your lamb rare to medium-rare, or an internal temperature of 125°F, remove from pan now. If you prefer your lamb more done, sear top of chop an additional 3 minutes to reach medium or an internal temperature of 130°F. Rest 3 minutes before serving.

Internal Temperature for Lamb

An instant-read thermometer is the best way to ensure your lamb is cooked properly. Rare is 120°F, medium-rare is 125°F, medium is 130°F, and medium-well is 140°F. Lamb cooked higher than an internal temperature of 145°F runs the risk of becoming tough and dry, so watch your temperature carefully the more you cook it.

PER SERVING

Calories: 178

Fat: 9g

Sodium: 247mg

Carbohydrates: 1g

Fiber: 0g

Sugar: 0g

Protein: 18g

MINUTE STEAK WITH GARLIC AND HERBS

PREP TIME: 25 MINUTES | COOK TIME: 2 MINUTES | SERVES: 1

 A minute steak is a steak, usually a sirloin cut ¼" thick, that cooks in a minute or two per side. These smaller steaks are a fun way to enjoy a steak on a Mediterranean diet, and they can be paired with a vegetable or grain side dish for a filling meal. Most grocery stores sell thin-cut steaks in their packaged meat department.

INGREDIENTS

1 teaspoon olive oil

½ teaspoon lemon juice

½ clove garlic, peeled and minced

2 teaspoons chopped fresh chives

1 teaspoon chopped fresh rosemary

½ teaspoon chopped fresh thyme leaves

⅛ teaspoon sea salt

⅛ teaspoon freshly cracked black pepper

1 (4-ounce) thin-cut sirloin

1. In a shallow dish, add olive oil, lemon juice, garlic, chives, rosemary, thyme, salt, and black pepper. Mix well. Set aside.

2. Remove steak from refrigerator 20 minutes before cooking. Heat an 8" skillet over medium-high heat. Once hot, add steak and sear both sides until browned, about 1 minute per side. Transfer steak to dish and turn to coat in oil and herbs. Let stand 2 minutes before serving.

PER SERVING

Calories: 233

Fat: 12g

Sodium: 250mg

Carbohydrates: 1g

Fiber: 0g

Sugar: 0g

Protein: 27g

LAMB STEW FOR ONE

PREP TIME: 20 MINUTES | COOK TIME: 1 HOUR 7 MINUTES | SERVES: 1

 Check your stew meat for tenderness by pulling a piece from the stew and pressing it with a fork. If it easily falls apart, it is ready. If it feels too firm, keep simmering it, covered, until it is your desired tenderness. If you prefer not to buy fresh rosemary for this dish, you can replace it with ¼ teaspoon dried rosemary.

INGREDIENTS

3 ounces lamb shoulder, cut into ½" pieces

1 teaspoon all-purpose flour

¼ teaspoon freshly cracked black pepper

⅛ teaspoon sea salt

1 teaspoon olive oil

⅓ cup roughly chopped white onion

⅓ cup roughly chopped celery

⅓ cup sliced carrots

½ clove garlic, peeled and minced

2 teaspoons tomato paste

1 cup low-sodium chicken stock

½ sprig rosemary

½ teaspoon dried thyme

½ bay leaf

1 small (about 4-ounce) russet potato, peeled and chopped

1. In a small bowl, add lamb, flour, black pepper, and salt. Toss until meat is evenly coated in flour and seasonings.

2. In a 1-quart Dutch oven or pot over medium heat, add olive oil and let it heat briefly, then swirl pan to coat. Add lamb cubes, leaving ½" between pieces, and brown on all four sides, about 3 minutes per side. You may need to work in batches. Once browned, transfer to a plate and set aside.

3. Return pot to heat and add onion, celery, and carrots. Cook, stirring often, until just tender, about 4 minutes. Add garlic and tomato paste and cook until garlic is fragrant, about 30 seconds.

4. Stir in stock, scraping any brown bits from bottom of pot, then add lamb with any juices on plate, rosemary, thyme, and bay leaf.

5. Bring mixture to a boil, reduce heat to medium-low, cover with lid, and let simmer 30 minutes. Remove lid and add potato. Cover pot and simmer 20 minutes or until potato pieces and meat are tender and falling apart.

6. Remove from heat and discard bay leaf and rosemary stem. Enjoy hot.

PER SERVING

*Calories: 361 | Fat: 12g | Sodium: 522mg | Carbohydrates: 40g
Fiber: 6g | Sugar: 7g | Protein: 22g*

PORK MEDALLIONS WITH MUSTARD SAUCE

PREP TIME: 10 MINUTES | COOK TIME: 9 MINUTES | SERVES: 1

 Pork tenderloin is leaner than the larger pork loin roast. It is easily overcooked, so keep an eye on your internal temperature. A whole pork tenderloin is generally about 1 pound, so be sure to slice the remainder of the loin into medallions and freeze them up to three months. Serve with the Olive Oil Mashed Potatoes from Chapter 5.

INGREDIENTS

6 ounces pork tenderloin

¼ teaspoon Italian seasoning

⅛ teaspoon smoked paprika

⅛ teaspoon sea salt

1 teaspoon olive oil, divided

½ clove garlic, peeled and minced

1 teaspoon unsalted butter

3 tablespoons low-sodium chicken broth

½ teaspoon Dijon mustard

1 teaspoon chopped fresh parsley

1. Slice pork loin into four medallions. Place between layers of plastic wrap and gently pound with a meat mallet until ½" thick. Season both sides with Italian seasoning, paprika, and salt. Set aside.

2. Heat an 8" skillet over medium heat. Once hot, add ½ teaspoon olive oil. Add pork and cook 3 minutes per side or until golden. Flip and add remaining ½ teaspoon olive oil and garlic and cook until pork reaches an internal temperature of 145°F, about 3–4 minutes. Remove from pan and set aside.

3. To the same skillet add butter. Once melted, reduce heat to medium-low and add broth and scrape up any brown bits from bottom of pan.

4. Add mustard and parsley and mix well, then add pork medallions with any juices and turn to coat them in sauce.

5. Transfer mixture to a serving plate and enjoy immediately.

PER SERVING

Calories: 243	Fiber: 0g
Fat: 13g	Sugar: 0g
Sodium: 595mg	Protein: 30g
Carbohydrates: 1g	

PHYLLO-WRAPPED BEEF TENDERLOIN

PREP TIME: 20 MINUTES | COOK TIME: 24 MINUTES | SERVES: 1

 This is a lower-fat version of beef Wellington that still packs in all the delicious flavor. The mushrooms, onion, and garlic should be very finely chopped.

INGREDIENTS

1 (4-ounce) beef tenderloin

⅛ teaspoon sea salt

⅛ teaspoon freshly cracked black pepper

1 teaspoon olive oil

4 ounces button mushrooms, finely minced

1 tablespoon finely minced yellow onion

¼ clove garlic, peeled and finely minced

1 teaspoon lemon juice

2 sheets phyllo dough

½ teaspoon extra-virgin olive oil

1. Season steak on both sides with salt and black pepper. Set aside.

2. Heat an 8" skillet over medium heat. Once hot, add olive oil. Add steak and sear on both sides until browned, about 2 minutes per side. Remove from pan and set aside.

3. To skillet, add mushrooms and onion. Cook, stirring often, until there is no moisture left in pan, about 5 minutes. Add garlic and lemon juice and stir well. Remove from heat and cool to room temperature.

4. Preheat oven to 375°F and line a small baking sheet with parchment.

5. Place one phyllo sheet on a work surface and brush with extra-virgin olive oil. Lay second sheet on top and brush with extra-virgin oil. Cut sheets in half vertically and place one square on top of the other, forming four sheets.

6. Spread half mushroom mixture in center of phyllo square. Place tenderloin on mushroom mixture and spoon reserved mushroom mixture over top. Bring sides of dough up over steak and pinch in center to form a bag shape. You may need to use a bit of butcher's twine to hold dough in place.

7. Bake 15–20 minutes or until phyllo is golden brown and crisp. Rest 2 minutes before serving.

PER SERVING

Calories: 397

Fat: 17g

Sodium: 435mg

Carbohydrates: 25g

Fiber: 2g

Sugar: 3g

Protein: 34g

PORK-STUFFED MUSHROOMS

PREP TIME: 20 MINUTES | COOK TIME: 26 MINUTES | SERVES: 1

 Stuffed mushrooms make a fun and unique meal that would be perfect served with soup, polenta or risotto, pasta, or roasted vegetables. Give these a Greek flair by swapping Italian seasoning for Greek and swapping mozzarella for crumbled feta or goat cheese.

INGREDIENTS

3 ounces ground pork

3 tablespoons panko bread crumbs

¼ teaspoon Italian seasoning

6 medium button mushrooms

1 teaspoon olive oil

2 tablespoons finely minced yellow onion

½ clove garlic, peeled and finely minced

¼ cup shredded part-skim mozzarella cheese

1. In a medium bowl, add pork, bread crumbs, and Italian seasoning. Gently mix until just combined. Set aside.

2. Preheat oven to 400°F and line a small baking sheet with foil lightly sprayed with nonstick cooking spray.

3. Remove stems from mushrooms and place mushroom caps on prepared baking sheet. Finely mince mushrooms stems.

4. Heat an 8" skillet over medium heat. Once hot, add olive oil. Add mushroom stems and onion and cook until onion is tender and mushroom stems are dry, about 5 minutes. Add garlic and cook until fragrant, about 30 seconds. Remove from heat and cool 10 minutes.

5. Add cooled mushroom mixture to pork and mix until well combined. Divide mixture between mushroom caps. Top with mozzarella.

6. Bake 20–25 minutes or until internal temperature of meat filling reaches 160°F and cheese is browned. Cool 2 minutes before serving.

PER SERVING

Calories: 320	Fiber: 1g
Fat: 12g	Sugar: 4g
Sodium: 240mg	Protein: 29g
Carbohydrates: 23g	

SALISBURY STEAK

PREP TIME: 20 MINUTES | COOK TIME: 17 MINUTES | SERVES: 1

 Ketchup and Dijon mustard do a lot of heavy lifting in the flavor department in this single-serving twist on the classic. Flipping the steak as it simmers in the sauce keeps it juicy in the center and keeps the outside from getting dry. Enjoy with creamy Olive Oil Mashed Potatoes (see Chapter 5).

INGREDIENTS

4 ounces 90/10 ground beef

3 tablespoons panko bread crumbs

¼ teaspoon Montreal steak seasoning

1 teaspoon ketchup

1 teaspoon Dijon mustard

¼ teaspoon Worcestershire sauce

1 tablespoon olive oil

⅓ cup sliced yellow onion

4 ounces button mushrooms, sliced

½ clove garlic, peeled and finely minced

1 teaspoon all-purpose flour

½ cup low-sodium beef broth

⅛ teaspoon freshly cracked black pepper

1. In a medium bowl, add beef, bread crumbs, Montreal steak seasoning, ketchup, mustard, and Worcestershire sauce. Gently mix until just combined. Form into a patty 1" thick.

2. Heat an 8" skillet over medium heat. Add patty and cook until browned on each side, about 2–3 minutes per side. Transfer patty to a plate and set aside. Steak is not cooked through at this stage.

3. To same skillet add olive oil. Swirl pan to coat, then add onion and mushrooms. Cook until vegetables are tender, about 4 minutes. Add garlic and cook until fragrant, about 30 seconds. Sprinkle flour and mix well. Cook 40 seconds, then stir in broth and mix well. Place steak into skillet, turn to coat, then simmer 7–9 minutes, flipping steak occasionally and stirring sauce, or until steak reaches 160°F and sauce has thickened.

4. Transfer steak to a plate. Stir gravy and season with black pepper. If gravy feels too thick, add water a teaspoon at a time until thinned to your preference. Pour gravy over steak. Enjoy immediately.

PER SERVING

Calories: 435

Fat: 22g

Sodium: 455mg

Carbohydrates: 28g

Fiber: 2g

Sugar: 5g

Protein: 29g

CHAPTER 11

DESSERTS

Stewed Cinnamon Apples with
  Dates 208
Spiced Poached Pear 209
Blueberry Compote 210
Grilled Peach with Yogurt
  and Honey 211
Frozen Fruity Yogurt Bark 213
Applesauce Mug Cake 214
Baked Stuffed Apple 215
Oatmeal Raisin Cookies 216
Dark Chocolate Mousse 217
Blueberry Crumble 218
White Wine–Poached Pear 220
Apple Oat Crisp 221
Lemon Loaf Cake 222
Chocolate Mug Cake 223
Banana Loaf Cake 225
Vanilla-Poached Apricots 226
Red Wine–Poached Figs with
  Ricotta and Almonds 227
Lemon Olive Oil Mug Cake 228

Life is better with a little sweetness, and who doesn't love a treat now and again? Dessert is a fun way to end a delicious meal, but the problem with most dessert recipes is the sugar, fat, and—when you are cooking for one—the waste. It's hard to justify sugar-laden treats while enjoying the Mediterranean lifestyle. Never fear! This chapter has tasty desserts that aren't loaded with sugar and fat, and recipes that do not make enough to feed the whole neighborhood. These recipes use minimal tools and bowls, so you don't have to stress about cleanup.

In this chapter you will find everything you need for tasty desserts that are as nourishing for the body as they are for the soul. When you want something simple and sweet, you can make Lemon Olive Oil Mug Cake or Frozen Fruity Yogurt Bark. If you want something warm and comforting, the Blueberry Crumble or Red Wine–Poached Figs with Ricotta and Almonds are just the ticket. Chocolate lovers will rejoice for Chocolate Mug Cake and Dark Chocolate Mousse. Ending your meal with a perfectly sized dessert makes Mediterranean cooking for one a pleasure!

STEWED CINNAMON APPLES WITH DATES

PREP TIME: 5 MINUTES | COOK TIME: 10 MINUTES | SERVES: 1

 These stewed apples are a lovely dessert any time of the year, but are especially nice in fall when apples are in season and the air is crisp. This can also be enjoyed as a topping for oatmeal for breakfast or served alongside Balsamic-Glazed Pork (see Chapter 10) as a sweet side dish.

INGREDIENTS

1 medium Granny Smith apple, peeled, cored, and cut into 1" pieces

2 pitted dates, finely chopped

1 tablespoon honey

1 tablespoon water

¼ teaspoon ground cinnamon

¹⁄₁₆ teaspoon sea salt

⅛ teaspoon pure vanilla extract

1. In a 1-quart saucepan over medium heat, add apple, dates, honey, water, cinnamon, and salt, stirring occasionally, until apple is tender, about 10 minutes. If apple pieces appear dry, add an additional tablespoon of water.

2. Once apples are tender, remove from heat and stir in vanilla. Enjoy warm or at room temperature.

Homemade Applesauce

You can make stewed apples into applesauce by cooking apple pieces until they're falling apart, about 20 minutes, then mashing them with a potato masher or puréeing them with an immersion blender. This applesauce should be refrigerated if not eaten right away and is good for up to five days.

PER SERVING

Calories: 182
Fat: 0g
Sodium: 97mg
Carbohydrates: 49g

Fiber: 4g
Sugar: 43g
Protein: 1g

SPICED POACHED PEAR

PREP TIME: 15 MINUTES | COOK TIME: 22 MINUTES | SERVES: 1

Poached pears are an elegant dessert that can be made ahead of time to be enjoyed later in the week. Simply refrigerate the pears once poached along with the reduced cooking liquid. When ready to serve, place pear and liquid over low heat until warm and then enjoy!

INGREDIENTS

½ cup water

½ cup red wine

1 tablespoon honey

¼ teaspoon ground cinnamon

¼ teaspoon pumpkin pie spice

¼ teaspoon pure vanilla extract

1 medium Bartlett pear, peeled, sliced in half, and core removed

1. In a 1-quart saucepan, combine water, wine, honey, cinnamon, pumpkin pie spice, and vanilla. Whisk well. Place over medium-low heat and add pear halves.

2. Bring mixture to a simmer and cook, turning every few minutes, until pear is tender, about 10 minutes. Transfer pear halves to a serving plate and set aside.

3. Increase heat to medium and bring mixture to a boil. Cook, stirring often, until reduced by half, about 12–15 minutes. Turn off heat and let cool 10 minutes, then spoon sauce over pear halves. Serve warm.

PER SERVING

Calories: 201

Fat: 0g

Sodium: 2mg

Carbohydrates: 43g

Fiber: 3g

Sugar: 35g

Protein: 1g

BLUEBERRY COMPOTE

PREP TIME: 5 MINUTES | COOK TIME: 8 MINUTES | SERVES: 1

 If you have fresh blueberries that are a little past their prime, you should use them to make this easy and delicious compote! You can use any fresh or frozen berries you have on hand, or you can use a mix if you only have a few of each kind.

INGREDIENTS

⅓ cup fresh or frozen blueberries

1 tablespoon water

1 tablespoon honey

⅛ teaspoon ground cinnamon

⅛ teaspoon pure vanilla extract

¼ teaspoon lemon juice

1. In a 1-quart saucepan, combine blueberries, water, honey, cinnamon, and vanilla. Mix well, then place over medium-low heat.

2. Bring mixture to a simmer and cook, stirring often, until blueberries have popped and mixture has thickened, about 8 minutes. If mixture is thinner than you like, you can reduce heat to low and continue to cook until thickened to your preference.

3. Remove from heat and stir in lemon juice. Serve warm or at room temperature.

PER SERVING

Calories: 92

Fat: 0g

Sodium: 0mg

Carbohydrates: 25g

Fiber: 1g

Sugar: 22g

Protein: 0g

GRILLED PEACH WITH YOGURT AND HONEY

PREP TIME: 5 MINUTES | COOK TIME: 6 MINUTES | SERVES: 1

Peaches make the perfect single-sized summer dessert! Use an unripe peach to ensure it holds its shape while grilling and is easy to handle. You can also make this recipe with any unripe stone fruits you like, such as plums or apricots.

INGREDIENTS

1 large unripe peach, sliced in half and pit removed

½ teaspoon olive oil

¼ teaspoon ground cinnamon

¼ cup plain low-fat Greek yogurt

2 teaspoons honey, divided

¼ teaspoon pure vanilla extract

1. Preheat grill to medium heat. Brush cut side of each peach half with olive oil. Grill 3–4 minutes per side or until peach is tender and has grill marks on flesh side. Transfer to a serving plate (placing the cut sides up). Dust with cinnamon.

2. In a small bowl, combine yogurt, 1 teaspoon honey, and vanilla. Mix well and spoon over peaches. Drizzle with remaining 1 teaspoon honey. Serve immediately.

Honey
Honey, if stored properly, does not spoil. Honey keeps indefinity when stored in a jar in a cool, dark place. If your honey has crystalized, it has not gone bad, even if it is very hard. Just gently warm the honey in a warm water bath to remelt it and use as usual.

PER SERVING

Calories: 175
Fat: 4g
Sodium: 18mg
Carbohydrates: 31g

Fiber: 3g
Sugar: 29g
Protein: 7g

FROZEN FRUITY YOGURT BARK

PREP TIME: 4 HOURS 5 MINUTES | COOK TIME: 0 MINUTES | SERVES: 1

 Single-serving cups of low-fat, low-sugar Greek yogurt are available in a wide range of flavors, so feel free to swap the vanilla yogurt used here if you'd like. Lemon yogurt with fresh blueberries, or vanilla yogurt with sliced banana and chocolate chips are just a couple options you can experiment with!

INGREDIENTS

1 (6-ounce) container vanilla low-fat Greek yogurt

¼ cup frozen mixed berries

2 tablespoons granola cereal

⅛ teaspoon ground cinnamon

1. Line a small rimmed baking sheet with parchment.

2. Spread yogurt over prepared baking sheet until it forms a ¼"-thick layer. Sprinkle berries and granola over the top and then dust with cinnamon.

3. Place in freezer 4 hours or until yogurt is firm. Once frozen, break into pieces and store in a freezer-safe airtight container in freezer until ready to enjoy.

Freezing Yogurt

You can absolutely freeze yogurt if you have more on hand than you can eat before spoiling. It's easiest to freeze it in single-serving portions, and you will want to thaw it overnight in the refrigerator. Once thawed, it may separate, but a quick whisk should smooth it back out. But once it's thawed, it can't be refrozen.

PER SERVING

Calories: 247
Fat: 4g
Sodium: 81mg
Carbohydrates: 40g

Fiber: 2g
Sugar: 27g
Protein: 14g

APPLESAUCE MUG CAKE

PREP TIME: 5 MINUTES | COOK TIME: 1 MINUTE | SERVES: 1

 Mug cakes are ideal when you are craving cake but don't want to bake a whole pan. This cake is the perfect size for one, is ready in mere minutes, and has a sweet, spicy apple flavor. If you use unsweetened *cinnamon* applesauce, be sure to reduce pumpkin pie spice to ⅛ teaspoon.

INGREDIENTS

¼ cup all-purpose flour

¼ teaspoon baking powder

¼ teaspoon pumpkin pie spice

1 tablespoon granulated sugar

3 tablespoons unsweetened applesauce

1 teaspoon olive oil

¼ teaspoon pure vanilla extract

1. In an 8-ounce microwave-safe mug, add flour, baking powder, pumpkin pie spice, and sugar. Mix with a fork, then add remaining ingredients and mix until smooth.

2. Microwave on high 60–90 seconds or until cake is puffed, the top is no longer shiny, and a toothpick inserted into the center of cake comes out clean.

3. Let cake rest in microwave 1 minute, then carefully remove. Serve immediately.

PER SERVING

Calories: 223

Fat: 5g

Sodium: 121mg

Carbohydrates: 42g

Fiber: 1g

Sugar: 17g

Protein: 3g

BAKED STUFFED APPLE

PREP TIME: 10 MINUTES | COOK TIME: 25 MINUTES | SERVES: 1

 This baked apple uses granola cereal to add flavor and help thicken the apple filling. Look for a granola cereal that is low in sugar and contains simple ingredients like oats, nuts, and dried fruit. If the top begins to get too dark while baking, cover it loosely with foil.

INGREDIENTS

1 tablespoon all-purpose flour

1 tablespoon rolled oats

2 teaspoons packed light brown sugar

⅛ teaspoon pumpkin pie spice

2 teaspoons unsalted butter

1 medium Fuji apple

1 tablespoon chopped pecans

1 tablespoon granola cereal

1. Preheat oven to 350°F and spray a 6" casserole dish with nonstick cooking spray.

2. In a small bowl, combine flour, oats, brown sugar, and pumpkin pie spice. Add butter and rub with fingers until mixture starts to clump. Set aside.

3. Cut top off apple. Use a small spoon to scoop out core and apple flesh, leaving ¼" of flesh around side of apple. Remove seeds and core, then chop flesh. Mix 3 tablespoons apple flesh with pecans and granola, then spoon mixture back into apple.

4. Place apple into prepared casserole dish, then top with oat topping. Bake 25–35 minutes or until apple is tender and topping is golden brown. Cool 10 minutes before serving. Enjoy warm or at room temperature.

PER SERVING

Calories: 340	*Fiber: 6g*
Fat: 13g	*Sugar: 33g*
Sodium: 7mg	*Protein: 3g*
Carbohydrates: 53g	

OATMEAL RAISIN COOKIES

PREP TIME: 1 HOUR 10 MINUTES | COOK TIME: 12 MINUTES | YIELDS: 6 COOKIES

 Greek yogurt and honey are the key to a cookie that stays moist and tender when baking with less butter. Salted butter in this recipe takes the place of added salt, and is needed to enhance the flavor of the brown sugar and cinnamon. These cookies stay fresh in an airtight container at room temperature for up to four days.

INGREDIENTS

2 tablespoons salted butter, softened

2 tablespoons plain low-fat Greek yogurt

¼ cup packed light brown sugar

1 teaspoon honey

1 large egg yolk

¼ teaspoon pure vanilla extract

½ cup whole-wheat pastry flour

¼ teaspoon ground cinnamon

¼ teaspoon baking soda

½ cup old-fashioned oats

¼ cup raisins

1. Preheat oven to 350°F and line a baking sheet with parchment.

2. In a medium bowl with an electric mixer on medium speed, cream together butter, yogurt, brown sugar, and honey until creamy, about 1 minute. Add egg yolk and vanilla and beat until well combined, about 30 seconds. Scrape down the sides of the bowl as needed.

3. Add flour, cinnamon, and baking soda and mix on low 10 seconds to just combine flour, then fold in oats and raisins with a spatula until evenly distributed and no dry flour remains. Cover the bowl and chill 1 hour.

4. Scoop batter into six balls and place on prepared baking sheet about 1" apart. Bake 12–14 minutes or until cookies are golden brown around the edges and just set in the center.

5. Cool on the pan 10 minutes before transferring cookies to a wire rack to cool another 10 minutes. Enjoy warm or at room temperature.

PER SERVING (1 COOKIE)

Calories: 168

Fat: 5g

Sodium: 59mg

Carbohydrates: 28g

Fiber: 2g

Sugar: 14g

Protein: 3g

DARK CHOCOLATE MOUSSE

PREP TIME: 3 HOURS 5 MINUTES | COOK TIME: 0 MINUTES | SERVES: 1

 Silken tofu is the key to this recipe's decadent, smooth texture. To store leftover silken tofu, place it in an airtight container and fill it with clean water. Cover and refrigerate up to three days. Silken tofu can be added to smoothies, soups, and sauces in place of dairy. You can use pure maple syrup in place of the honey if you prefer.

INGREDIENTS

4 ounces silken tofu, drained, at room temperature

2 teaspoons honey

1 teaspoon cocoa powder

¼ teaspoon pure vanilla extract

1 ounce 70% dark chocolate, melted and cooled

1. In a food processor or blender, add tofu, honey, cocoa powder, and vanilla. Blend until smooth and no lumps remain, about 1 minute.

2. Scrape down sides of bowl and add melted chocolate. Process again 30–40 seconds until well combined, scraping down the sides of bowl as needed. The mixture may seem thin. This is normal.

3. Transfer mixture to a serving bowl and chill at least 3 hours or overnight. Serve chilled.

PER SERVING

Calories: 274
Fat: 11g
Sodium: 46mg
Carbohydrates: 33g

Fiber: 3g
Sugar: 26g
Protein: 10g

BLUEBERRY CRUMBLE

PREP TIME: 15 MINUTES | COOK TIME: 30 MINUTES | SERVES: 1

 You can use fresh or frozen blueberries for this dessert. If you use frozen, let them thaw in a strainer over a bowl to collect the excess juices. These juices can be added to smoothies, mixed into yogurt, or mixed with club soda to make a refreshing blueberry soda.

INGREDIENTS

2 tablespoons whole-wheat pastry flour

2 tablespoons rolled oats

2 tablespoons granulated sugar, divided

⅛ teaspoon ground cinnamon

1 tablespoon cubed salted butter, chilled

1 cup fresh blueberries

2 teaspoons cornstarch

¼ teaspoon pure vanilla extract

1. In a medium bowl, combine flour, oats, 1 tablespoon sugar, and cinnamon. Whisk well to combine. Add butter and use your fingers to rub mixture until it resembles coarse sand. Set aside.

2. Preheat oven to 350°F and place a baking sheet on bottom rack of oven.

3. In a separate medium bowl, add blueberries, remaining 1 tablespoon sugar, cornstarch, and vanilla. Toss well to coat. Transfer mixture to a 6" pie pan. Top with prepared oat topping.

4. Bake on heated baking sheet 30–35 minutes or until topping is golden brown and filling is bubbling. Remove from oven and let cool 30 minutes before enjoying.

PER SERVING

Calories: 396	Fiber: 7g
Fat: 12g	Sugar: 40g
Sodium: 92mg	Protein: 4g
Carbohydrates: 70g	

WHITE WINE–POACHED PEAR

PREP TIME: 5 MINUTES | COOK TIME: 32 MINUTES | SERVES: 1

 Sauvignon blanc has a zippy, bright flavor that has notes of apple, peach, and passion fruit. Here it is used to make a refreshing, light-flavored poached pear that is perfect served with a little vanilla low-fat Greek yogurt, a drizzle of raspberry sauce, or a sprinkle of granola for crunch.

INGREDIENTS

½ cup water

½ cup sauvignon blanc

1 tablespoon honey

1 teaspoon freshly grated lemon zest

¼ teaspoon pure vanilla extract

⅛ teaspoon ground cinnamon

1 medium Bartlett pear, peeled, sliced in half, and core removed

1. In a 1-quart saucepan, combine water, wine, honey, lemon zest, vanilla, and cinnamon. Whisk well. Place over medium-low heat and add pear halves.

2. Bring mixture to a simmer and cook, turning pear halves every few minutes, until tender, about 10 minutes. Transfer pear halves to a serving plate and set aside.

3. Increase heat to medium and bring mixture to a boil. Cook, stirring often, until reduced by half, about 12–15 minutes. Turn off heat and let cook 10 minutes, then spoon sauce over pear. Serve warm.

Fresh Raspberry Sauce for One

In a 1-quart saucepan over medium heat, add ⅓ cup fresh raspberries, 2 teaspoons granulated sugar, 2 teaspoons water, and ⅛ teaspoon cornstarch. Cook, mashing berries with a spatula, until mixture starts to bubble and thicken. Strain mixture through a fine-mesh strainer into a bowl. Enjoy warm or at room temperature.

PER SERVING

Calories: 198

Fat: 0g

Sodium: 1mg

Carbohydrates: 42g

Fiber: 3g

Sugar: 35g

Protein: 1g

APPLE OAT CRISP

PREP TIME: 15 MINUTES | COOK TIME: 30 MINUTES | SERVES: 1

 This personal-sized crisp has a lot of added nutrition from the oats, raisins, and apple. It serves one, but you can split this into two servings and enjoy them with a scoop of low-fat frozen yogurt or ice cream for a special treat. Reheat leftovers in a 200°F oven for 10 minutes.

INGREDIENTS

2 tablespoons whole-wheat pastry flour

1 tablespoon granulated sugar

1 tablespoon cubed salted butter, chilled

1 medium Granny Smith apple, peeled, cored, and cut into ½" pieces

2 tablespoons golden raisins

1 tablespoon rolled oats

2 teaspoons honey

1 teaspoon cornstarch

¼ teaspoon ground cinnamon

1. In a medium bowl, combine flour and sugar. Whisk well to combine. Add butter and use your fingers to rub mixture until it resembles coarse sand. Set aside.

2. Preheat oven to 350°F and place a baking sheet on bottom rack of oven.

3. In a separate medium bowl, add apple, raisins, oats, honey, cornstarch, and cinnamon. Toss well to coat. Transfer mixture to a 6" pie pan. Top with flour mixture.

4. Bake on heated baking sheet 30–35 minutes or until topping is golden brown and filling is bubbling. Remove from oven and let cool 30 minutes before enjoying.

PER SERVING

Calories: 414
Fat: 11g
Sodium: 93mg
Carbohydrates: 79g

Fiber: 6g
Sugar: 53g
Protein: 3g

LEMON LOAF CAKE

PREP TIME: 10 MINUTES | COOK TIME: 20 MINUTES | SERVES: 2

 This moist lemon cake keeps up to four days if kept in an airtight container at room temperature thanks to the olive oil, which helps it retain moisture. If your produce department has Meyer lemons available, you can use them here for a milder, sweeter lemon flavor.

INGREDIENTS

½ cup whole-wheat pastry flour

3 tablespoons granulated sugar

¼ teaspoon baking powder

⅛ teaspoon baking soda

⅛ teaspoon salt

3 tablespoons 1% milk

1 tablespoon lemon juice

1 large egg, at room temperature

1 tablespoon olive oil

1 teaspoon freshly grated lemon zest

¼ teaspoon pure vanilla extract

1. Preheat oven to 350°F and spray a 5" × 3" mini-loaf pan with nonstick cooking spray.

2. In a medium bowl, add flour, sugar, baking powder, baking soda, and salt. Whisk to combine. Set aside.

3. In a small bowl, add milk, lemon juice, egg, olive oil, lemon zest, and vanilla. Whisk to combine. Pour wet ingredients into dry ingredients and use a spatula to mix until just combined, about ten strokes. Do not overmix.

4. Transfer batter to prepared pan. Bake 20–22 minutes or until top is golden brown and cake springs back when gently pressed in the center. Cool in pan 5 minutes, then turn cake out of pan and transfer to a wire rack to cool completely before serving.

PER SERVING

Calories: 290
Fat: 9g
Sodium: 329mg
Carbohydrates: 44g

Fiber: 4g
Sugar: 20g
Protein: 7g

CHOCOLATE MUG CAKE

PREP TIME: 5 MINUTES | COOK TIME: 1 MINUTE | SERVES: 1

 It may feel strange to use mayonnaise in a cake, but it replaces oil and adds a little tanginess that makes the cake irresistible. You can use regular cocoa powder instead of the Dutch-processed cocoa powder called for in the recipe as either one will give this cake a rich chocolate flavor.

INGREDIENTS

3 tablespoons all-purpose flour

3 tablespoons Dutch-processed cocoa powder

2 tablespoons packed light brown sugar

⅛ teaspoon baking powder

1 tablespoon olive oil mayonnaise

1 tablespoon unsweetened applesauce

2 tablespoons 1% milk

1 tablespoon water

¼ teaspoon pure vanilla extract

1. In an 8-ounce microwave-safe mug, add flour, cocoa powder, brown sugar, and baking powder. Whisk well to combine, then add remaining ingredients and stir until mixture is smooth. Be careful not to overmix. Use a small spatula to scrape batter from the edges of the mug.

2. Microwave on high 1–1½ minutes or until cake rises and center is firm and a toothpick inserted into center comes out clean.

3. Cool 30 seconds before removing from microwave and enjoying.

Mastering Mug Cakes

Never fill your mug more than halfway with batter, and be sure you are using a mug with the correct volume for your recipe. Mug cakes will puff when cooking but sink when removed from the microwave. They will not brown, so a pale cake is normal. Err on the side of cooking for the shortest directed time and only add more time as needed to prevent overcooking.

PER SERVING

Calories: 320
Fat: 5g
Sodium: 185mg
Carbohydrates: 58g

Fiber: 4g
Sugar: 30g
Protein: 7g

BANANA LOAF CAKE

PREP TIME: 10 MINUTES | COOK TIME: 30 MINUTES | SERVES: 2

 Do you have a banana on the counter that is past its prime for snacking on? Use it to make this delicious and healthful loaf cake! You can top slices of this cake with vanilla low-fat Greek yogurt or a smear of whipped cream cheese sprinkled with a little cinnamon.

INGREDIENTS

½ cup whole-wheat pastry flour

2 tablespoons packed dark brown sugar

¼ teaspoon baking powder

¼ teaspoon pumpkin pie spice

⅛ teaspoon baking soda

⅛ teaspoon salt

½ cup mashed very ripe banana (about 1 medium banana)

2 tablespoons 1% milk

1 tablespoon honey

1 large egg, at room temperature

¼ teaspoon pure vanilla extract

1. Preheat oven to 350°F and spray a 5" × 3" mini-loaf pan with nonstick cooking spray.

2. In a medium bowl, add flour, brown sugar, baking powder, pumpkin pie spice, baking soda, and salt. Whisk to combine. Set aside.

3. In a small bowl, add banana, milk, honey, egg, and vanilla. Whisk to combine. Pour wet ingredients into dry ingredients and use a spatula to mix until just combined, about ten strokes. Do not overmix.

4. Transfer batter to prepared pan. Bake 30–35 minutes or until top is golden brown and cake springs back when gently pressed in the center. Cool in pan 3 minutes, then turn cake out of pan and transfer to a wire rack to cool to room temperature.

PER SERVING

Calories: 287
Fat: 2g
Sodium: 330mg
Carbohydrates: 59g

Fiber: 6g
Sugar: 30g
Protein: 7g

VANILLA-POACHED APRICOTS

PREP TIME: 10 MINUTES | COOK TIME: 5 MINUTES | SERVES: 1

 Strain the syrup used for poaching these apricots and use it for flavoring hot or iced tea, oatmeal, or in place of vanilla extract in citrus-flavored desserts like the Lemon Loaf Cake in this chapter. You can also mix 2 tablespoons with 8 ounces of sparkling water for a refreshing drink!

INGREDIENTS

½ cup water

¼ cup orange juice

2 tablespoons lemon juice

1 tablespoon honey

1 (2") strip fresh lemon zest

1 (2") strip fresh orange zest

¼ teaspoon pure vanilla extract

2 medium apricots, sliced in half and pit removed

1. In a 1-quart saucepan combine water, orange juice, lemon juice, honey, lemon zest, orange zest, and vanilla. Whisk well. Place pan over medium heat and cook until mixture starts to simmer, then reduce heat to medium-low and add apricots.

2. Simmer, turning apricots occasionally, until tender, about 5 minutes. Transfer apricots to a serving plate and serve warm.

Preserving Zested Citrus
If your recipe calls for citrus zest but not the juice, you will need to wrap the fruit in plastic wrap, or other airtight food-safe wrap, and refrigerate to keep it fresh. The zest acts as a barrier, and once it's removed the citrus will start to dry out and spoil very quickly unless wrapped up tight.

PER SERVING

Calories: 41

Fat: 0g

Sodium: 0mg

Carbohydrates: 10g

Fiber: 1g

Sugar: 9g

Protein: 1g

RED WINE–POACHED FIGS WITH RICOTTA AND ALMONDS

PREP TIME: 5 MINUTES | COOK TIME: 10 MINUTES | SERVES: 1

 Dried figs keep fresh up to a year if stored in a cool, dry place in an airtight container. Compared to the shelf life of fresh figs, which is just two or three days, it makes a lot of sense to buy them dry. Here they are poached in red wine to make them soft and succulent!

INGREDIENTS

⅓ cup water

⅓ cup red wine

1 tablespoon honey, divided

1 teaspoon orange juice

1 (2") strip fresh orange zest

¼ teaspoon pure vanilla extract

4 dry mission figs, stems trimmed and cut in half

¼ cup reduced-fat ricotta cheese

1 tablespoon toasted sliced almonds

1. In a 1-quart saucepan, combine water, wine, 2 teaspoons honey, orange juice, orange zest, and vanilla. Whisk well. Add figs and place over medium heat until mixture starts to simmer. Cook, turning figs often, until they are rehydrated and tender, about 5 minutes. Transfer figs to a serving plate and set aside.

2. Continue to simmer poaching liquid until reduced by half, about 5 minutes. Remove from heat and cool.

3. In a small bowl, combine ricotta with remaining 1 teaspoon honey. Mix well.

4. To serve, arrange figs on plate and top with ricotta mixture. Drizzle with reduced poaching liquid and garnish with toasted almonds. Serve immediately.

PER SERVING

Calories: 293
Fat: 8g
Sodium: 65mg
Carbohydrates: 45g

Fiber: 4g
Sugar: 34g
Protein: 10g

LEMON OLIVE OIL MUG CAKE

PREP TIME: 5 MINUTES | COOK TIME: 1 MINUTE | SERVES: 1

 Extra-virgin olive oil has a grassy, earthy flavor that is enhanced when paired with lemon. Here they are combined in a personal-sized mug cake that tastes elegant but is ready in a flash. Like most mug cakes, this is best enjoyed while it is still warm. Feel free to swap lemon zest for orange zest if you like!

INGREDIENTS

¼ cup all-purpose flour

¼ teaspoon baking powder

¼ teaspoon freshly grated lemon zest

1 tablespoon granulated sugar

3 tablespoons unsweetened applesauce

2 teaspoons extra-virgin olive oil

¼ teaspoon pure vanilla extract

1. In an 8-ounce microwave-safe mug, add flour, baking powder, lemon zest, and sugar. Mix with a fork, mashing against the sides until lemon zest is fragrant. Add remaining ingredients and mix until smooth.

2. Microwave on high 60–90 seconds or until cake is puffed, the top is no longer shiny, and a toothpick inserted in center comes out clean.

3. Let cake rest in microwave 1 minute, then carefully remove. Serve immediately.

PER SERVING

Calories: 262

Fat: 9g

Sodium: 121mg

Carbohydrates: 42g

Fiber: 1g

Sugar: 17g

Protein: 3g

US/METRIC CONVERSION CHARTS

OVEN TEMP CONVERSIONS

Degrees Fahrenheit	Degrees Celsius
200 degrees F	95 degrees C
250 degrees F	120 degrees C
275 degrees F	135 degrees C
300 degrees F	150 degrees C
325 degrees F	160 degrees C
350 degrees F	180 degrees C
375 degrees F	190 degrees C
400 degrees F	205 degrees C
425 degrees F	220 degrees C
450 degrees F	230 degrees C

VOLUME CONVERSIONS

US Volume Measure	Metric Equivalent
⅛ teaspoon	0.5 milliliter
¼ teaspoon	1 milliliter
½ teaspoon	2 milliliters
1 teaspoon	5 milliliters
½ tablespoon	7 milliliters
1 tablespoon (3 teaspoons)	15 milliliters
2 tablespoons (1 fluid ounce)	30 milliliters
¼ cup (4 tablespoons)	60 milliliters
⅓ cup	90 milliliters
½ cup (4 fluid ounces)	125 milliliters
⅔ cup	160 milliliters
¾ cup (6 fluid ounces)	180 milliliters
1 cup (16 tablespoons)	250 milliliters
1 pint (2 cups)	500 milliliters
1 quart (4 cups)	1 liter (about)

WEIGHT CONVERSIONS

US Weight Measure	Metric Equivalent
½ ounce	15 grams
1 ounce	30 grams
2 ounces	60 grams
3 ounces	85 grams
¼ pound (4 ounces)	115 grams
½ pound (8 ounces)	225 grams
¾ pound (12 ounces)	340 grams
1 pound (16 ounces)	454 grams

BAKING PAN SIZES

American	Metric
8 x 1½ inch round baking pan	20 x 4 cm cake tin
9 x 1½ inch round baking pan	23 x 3.5 cm cake tin
11 x 7 x 1½ inch baking pan	28 x 18 x 4 cm baking tin
13 x 9 x 2 inch baking pan	30 x 20 x 5 cm baking tin
2 quart rectangular baking dish	30 x 20 x 3 cm baking tin
15 x 10 x 2 inch baking pan	30 x 25 x 2 cm baking tin (Swiss roll tin)
9 inch pie plate	22 x 4 or 23 x 4 cm pie plate
7 or 8 inch springform pan	18 or 20 cm springform or loose bottom cake tin
9 x 5 x 3 inch loaf pan	23 x 13 x 7 cm or 2 lb narrow loaf or pâté tin
1½ quart casserole	1.5 liter casserole
2 quart casserole	2 liter casserole

HOW TO REDUCE A RECIPE

Original Amount	Half the Amount	One-Third the Amount
1 cup	½ cup	⅓ cup
¾ cup	6 tablespoons	¼ cup
⅔ cup	⅓ cup	3 tablespoons + 1½ teaspoons
½ cup	¼ cup	2 tablespoons + 2 teaspoons
⅓ cup	2 tablespoons + 2 teaspoons	1 tablespoon + 2¼ teaspoons
¼ cup	2 tablespoons	1 tablespoon + 1 teaspoon
1 tablespoon	1½ teaspoons	1 teaspoon
1 teaspoon	½ teaspoon	¼ teaspoon
½ teaspoon	¼ teaspoon	⅛ teaspoon
¼ teaspoon	⅛ teaspoon	dash

INDEX

Note: Page numbers in **bold** indicate recipe category lists.

A

Alcohol, cooking without, 107. *See also* Wine
Apples
    about: homemade applesauce, 208
    Apple Oat Crisp, 221
    Applesauce Mug Cake, 214
    Baked Stuffed Apple, 215
    Stewed Cinnamon Apples with Dates, 208
Apricots, vanilla-poached, 226
Artichokes
    Lentils with Tomato, Artichoke, and Feta,
      138
    Olive Oil Pasta with Marinated Artichokes
      and Spinach, 101
    Spinach and Artichoke–Stuffed Mushroom,
      128–29
Asparagus, 84, 164
Avocados
    about: storing cut avocado, 21
    Avocado Toast with Balsamic-Marinated
      Tomatoes, 21
    Mediterranean-Style Avocado Dip, 49

B

Baba Ghanoush, 39
Balsamic vinegar, buying, 127
Banana Loaf Cake, 225
Barley soups, 68, 69
Basil Pesto Rice with Olives and Goat Cheese,
    78
Beans and lentils. *See also* Green beans
    about: canned, 35, 63; storing chickpeas,
      52; storing cooked lentils, 19; swapping
      lentils, 124
    Beef and Black Bean Enchilada Casserole,
      194
    Black Bean Sliders, 119
    Black Bean Tostadas with Corn and Tomato,
      123
    Brown Rice and Chickpea Salad, 57
    Chickpea Hash with Hard-Boiled Egg, 19
    Creamy Pasta with Chickpeas, 109
    Crispy Seasoned Chickpeas, 52
    Garlicky Lentil Dip, 42
    Kale and Lentil Stew, 124
    Lentil and Zucchini Boats, 139
    Lentil Balls, 121
    Lentil Curry with Spinach and Tomato, 133
    Lentils with Tomato, Artichoke, and Feta,
      138
    Minestrone Soup, 73
    Pinto Bean Dip with Cilantro, Cumin, and
      Lime, 36
    Three-Bean Salad, 63
    Three-Bean Vegetarian Chili, 126
    Tofu and Chickpea–Stuffed Pepper, 134
    Vegetable Bowls with Turkey and Hummus,
      169
    White Bean Cassoulet, 125
    White Bean Dip with Garlic and Herbs, 35
    White Beans with Garlic and Fresh
      Tomatoes, 118
    Whole-Grain Pancakes with Berry Sauce,
      23
Beef
    about: making steak seasoning blend, 185
    Beef and Black Bean Enchilada Casserole,
      194
    Beef and Mushroom Stroganoff, 192
    Beef and Vegetable Stew with Olives,
      186–87
    Beef Stew with Red Wine, 189
    Beefy Stuffed Peppers, 193
    Minute Steak with Garlic and Herbs, 200
    Phyllo-Wrapped Beef Tenderloin, 204

Salisbury Steak, 206
Spaghetti with Meat Sauce, 115
Spaghetti with Meaty Mushroom Sauce, 188
Unstuffed Cabbage Rolls in a Bowl, 198
Berries
Berry and Yogurt Smoothie, 27
Blueberry Almond Butter Smoothie Bowl, 32
Blueberry Compote, 210
Blueberry Crumble, 218–19
Fresh Raspberry Sauce for One, 220
Greek Yogurt Parfait, 12
Ricotta Berry Toast, 25
Whole-Grain Pancakes with Berry Sauce, 23
Bread and such
Ricotta Berry Toast, 25
Spiced Pita Chips, 34
Veggie Lover's Pita Pizza Bites, 51
Breakfast, 11–32. See also Eggs
about: overview of recipes, 11
Almond Date Oatmeal, 13
Avocado Toast with Balsamic-Marinated Tomatoes, 21
Berry and Yogurt Smoothie, 27
Blueberry Almond Butter Smoothie Bowl, 32
Fruit and Nut Overnight Oatmeal, 20
Greek Yogurt Parfait, 12
Ricotta Berry Toast, 25
Broccoli, roasted with feta, 85

C

Cabbage rolls and coleslaw, 198
Canned food safety, 63
Carrots, in Roasted Carrot Tahini Bisque, 66
Cauliflower purée, garlic, 89
Cauliflower Steak with Balsamic Glaze, 127
Cheese
about: Halloumi, 60; to stock, 8; strained yogurt cheese, 37
Basil Pesto Rice with Olives and Goat Cheese, 78
Brown Rice Bowl with Fried Halloumi and Mint Dressing, 60
Creamy Cheese Polenta, 88
eggs with (See Eggs)
Feta and Spinach–Stuffed Chicken Breast, 172
Israeli Couscous with Red Pepper and Goat Cheese, 67
pasta with (See Pasta)
Ricotta Berry Toast, 25
Roasted Broccoli with Feta, 85
Chicken. See Poultry
Chickpeas. See Beans and lentils
Chips, 34, 47. See also Dips and snacks
Chocolate. See Desserts
Chocolate Mug Cake, 223
Cilantro Lime Rice, 91
Citrus
about: preserving zested citrus, 226
Baked Lemon Parmesan Asparagus, 84
Chicken and Lemon Asparagus, 164
Cilantro Lime Rice, 91
Citrus Mashed Sweet Potatoes, 93
Lemon Garlic Rice Pilaf, 77
Lemon Loaf Cake, 222
Lemon Olive Oil Mug Cake, 228
Lemon Parmesan Risotto, 90
seafood dishes with, 104, 110, 158–59, 160
Cooking for one, 7
Corn and polenta
about: selecting fresh corn, 86
Creamy Cheese Polenta, 88
Polenta Cakes with Fresh Tomato Sauce, 132
Spiced Corn on the Cob, 86–87
Couscous, 67, 72, 135
Cucumbers
Creamy Cucumbers with Red Onion and Dill, 83
Tzatziki Sauce, 37

D

Daily foods, 6
Dairy, 8

Date Nut Energy Bites, 48
Dates, in Almond Date Oatmeal, 13
Desserts, **207**–28. *See also* Apples
   about: overview of recipes, 207
   Banana Loaf Cake, 225
   Blueberry Compote, 210
   Blueberry Crumble, 218–19
   Chocolate Mug Cake, 223
   Dark Chocolate Mousse, 217
   Fresh Raspberry Sauce for One, 220
   Frozen Fruity Yogurt Bark, 213
   Grilled Peach with Yogurt and Honey, 211
   Lemon Loaf Cake, 222
   Lemon Olive Oil Mug Cake, 228
   Oatmeal Raisin Cookies, 216
   Red Wine–Poached Figs with Ricotta and Almonds, 227
   Spiced Poached Pear, 209
   Vanilla-Poached Apricots, 226
   White Wine–Poached Pear, 220
Dips and snacks, **33**–53. *See also* Sauces
   about: overview of, 33
   Baba Ghanoush, 39
   Baked Vegetable Chips, 47
   Crispy Seasoned Chickpeas, 52
   Date Nut Energy Bites, 48
   Fresh Tomato Salsa (Pico de Gallo), 40
   Garlicky Lentil Dip, 42
   Mediterranean Deviled Egg, 44–45
   Mediterranean-Style Avocado Dip, 49
   Muhammara (Roasted Red Pepper Spread), 46
   Olive Spread, 41
   Pinto Bean Dip with Cilantro, Cumin, and Lime, 36
   Seasoned Mixed Nuts, 43
   Smoked Salmon Spread, 53
   Spiced Pita Chips, 34
   Tzatziki Sauce, 37
   Veggie Lover's Pita Pizza Bites, 51
   White Bean Dip with Garlic and Herbs, 35

E

Eggplant, in Baba Ghanoush, 39
Eggs
   about: benefits of, 15; poaching in advance, 31
   Baked Egg in a Bell Pepper, 26
   Baked Egg with Dill and Tomato, 15
   Chickpea Hash with Hard-Boiled Egg, 19
   Egg Poached in Tomato Sauce (Shakshuka), 16–17
   Eggs Florentine with Greek Yogurt Hollandaise, 30–31
   Farmer's Omelet, 24
   Mediterranean Deviled Egg, 44–45
   Red Pepper and Feta Omelet, 14
   Spanakopita Frittata, 28–29
   Spinach and Mozzarella Frittata, 18
Enchilada casserole, 194

F

Figs, red wine–poached, 227
Freezer items, 9
Freezing foods, 40, 182, 195, 213
Frittata, 18
Fruit. *See also* Desserts; *specific fruit*
   about: produce to stock, 8–9; storing dry fruit, 58
   Frozen Fruity Yogurt Bark, 213
   Fruit and Nut Brown Rice Salad, 58–59
   Fruit and Nut Overnight Oatmeal, 20

G

Garlic
   about: shortcut using purée, 77
   Garlic Butter Dipping Sauce, 153
   Garlic Cauliflower Purée, 89
   Garlicky Lentil Dip, 42
   Lemon Garlic Rice Pilaf, 77
Green beans, 81, 95
Grocery shopping, 7–8

H

Hash (chickpea), 19
Herbs, freezing fresh, 40
Honey, storing, 211

I

Ingredients
  freezing, 10
  fresh, 8–9
  keeping inventory of, 10
  pantry staples, 9
  prepping ahead, 10
Inventorying ingredients, 10

K

Kale and Lentil Stew, 124
Kale and Orzo Chicken, 170

L

Lamb
  about: internal temperature for, 199
  Greek Meatballs, 195
  Herbed Lamb Chop, 199
  Lamb Stew for One, 201
  Minty Lamb Meatballs in Spicy Red Pepper
    Ragu, 190–91
Lasagna Rolls, 112–13
Lettuce wraps, 174–75

M

Meal planning and prep, 9–10
Measurement conversion charts, 229–30
Meatballs, 173, 190–91, 195, 197
Meatloaf, turkey, 178
Mediterranean diet
  about: overview and focus of, 4, 5; this
    book and, 5
  base (daily foods), 6
  cooking for one, 7
  fresh ingredients and pantry staples, 8–9
  level 2 (weekly foods), 6
  level 3 (foods in moderation), 6
  level 4 (monthly foods), 6
  meal prep/avoiding waste, 9–10
  other elements of, 6–7
  shopping tips, 7–8
  tools for cooking, 7

Minestrone Soup, 73
Moderation, foods in, 6
Mushrooms
  about: storing, 99
  Beef and Mushroom Stroganoff, 192
  Chicken and Mushroom Marsala, 165
  Creamy Mushroom Risotto, 82
  Farmer's Omelet, 24
  Mushroom Barley Soup, 68
  Pork-Stuffed Mushrooms, 205
  Spaghetti with Meaty Mushroom Sauce,
    188
  Spicy Mushroom Penne, 99
  Spinach and Artichoke–Stuffed Mushroom,
    128–29
  Wild Rice and Mushroom Soup, 56

N

Nuts and seeds. See also Tahini
  Almond Date Oatmeal, 13
  Blueberry Almond Butter Smoothie Bowl,
    32
  Date Nut Energy Bites, 48
  Fruit and Nut Brown Rice Salad, 58–59
  Fruit and Nut Overnight Oatmeal, 20
  Miso Green Beans with Almonds, 95
  Pistachio-Crusted Halibut, 154
  Seasoned Mixed Nuts, 43

O

Oats
  about: storing, 13
  Almond Date Oatmeal, 13
  Apple Oat Crisp, 221
  Fruit and Nut Overnight Oatmeal, 20
  Oatmeal Raisin Cookies, 216
Olive Oil Mashed Potatoes, 96
Olive Oil Pasta with Marinated Artichokes
  and Spinach, 101
Olive oil vs. extra-virgin olive oil, 138
Olive Spread, 41
One, cooking for, 7

P

Pancakes, whole-grain with berry sauce, 23
Pantry staples, 9
Pasta, **97**–116
    about: measuring without scale, 102; overview of dishes, 97
    Angel Hair Pasta with Shrimp and Lemon, 110
    Baked Spaghetti Nests with Mozzarella, 140
    Baked Ziti, 114
    Bow Tie Pesto Pasta, 108
    Chicken and Noodles Casserole, 176
    Chicken with Toasted Orzo, 167
    Creamy Pasta with Chickpeas, 109
    Fettuccine with Crab and Lemon, 104
    Fettuccine with Greek Yogurt Alfredo Sauce, 98
    Herbed Orzo, 79
    Kale and Orzo Chicken, 170
    Lasagna Rolls, 112–13
    Linguine with Clams, 142
    Macaroni and Cheese, 116
    Olive Oil Pasta with Marinated Artichokes and Spinach, 101
    Orzo and Mozzarella–Stuffed Tomato, 102–3
    Pasta Primavera, 107
    Rotini with Charred Tomatoes and Mozzarella, 111
    Rotini with Roasted Vegetable Tomato Sauce, 100
    Shrimp Pasta with Basil and Feta, 146–47
    Spaghetti with Meat Sauce, 115
    Spaghetti with Meaty Mushroom Sauce, 188
    Spanakopita-Stuffed Shells, 105
    Spicy Mushroom Penne, 99
    Zucchini Lasagna, 120
Peach, grilled with yogurt and honey, 211
Pear, poached, 20, 209
Peppers
    Baked Egg in a Bell Pepper, 26
    Beefy Stuffed Peppers, 193
    Farmer's Omelet, 24

    Israeli Couscous with Red Pepper and Goat Cheese, 67
    Muhammara (Roasted Red Pepper Spread), 46
    Red Pepper and Feta Omelet, 14
    Red Pepper Dressing, 76
    Tofu and Chickpea–Stuffed Pepper, 134
Pesto dishes, 78, 108, 182
Pizza bites, 51
Polenta. *See* Corn and polenta
Pork
    Balsamic-Glazed Pork, 185
    Pork Medallions with Mustard Sauce, 202–3
    Pork-Stuffed Mushrooms, 205
    Vegetable-Packed Pork Meatball Sub, 197
Potatoes
    Green Beans with Potatoes and Tomatoes, 81
    Herb Vinaigrette Potato Salad, 94
    Mediterranean Twice-Baked Potato, 130–31
    Olive Oil Mashed Potatoes, 96
    Potato and Spinach Soup, 62
Poultry, **163**–83
    about: chicken cutlets, 165
    Balsamic Chicken Thigh with Tomato and Basil, 177
    Chicken and Lemon Asparagus, 164
    Chicken and Mushroom Marsala, 165
    Chicken and Noodles Casserole, 176
    Chicken Cacciatore, 166
    Chicken Lettuce Wraps, 174–75
    Chicken Scallopine, 171
    Chicken with Toasted Orzo, 167
    Easy Pesto Chicken, 182
    Feta and Spinach–Stuffed Chicken Breast, 172
    Fig-Glazed Chicken Breast, 179
    Kale and Orzo Chicken, 170
    Mini Turkey Meatloaf, 178
    Turkey Burger, 181
    Turkey Meatballs in Red Pepper Sauce, 173
    Vegetable Bowls with Turkey and Hummus, 169
    Wine-Braised Chicken Thigh, 183

Prepping ingredients, 10
Produce, 8–9
Proteins, 8. *See also specific proteins*

R

Rice and wild rice
  about: brown vs. white, 55
  Basil Pesto Rice with Olives and Goat
    Cheese, 78
  Brown Rice and Chickpea Salad, 57
  Brown Rice and Vegetables with Red
    Pepper Dressing, 76
  Brown Rice Bowl with Fried Halloumi and
    Mint Dressing, 60
  Brown Rice Salad with Zucchini and
    Tomato, 55
  Cilantro Lime Rice, 91
  Creamy Mushroom Risotto, 82
  Fruit and Nut Brown Rice Salad, 58–59
  Lemon Garlic Rice Pilaf, 77
  Lemon Parmesan Risotto, 90
  Wild Rice and Mushroom Soup, 56

S

Salads
  about: coleslaw for one, 198; overview
    of recipes, 54; saving time buying
    ingredients, 118
  Brown Rice and Chickpea Salad, 57
  Brown Rice Bowl with Fried Halloumi and
    Mint Dressing, 60
  Brown Rice Salad with Zucchini and
    Tomato, 55
  Farro Salad with Tomatoes and Olives, 61
  Fruit and Nut Brown Rice Salad, 58–59
  Herb Vinaigrette Potato Salad, 94
  Israeli Couscous with Red Pepper and Goat
    Cheese, 67
  Italian Mixed Green Salad, 65
  Mediterranean Couscous Salad, 72
  Three-Bean Salad, 63
Sandwiches and wraps
  about: meatloaf sandwiches, 178

Black Bean Sliders, 119
Chicken Lettuce Wraps, 174–75
Seasoned Tofu Gyro, 137
Turkey Burger, 181
Sauces
  Fresh Tomato Salsa (Pico de Gallo), 40
  Garlic Butter Dipping Sauce, 153
  Greek Yogurt Hollandaise, 30–31
  Red Pepper Dressing, 76
  Roasted Vegetable Tomato Sauce, 100
  Small-Batch Fresh Pesto, 78
  Tzatziki Sauce, 37
Seafood, **141–62**
  about: cooking frozen shrimp, 146;
    preparing mussels, 144; saving/using
    shrimp scraps, 110; smoked salmon, 53;
    whitefish, 151
  Angel Hair Pasta with Shrimp and Lemon,
    110
  Baked Crab Cake, 149
  Fettuccine with Crab and Lemon, 104
  Lemon Herb Fish Packet, 160
  Lemon Salmon with Dill, 158–59
  Linguine with Clams, 142
  Lobster Tail with Olive Oil and Herbs, 150
  Mediterranean Cod, 157
  Mediterranean Seafood Chowder, 143
  Mussels Saganaki, 148
  Mustard Herb Whitefish, 151
  Pistachio-Crusted Halibut, 154
  Rosemary Salmon, 161
  Seasoned Steamed Crab Legs, 153
  Shrimp Pasta with Basil and Feta, 146–47
  Shrimp Scampi, 145
  Smoked Salmon Spread, 53
  Steamed Cod with Capers and Lemon, 155
  Steamed Mussels, 144
  Tomato-Poached Fish, 156
  Whitefish Stew, 162
Shakshuka, 16–17
Shopping tips, 7–8
Side dishes, **75–96**. *See also* Salads
  about: overview of recipes, 75
  Baked Lemon Parmesan Asparagus, 84
  Basil Pesto Rice with Olives and Goat

Cheese, 78
Brown Rice and Vegetables with Red Pepper Dressing, 76
Cilantro Lime Rice, 91
Citrus Mashed Sweet Potatoes, 93
Creamy Cheese Polenta, 88
Creamy Cucumbers with Red Onion and Dill, 83
Creamy Mushroom Risotto, 82
Garlic Cauliflower Purée, 89
Green Beans with Potatoes and Tomatoes, 81
Herbed Orzo, 79
Herb Vinaigrette Potato Salad, 94
Lemon Garlic Rice Pilaf, 77
Lemon Parmesan Risotto, 90
Miso Green Beans with Almonds, 95
Olive Oil Mashed Potatoes, 96
Roasted Broccoli with Feta, 85
Spiced Corn on the Cob, 86–87
Smoothies
about: prepping for, 27
Berry and Yogurt Smoothie, 27
Blueberry Almond Butter Smoothie Bowl, 32
Snacks. See Dips and snacks
Soups and stews
about: overview of recipes, 54
Beef and Vegetable Stew with Olives, 186–87
Beef Stew with Red Wine, 189
Kale and Lentil Stew, 124
Lamb Stew for One, 201
Mediterranean Seafood Chowder, 143
Minestrone Soup, 73
Mushroom Barley Soup, 68
Potato and Spinach Soup, 62
Roasted Carrot Tahini Bisque, 66
Three-Bean Vegetarian Chili, 126
Tomato Basil Soup, 70–71
Vegan Avgolemono, 74
Vegetable Barley Soup, 69
Whitefish Stew, 162
Wild Rice and Mushroom Soup, 56
Spinach

Feta and Spinach–Stuffed Chicken Breast, 172
Potato and Spinach Soup, 62
Spanakopita Frittata, 28–29
Spanakopita-Stuffed Shells, 105
Spinach and Artichoke–Stuffed Mushroom, 128–29
Spinach and Mozzarella Frittata, 18
Stroganoff, 192
Sweet potatoes, citrus mashed, 93

T
Tahini
Baba Ghanoush, 39
Roasted Carrot Tahini Bisque, 66
Vegan Avgolemono, 74
Tofu
Dark Chocolate Mousse, 217
Seasoned Tofu Gyro, 137
Tofu and Chickpea–Stuffed Pepper, 134
Tomatoes
Avocado Toast with Balsamic-Marinated Tomatoes, 21
Egg Poached in Tomato Sauce (Shakshuka), 16–17
Fresh Tomato Salsa (Pico de Gallo), 40
Green Beans with Potatoes and Tomatoes, 81
Mediterranean Stuffed Tomato, 135
Orzo and Mozzarella–Stuffed Tomato, 102–3
Roasted Vegetable Tomato Sauce, 100
Rotini with Charred Tomatoes and Mozzarella, 111
salads with (See Salads)
Tomato Basil Soup, 70–71
Tomato-Poached Fish, 156
Tools, cooking, 7
Tostadas, 123
Turkey. See Poultry

U
Umami, adding, 74

V

Vanilla-Poached Apricots, 226
Vegan Avgolemono, 74
Vegetables. *See also* Side dishes; *specific vegetables*
  about: produce to stock, 8–9
  Brown Rice and Vegetables with Red Pepper Dressing, 76
  pasta with (See Pasta)
  Vegetable Barley Soup, 69
  Vegetable Bowls with Turkey and Hummus, 169
  Vegetable-Packed Pork Meatball Sub, 197
  Veggie Lover's Pita Pizza Bites, 51
Vegetarian main dishes, **117**–40
  Baked Spaghetti Nests with Mozzarella, 140
  Black Bean Sliders, 119
  Black Bean Tostadas with Corn and Tomato, 123
Cauliflower Steak with Balsamic Glaze, 127
  Kale and Lentil Stew, 124
  Lentil and Zucchini Boats, 139
  Lentil Balls, 121
  Lentil Curry with Spinach and Tomato, 133
  Lentils with Tomato, Artichoke, and Feta, 138
  Mediterranean Stuffed Tomato, 135
  Mediterranean Twice-Baked Potato, 130–31
  Polenta Cakes with Fresh Tomato Sauce, 132
  Seasoned Tofu Gyro, 137
  Spinach and Artichoke–Stuffed Mushroom, 128–29
  Three-Bean Vegetarian Chili, 126
  Tofu and Chickpea–Stuffed Pepper, 134
  White Bean Cassoulet, 125
  White Beans with Garlic and Fresh Tomatoes, 118
  Zucchini Lasagna, 120

W

Weekly foods, 6
Whole-Grain Pancakes with Berry Sauce, 23
Wild Rice and Mushroom Soup, 56
Wine
  about: boxed wine benefits, 189; cooking without, 107
  Beef Stew with Red Wine, 189
  Red Wine–Poached Figs with Ricotta and Almonds, 227
  Wine-Braised Chicken Thigh, 183

Y

Yogurt
  about: freezing, 213; strained yogurt cheese, 37
  Berry and Yogurt Smoothie, 27
  Blueberry Almond Butter Smoothie Bowl, 32
  Eggs Florentine with Greek Yogurt Hollandaise, 30–31
  Fettuccine with Greek Yogurt Alfredo Sauce, 98
  Frozen Fruity Yogurt Bark, 213
  Greek Yogurt Parfait, 12
  Grilled Peach with Yogurt and Honey, 211
  Tzatziki Sauce, 37

Z

Zucchini
  Baked Vegetable Chips, 47
  Brown Rice Salad with Zucchini and Tomato, 55
  Lentil and Zucchini Boats, 139
  Zucchini Lasagna, 120

ABOUT THE AUTHOR

Kelly Jaggers is a cookbook author, recipe developer, and founder of the recipe blog *Evil Shenanigans* (EvilShenanigans.com). She is the author of ten cookbooks, including *The Everything® Mediterranean Instant Pot® Cookbook*, *The Everything® Easy Instant Pot® Cookbook*, and *The Ultimate Baking for One Cookbook*. Kelly is also a food stylist and photographer who has provided photography for various cookbooks and websites. When she is not busy cooking up a storm in her own kitchen, she teaches in-person and virtual cooking classes and is a small event caterer. Kelly lives in Dallas with her husband and two hound dogs.

COOKING SOLO
Will Never Be Boring Again!